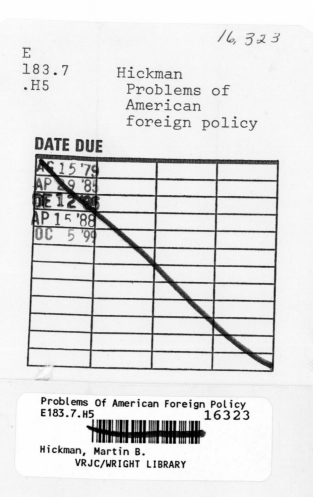

PROBLEMS OF
AMERICAN FOREIGN POLICY

The Insight Series

Studies in Contemporary Issues

from Glencoe Press

PROBLEMS OF AMERICAN FOREIGN POLICY, 2nd edition
Martin B. Hickman

THE OPPENHEIMER AFFAIR: a political play in three acts
Joseph Boskin and Fred Krinsky

THE POLITICS OF RELIGION IN AMERICA
Fred Krinsky

THE WELFARE STATE: who is my brother's keeper?
Fred Krinsky and Joseph Boskin

OPPOSITION POLITICS: the anti–new deal tradition
Joseph Boskin

IS AMERICAN DEMOCRACY EXPORTABLE?
Edward G. McGrath

PROTEST FROM THE RIGHT
Robert A. Rosenstone

DEMOCRACY AND COMPLEXITY: who governs the governors?
Fred Krinsky

FERMENT IN LABOR
Jerome Wolf

AMERICAN ANTI-WAR MOVEMENTS
Joseph Conlin

THE POLITICS AND ANTI-POLITICS OF THE YOUNG
Michael Brown

URBAN RACIAL VIOLENCE IN THE TWENTIETH CENTURY
Joseph Boskin

POSTWAR AMERICA: the search for identity
Donald G. Baker and Charles H. Sheldon

AN AWAKENED MINORITY: the Mexican-Americans, 2nd edition
Manual P. Servin

THE SUPREME COURT: politicians in robes
Charles H. Sheldon

DEPRIVATION IN AMERICA
Victor B. Ficker and Herbert S. Graves

BOYS NO MORE: a black psychologist's view of community
Charles W. Thomas

POLITICS OF THE NEW LEFT
Matthew Stolz

THE MILITARY AND AMERICAN SOCIETY
Martin B. Hickman

Series Editors: Fred Krinsky and Joseph Boskin

PROBLEMS OF AMERICAN FOREIGN POLICY
SECOND EDITION

Martin B. Hickman

Professor
Department of Political Science
Brigham Young University

GLENCOE PRESS
A division of Benziger Bruce & Glencoe, Inc.
Beverly Hills

GLENCOE PRESS
A division of Benziger Bruce & Glencoe, Inc.
8701 Wilshire Boulevard
Beverly Hills, California 90211
Collier-Macmillan Canada, Ltd.

Library of Congress Catalog Card Number: 74-10312

First printing, 1975

Contents

Preface

Much has happened in the years since the first edition of this reader appeared. The American armed forces have left Vietnam, although the war continues; President Nixon has sipped tea with Mao Tse-tung and toasted détente with Brezhnev; Charles DeGaulle and Willy Brandt have left the international scene; America has a new hero, Henry Kissinger, whose diplomatic triumphs in China, Vietnam, and the Middle East have dazzled not only his countrymen but also the sophisticated diplomatic community; the energy crisis and inflation have sharply reminded us that the transition from isolation to international interdependence is not without its costs; and finally, President Nixon's resignation has caused us to reflect on the "insolence of office" as well as on the "arrogance of power," and that constitutional crisis has belatedly called us to a defense of those liberties the Founding Fathers esteemed so highly.

President Nixon and Secretary Kissinger introduced a number of changes not only in the substance of foreign policy but in its structure and process as well. The office of the president's assistant for national security affairs became the base from which Kissinger reorganized the policy process at the presidential level and gave new impetus to the National Security Council system as a means of coordinating the military and political aspects of foreign policy. The selections in this edition reflect those changes and attempt to assess them against the background of our increasing knowledge and understanding of the foreign policy process.

Although a number of selections included in the earlier edition have been replaced, the major themes treated in the reader remain essentially the same: the nature of the foreign policy, the impact of our constitutional system on the policy process, the roles of the president and the Congress, the effectiveness of the State Department, and the integration of military, intelligence, and diplomatic agencies into a single policy process. These themes remain central to the problems of making foreign policy, and for thirty years they have been the main concerns of public discussion of foreign policy making. American involvement in Vietnam accentuated this continuing concern and resulted in a debate that challenged concepts that had been accepted as basic truths. The most important of the concepts thus questioned was the notion that the president needs maximum freedom in conducting foreign policy. Opponents of American policy in Vietnam, many of whom espoused the concept of executive freedom in foreign policy, have argued that the Congress must reassert its constitutional prerogative to check and supervise foreign policy. Hence the issues raised by the readings retain their relevance. Indeed, perhaps at no time in American history have students of the foreign policy process had a better opportunity to subject the accepted truths about making foreign policy to the searching test of experience.

Concentration on a few major themes could lead to dangerous over-simplification. Some of my friends in the State Department doubt whether it is possible to reduce the complexities of the foreign policy process to understandable patterns without robbing the description of all meaning. These people are struck by how often policy is determined by chance, caprice, and personality conflicts. Unless the student sees such forces at work, they argue, he will never fully understand the way foreign policy is made. I recognize the legitimacy of their fears without fully sharing them. Decision making is necessarily a dynamic process, difficult to describe in full detail. When asked to reconstruct the process, even the decision makers are apt to "tidy up" the thoughts and connections that led to action. The task of the analyst or observer is to see whether there are patterns underlying the apparent confusion. Moreover, the grasp of these patterns is often more important to an understanding of the decision-making process than the details, because these patterns give the details their full meaning.

Without some central organizing concepts, students will mistake confusion and caprice, so easy to identify in the policy process, as the whole of reality. The readings in this book present, for the most part, such organizing concepts and tend, therefore, to obscure the complexity of the foreign policy process; they were selected in full recognition of this limitation. I hoped that the student provided with a conceptual framework would be better prepared to see the details of the policy process in their proper perspective. The learning process is in essence the task of applying general concepts to specific situations and thereby discovering not only the limitations of the generalizations but also how they can be reformulated to improve their usefulness. The organizing concepts found in this collection of readings are, therefore, not the final word but a useful starting point.

Chapter One

Thinking about Foreign Policy

The formulation of foreign policy poses a set of special problems for the policy maker. In the first instance, he is faced with a policy environment that has been shaped not by rational choice but by the clash of opposing political, economic, and ultimately military, forces. This environment determines to a large measure the range of his policy options. An American president might well deplore the existence of an international system dominated by two superpowers, each with a formidable arsenal of thermonuclear weapons, but his policy choices must deal with that specific reality. Likewise, a president might hope and work for a "generation of peace" but find that goal elusive because other policy makers over whom he has no control have interests that cannot be achieved without the use of force. The "real" world, then, must be dealt with on its own terms; the hoary definition of politics as the "art of the possible" applies with even greater force in international affairs than it does in domestic politics.

A corollary of this environmental constraint on the making of foreign policy is the dilemma of power. All too often students conceive of power as being a measurable quantity and consequently believe that power will always be an effective instrument of foreign policy. Obviously, this is true in the abstract, but in the real world of foreign policy making this abstract power is not always the ready handmaiden of effective foreign policy. Why should this be so? Because in the final analysis power is not a quantity but a relation and relations are defined by concrete situations, not by measuring abstract power indicators.

The problem the true nature of power sets for the foreign policy maker is starkly revealed in the *Pueblo* affair. The *Pueblo* was an American naval vessel carrying out a surveillance mission in international waters off the coast of North Korea. It strayed into North Korean territorial waters, where its crew as well as the vessel were captured by North Korean naval forces. This action by the North Koreans posed a twofold problem for American policy makers: (1) What should be the goal of American policy? (2) What means should be employed to achieve this goal? Very soon after the capture, it became apparent that American policy was to obtain the release of the crew as rapidly as possible. That policy goal defined the situation and determined the power relations between the two nations. Therefore, the behavior of the United States could not be predicted by reference to its relative power position vis-à-vis North Korea as measured by the traditional standards of power. Its behavior was determined by its policy goal, i.e., the return of the crewmen alive and well. Had American policy makers decided to punish the North Koreans without regard for the safety or return of the crew, they could have easily done so because of American naval and air superiority. But they opted instead for return of the crewmen and by so doing rendered the overwhelming military power of the United States irrelevant, for although it could be used to punish or gain revenge, it could not be used to assure the safe return of the crew members.

Foreign policy makers must cope not only with the intransigence of the environment and the dilemma of power but also with the rapidly expanding scope of foreign policy. A century ago, even a half century ago, scholars and statesmen could draw relatively clear lines between foreign and domestic policy. That line has become increasingly obscured, partly by the emergence of the cold war in the early post–World War II era but most importantly by the growing interdependence in the world. Almost every domestic problem has some international implication: the price of fuel depends to a large measure on the price at which the Arab nations are willing to sell their oil; the rate of inflation is affected in part by the demand for American exports; the domestic success of President Johnson did not compensate for his foreign policy failures, and President Nixon hoped in vain that his foreign policy success would save him from the tragedy of Watergate.

The time, therefore, when one could answer that foreign policy is the official acts of a government in relation to other governments is long gone. Foreign policy now not only encompasses the nation's political and military relations with other nations but reaches deep into all aspects of international economics in both the public and the private sectors. Furthermore, humanitarian issues are thrusting their way into foreign policy. In the 1950s the refusal to serve a foreign diplomat at a drive-in in Maryland, as well as a freedom march in Alabama and civil rights legislation, all had their impact on American foreign policy. In the 1970s Senator Jackson hopes to use the Soviet Union's desire for increased trade with the United States as a means of inducing the Russian government to relax its restrictions on Jewish emigration to Israel.

The expanding scope of foreign policy has caused us to look more closely at the truism that, in the United States, foreign policy is made by the president. Knowing this tells little about the way in which the president obtains the information and advice on which foreign policy is based, or about the tugging and hauling between various interest groups and bureaucratic offices that precedes those decisions. If one looks at a chart showing the organization of the United States government, it is obvious that the secretary of state and the State Department advise the president on matters of foreign policy. But experience since World War II has taught us that the organizational units to which the president turns for advice and information vary from situation to situation. The easy answer, then, that the secretary of state is the president's principal adviser on questions of foreign policy, conceals the influence that the secretary of defense and the presidential assistant for national security affairs have over foreign policy decisions. Unless we look beyond the Department of State to the Department of Defense, to the Central Intelligence Agency, to the Department of Commerce, to the Treasury Department, and to the fifty-odd departments and agencies with foreign policy interests, we will not see the whole picture. Furthermore, we must look beyond the governmental officials to those public and private citizens who have the president's ear, if we are to find the threads of influence out of which the president eventually weaves the policy fabric.

Finally, there is the relation of the internal structure of the nation to the making of foreign policy. Clearly, internal politics influences foreign policy. The antiwar movement in the United States profoundly influenced American policy in Vietnam. Great Britain's need to trade in order to live has a profound influence on the kind of foreign policy it adopts. DeGaulle's vision of French glory was more than mere rhetoric; it shaped the substance and form of French foreign policy. The military power of the Soviet Union permits it to undertake one kind of foreign policy, the military weakness of Belgium dictates another. Although there is much dispute about the precise nature of the relationship, ideology certainly affects foreign policy. Economic growth and political stability also are related to foreign policy.

Although it is generally recognized that these internal factors influence the content of foreign policy, it is not always clear that the same is true of the way in which governments are organized and operated. The impact of governmental structure on the foreign policy process is perhaps sharper in the United States than in any other major country. The Constitution of the United States divides and separates governmental powers in a complex pattern. This division of power—federalism and separation of powers—has had a significant impact on our internal political life. Federalism has not directly affected the formulation and conduct of foreign policy, for the Constitution assigns full power over this phase of the nation's life to the federal government. Separation of powers is, however, a fact of political life that has profoundly influenced the making of foreign policy. Indeed, it is not far from the mark to say that the implications of that concept have been the principal preoccupation of most analysts of the foreign policy process in the United States.

The readings in this section, and the questions that follow each reading, have been selected to raise issues surrounding these problems. The first selection, "The Distinctive Environment of Foreign Policy," by Martin B. Hickman, provides intellectual scaffolding. The article emphasizes the differences between the environments of foreign and of domestic policy. It also assesses the impact of this difference on the foreign policy process and on the national interest as a guide to foreign policy.

The second selection, "The Constitutional Setting of Policy," by Paul Seabury, shows that the relations between the internal structure of a nation and its foreign policy are profound. Our government's internal nature exerts more than a temporary influence on efforts to solve a current problem; it reaches into the very heart of our democratic society and underlies all our relationships throughout the world.

The Distinctive Environment of Foreign Policy

Martin B. Hickman

In matters of foreign policy, most Americans know what they would do if they were the president, and they confidently expect that fidelity to principles and application of common sense will yield the right answers. The serious student of the foreign policy process must look beyond the generalities of "conventional wisdom" for a guide to understanding foreign policy. At the beginning, he must grasp the simple yet decisive difference between the environment in which *domestic policy* is carried out and that in which *foreign policy* operates. He should see that, although these environments are similar because their components are the same, they are also different because these components function in sharply different ways. He must understand that, because the environments are different, guides to successful foreign policy are often ambiguous, and that the foreign policy process is frequently hampered by the absence of information and by the pressure of time. In the course of this article we will examine each of these problems.

A comparison of the domestic and the foreign policy environments must focus on the interaction among three components—norms, interests, and force—for these interactions determine the nature of the environment. But before examining these relationships, it is necessary to define with some care each component. (1) Norms are values shared by the individuals or groups in the environment. These values are expressed as legal norms, which we call laws, or as ideas about the way individuals and groups ought to behave in society, which we call ethical, moral, or social norms. The primary distinction between legal and other norms rests on the way they are enforced. Legal norms are generally enforced by the political community, while other norms are enforced through the pressure of family, peer groups, or public opinion. (2) Interests are goals that individuals or groups believe are necessary to their existence, prosperity, or prestige. In the domestic environment, the groups may be business, social, professional, labor, or religious; in the international environment, interest groups are primarily nations. (3) Force is the use of coercive measures to obtain compliance with a legal norm when voluntary compliance is not forthcoming. It also is used to realize an interest.

The Domestic Environment

In the domestic environment, law is the fundamental determinant wherever conflict arises between interests and law. The conflict is ordinarily resolved in favor of law. Ownership of property, for example, is determined by which party satisfies the legal norms governing the ownership and transfer of property. Neither the interests of the parties nor the ability of one party to physically coerce the other is relevant to the question of ownership. Enforcement of law is the responsibility of a central decision maker who can use the full power of the community to ensure compliance.

Although legal norms are preeminent in the domestic environment, interests also are important. Indeed, the competition among various interests on the domestic scene constitutes what we call politics. Interests cannot be realized unless they are transformed into norms through the legislative process. Where individuals or groups seek to impose their interests on others without transforming them into legal norms the power of the community is interposed. This means that, at least in a democracy, interests cannot become norms until a substantial number of individuals or groups are prepared to accept them as the common interest and, therefore, binding on the whole community. This process is clearly seen in the attempt to prohibit the making, selling, and transporting of alcoholic beverages in the United States. In the early 1920s, a substantial pressure group was successful in convincing the majority of the nation that prohibition was really the common interest. The Eighteenth Amendment was adopted, transforming the interest of this pressure group into the legal norm for the nation. Prohibition went from a legal norm to an interest when opponents of prohibition were successful in obtaining the repeal of the Eighteenth Amendment in 1933.

In the domestic environment, the right to use force is limited to a central authority, government, in accordance with the legal norms of the community. Force is used to enforce legal norms, to maintain internal law and order, and to protect the community from external enemies. Those who encroach on the government's right to use force are labeled criminals and punished. Only when people are willing to obey the laws can force be used effectively, because the potential effectiveness of force depends significantly on the extent to which it does not have to be used. In the domestic environment, compliance can be relied on because a majority of citizens prefer their own country over all other political units, both internal and external, that compete for their loyalty.

The International Environment

In the international environment, unlike in the domestic environment, the legal norm, i.e., international law, does not ultimately determine behavior. International law does exist, it is true, but each nation in the international community retains full power to determine the extent of its own responsibility under international law, unless the nation has specifically delegated its power to an international organization. This decentralization introduces an element of caprice into international law, for there is no final arbiter of its meaning. A nation, therefore, cannot assume that its interpretation of international law will coincide with the interpretation made by other nations. Consequently, although nations may prefer to comply with international law as they see it, they realize that different interpretations by other nations may well jeopardize their most vital interests.

This decentralization gives the relationship between norms and interests in the foreign environment a character entirely different from that in the domestic environment. Whereas in the domestic environment norms regulate and control interests, in the international environment norms and interests are coordinate and competitive guides to action. The dictates of interests and of international law are frequently compatible and, when this is so, making foreign policy is relatively easy. Where they are incompatible, making foreign policy is more difficult; then, the merits of these competitive guides must be weighed. In the past, the tendency has been for nations to follow national interests rather than international law whenever their power has been sufficient to make this decision feasible. Of course, nations advance an interpretation of international law that justifies their behavior, but, as we have seen, each country decides for itself how to apply international law. The situation is fundamentally different from that of the domestic environment, where the interpretation and enforcement of the law is in the hands of the central government.

In the international environment, the right to use force is not concentrated in a single authority but is retained by each nation. International law provides that nations may legitimately use force in certain circumstances, the most familiar of which is self-defense. However, self-defense may be used by a nation to justify almost any action. In 1939, World War II began when Hitler asserted that Poland had attacked Germany and that Germany's counterattack was clearly self-defense. In 1967, after the outbreak of hostilities between Egypt and Israel, each country charged the other with aggression; each was sure that its own use of force was justified by its right of self-defense under international law. It is clear then that as long as the power to interpret international law is not given to a central authority, each country is free to decide whether to use force for the maintenance of international law and order or for the advancement of its own interests. Each nation also decides whether it will take action unilaterally or in cooperation with other nations through international organizations such as the Organization of American States, the North Atlantic Treaty Organization, or the United Nations.

Because international law and national interests are coordinate and competing standards of behavior in the international environment, ever present is the possibility that a nation will use force either to obtain its version of international law or to assure the realization of its national interests. Stanley Hoffmann has pointed out that, while "procedures for cooperation, for the creation and expression of consent, exist in both domestic and world politics, the permanent possibility of free and legitimate recourse to violence remains the mark of international relations."[1]

In recapitulation, then, we see that domestic policy operates in an environment where legal norms receive substantial compliance or are systematically enforced where necessary. Interests exist but are not controlling, unless they become transformed into norms by the legislative process. Force is controlled by a central authority that possesses a legitimate monopoly over its use. On the other hand, foreign policy operates in an arena where legal norms are not controlling, where national interests may be used to justify violation of the legal norms, and where no central authority has the monopoly over the use of force.

Guides to Policy

It has been frequently asserted that, in the international environment described above, a healthy concern for the national interest is the cornerstone of a successful foreign policy. Hans Morgenthau and George Kennan assert that this concern has been absent in the making of American foreign policy. American policy makers, they allege, have mistakenly supposed that the moral and legal values on the domestic scene prevail to the same extent in the international arena. This "moral-legalistic" approach, they say, has obscured the national interest and has led the United States into questionable policies during the past half-century. These critics argue that the national interest must be the basis of any rational policy in a world where there is no central authority and where there are deep-rooted disputes over the existence and meaning of common norms.

---

1. In *The State of War* (New York: Praeger, 1965), p. 89.

There is, of course, a good deal of justice in this criticism. However, it raises a number of questions that must be answered before the criticism can be assessed. First, what is the national interest? This term has as many meanings as there are people who use it. In an attempt to make the concept a guide to policy makers, it has been redefined as "national security." But this redefinition is not without a certain ambiguity of its own. Some military leaders and their supporters believe that national security can be achieved only when a nation is sufficiently strong to cope with any possible military threat. As has been often noted, such efforts in the past generally have been interpreted by other nations as creating new threats to their own security, and they have countered by increasing armaments. This reaction has spurred the first nation to redouble its own efforts, and an arms race, accompanied by an increased possibility of armed conflict, has resulted. Other policy makers believe that national security is more likely to be won when all nations voluntarily comply with international law, that a rational foreign policy should rely more heavily on the rule of law than on military might. It must be clear, therefore, that national interest, defined as national security, is not an infallible guide to policy making but rather an all-encompassing goal that leaves the question of means open.

One cannot escape the conclusion that neither the national interest nor international law can alone provide a sure guide to foreign policy. Just as reliance on legal norms in international affairs without regard for interest can lead to unrealistic foreign policies, so reliance on interest to the exclusion of international law leads to an increase in conflict among nations; the scales become heavily weighted on the side of the strong and cynical, which in turn, as we have noted, leads to an increase in the instability of the international system. It becomes necessary, then, to judge the relevance of each of these components in a given historical situation. There are no hard-and-fast rules to assure the success of this effort. But recognition that foreign and domestic policies exist in substantially different environments permits sounder conceptualization than does the assumption that the two environments are the same.

The Policy Process

The first step in understanding foreign policy is to grasp the basic distinction between the domestic and the foreign environments; the second is to see how this difference influences the policy process.

The integrated relationship of norms, interests, and force in the *domestic* environment provides the policy maker with a substantial degree of control over the environment. As a consequence, the policy process is essentially legislative and is characterized by investigation, discussion, and careful weighing of the evidence. In most cases there is sufficient time for exhaustive hearings, where competing interests have their day in court, and there is also sufficient time for extensive debate on the relative merits of these interests. Clearly, domestic policy makers do not have perfect information and unlimited time. If they did, the whole task could be assigned to a computer complex. But time pressure and lack of information are not the principal problems that confront domestic policy makers; their crucial concerns are determining the meaning of the evidence and deciding among competing interests. Because this task cannot be performed without adequate information and sufficient time, the tendency in making domestic policy is to delay decisions until the necessary information is at hand and until time has been taken to consider that information.

The nonintegrated relationship of norms, interests, and force in the international environment deprives the *foreign* policy maker of substantial control over the environment. Foreign policy frequently has to be made on the basis of inadequate information and under severe time pressure. Consequently, the policy process is executive in nature. The decision maker must be given authority to handle information as he sees fit, including the right to conceal information from potential external enemies and from citizens of his own nation. The foreign policy maker also needs wide discretion because he must reach decisions rapidly. It is important then, to examine closely how the lack of information and the lack of time affect the foreign policy process.

Foreign policy often has to be made in the absence of all the relevant information. What was the intention of the USSR in placing missiles in Cuba in 1962? Was this move meant to upset the existing power relationship in the Caribbean, or did the Soviets really believe these missiles to be defensive weapons against an attack from the United States? What would be the Russian reaction to a blockade, to an air strike, or to an invasion? Although definitive answers to these questions were not at hand, a decision would have been made with greater certainty had more reliable information been available.

In the international environment, information is often inadequate for a number of reasons, but the following are particularly important: (1) In each country, the foreign policy makers do everything they can to conceal the extent of their information from the policy makers of other countries. Indeed, most nations have elaborate security systems to protect classified information and complicated codes to assure this secrecy during transmission. Conversely, nations expend considerable time, money, and manpower to penetrate other nations' security systems. (2) Information may be fragmented, and a good deal of effort is required to piece the puzzle together. Thus, most of the Central Intelligence Agency staff is assigned to the difficult and time-consuming task of putting together overt but fragmented information about the rest of the world. (3) Obviously, all the information available cannot be processed by the policy maker. The important information must be separated from the unimportant, the reliable from the unreliable, and the relevant from the irrelevant before the policy maker sees it. But this selection and sifting process may operate to hide information from the policy maker rather than bring it to his attention. The Bay of Pigs[2] is perhaps the most recent case where a president has had cause to complain about the selection process; Pearl Harbor is perhaps the most dramatic. (4) Closely related to the selection problem is that of conceptualization. There is a popular belief that the facts have one and only one meaning, readily apparent to all observers. "Let the facts speak," we are fond of saying. The truth is, of course, that facts generally have meaning only within the conceptual framework the observer brings to the problem. There is no dispute about the fact of the American Civil War, but the meaning of that fact is still being debated long after its close. At Pearl Harbor, our intelligence system produced more than sufficient information in terms of quantity but failed to provide answers to pressing questions because the interpreters of that information brought a faulty conceptual framework to their task. Nor is there any dispute about the fact that, at the Munich conference of 1938, European leaders sacrificed Czechoslovakia to Hitler's territorial demands. In retrospect, this sacrifice represents the folly of appeasement; in 1938, to Sir Neville Chamberlain, British prime minister, it meant "peace in our time."

The possibility of error in the information process is rather large, and foreign policy makers must constantly be on the alert that both

---

2. On April 17, 1961, a landing force of 1,400 anti-Castro Cuban exiles, organized, financed, trained, and directed by the United States Central Intelligence Agency, was crushed in less than three days by superior numbers of Castro's army. Defeat was blamed on the fact that the CIA underestimated Cuba's military strength, did not coordinate its plans with the United States Department of Defense, and misjudged the extent of the support that the Cuban people were prepared to give the invasion.

the factual data and the conceptualizations they bring to the study of that data are relevant to the problem to be solved. In the study of foreign policy making, it is apparent to the historian or critic that, in most cases where errors have been made, sufficient information was at hand to solve the problem if only it had been seen in the proper perspective. The essential problem, then, is not the raw data, although this must be a central concern of the information process. It is the continued reevaluation of the conceptualizations the policy maker brings to the problem at hand.

The problem of adequate information cannot be separated from the second variable we are considering—time. If time were not in short supply, the problem of gathering and analyzing information would be substantially easier. But foreign policy makers are constantly bedeviled by time pressures; decisions often cannot be postponed. The reasons for this constant time pressure are not always made explicit, and therefore it is worthwhile to examine three general situations in which time is an acute factor for foreign policy makers.

The first occurs when there is a reduction in the absolute time within which a decision must be reached. The most common example occurs when one nation presents another with an ultimatum that must be answered by a given date. The fixing of a specific termination point on the decision-making process forces a reduction in the number of alternatives considered and the extent to which each can be analyzed.

A second situation arises in crises characterized by a sharp increase in the number and variety of transactions between the parties to the dispute. Indeed, the interactions can occur so rapidly that the decision maker becomes confused about the sequence. There is some evidence that the key to the solution to the Cuban missile crisis was the decision by the United States policy makers that Khrushchev's letters to President Kennedy were written in inverse order from their receipt.[3]

---

3. Two messages were received by the president. The first, dated Friday October 26, was a personal letter from Chairman Khrushchev proposing a generally acceptable outline for the resolution of the crisis. The second was broadcast on Saturday morning, the 27th. Its style suggested the handiwork of the Soviet Foreign Office, and it contained terms unacceptable to the president. Attorney General Kennedy suggested that the Saturday message be ignored—that the president should respond only to the October 26 letter. The president accepted this advice and communicated with the chairman on the basis of the proposals in the Friday message. This tactic proved to be successful. It was later determined that the Saturday message was written before the Khrushchev letter, but, because of delays in the Soviet Foreign Office, was broadcast after the Friday letter had been received.

Such a sudden increase in transactions means that, although no specific time limit is placed on the decision-making process, the amount of time allowed for each decision must be reduced, for time is not an infinite resource. Moreover, the fact that the decision-making process is open-ended does not mean that the making of the decision can be postponed indefinitely. The flow of time forces changes in the alternatives open to the decision maker; if he wishes to retain some options, he must move rapidly. In the Cuban missile crisis, the need to act before the missiles became operational was necessary if some desirable alternatives were to be kept open.

A third situation occurs when the problems are complex. The amount of time available for the decision may be, in absolute terms, relatively long, but, in terms of the problems facing the decison maker, the absolute time may be relatively short. The acute crisis usually involves critical but fairly simple questions. The threat tends to be straightforward rather than ambivalent, the dangers clearly outlined, and the range of decision alternatives limited. President Truman's decision to use American forces in Korea in 1950 illustrates this type of situation. The problem of emerging Chinese power exemplifies a situation in which the issues are so complex that no guess can be made as to what would be a reasonable length of time in which to reach a decision. Frequently, such situations are called permanent crises to underline the fact that the amount of time in which to solve the problem will always be in short supply.

Insufficient time, inadequate information, and the ever-present possibility that nations will resort to the use of force profoundly influence the environment in which foreign policy is made. The result is that foreign policy makers must reach decisions in a much more uncertain environment than that in which domestic policy makers operate. In reaching decisions about domestic policy, Americans have at least the great fundamentals of the Constitution to guide them. In making foreign policy, the environment provides only the signposts of international law and national interests, where ambiguities are as likely to confuse the decision maker as to guide him. So formidable, therefore, are the problems of foreign policy makers that one would like to name irony and pity as their judges. But this cannot be; more trenchant performance standards must be imposed where questions of foreign policy are involved. As President Kennedy told his aides after the Bay of Pigs, "Domestic policy can only defeat us; foreign policy can kill us."

Questions

1. How does Professor Hickman distinguish between the domestic and the international environment? What are the characteristics of each, and how do they differ?
2. "Enforcement of norms in the international environment is difficult because of conflicting national interests." Is "national interest" the only determinant of differences in perceptions of international law?
3. Discuss the time factor in domestic and international policy making.
4. What is a "permanent crisis"?
5. "If only the president and the Department of State would just use common sense, we would be a lot better off." Comment.

The Constitutional Setting of Policy*

Paul Seabury

Paul Seabury is professor of political science at the University of California, Berkeley, and the author of *The Wilhelmstrasse, A Study of German Diplomats under the Nazi Regime* and *The Waning of Southern Internationalism.* He has been chairman of the executive committee of Americans for Democratic Action, visiting fellow at the Center for International Studies at Princeton University, resident professor at the Brookings Institution, and a Guggenheim Fellow.

Order is the first desideratum for the simple reason that chaos means non-existence. —REINHOLD NIEBUHR

In the past twenty years, organizational innovations to cope with international crisis have profoundly affected all spheres of American government and policies. The kinds of public transactions occurring between the United States and other nations have grown. Traditional American diplomatic and military establishments have been enlarged

*From *Power, Freedom and Diplomacy*, by Paul Seabury. Copyright © 1963 by Random House, Inc. Reprinted by permission of the publisher.

beyond belief, and their tasks both diversified and intensified. Secret intelligence and propaganda have been added to them. The overseas activities of once domestic governmental agencies like the Departments of Labor, Agriculture, and Treasury have become global in scope. Requirements of speed, flexibility, and adaptability have greatly strained traditional modes of administration. New international organizations add a further multilateral dimension to the encounters and transactions of states. Everything is related to everything else. This organizational revolution is hardly unique to the United States. But due to the central position of the United States in the non-Communist world, the making of American foreign policy, never an easy task, has been altered beyond belief.

The management of foreign affairs seems to many people an arcane and obscure affair. Not secrecy alone (a perpetual problem of democracies in foreign affairs), but also complexity, have made it virtually incomprehensible to the man in the street, and deeply puzzling at times even to many men who work within the labyrinthine corridors of government itself. American social scientists and journalists today attempt to light up these corridors by crystallizing or photographing the complex processes of decision making. But they constantly run up against the extraordinary difficulty that the processes appear so ephemeral, and so contingent upon changing global political problems. The processes seemingly depend too upon constant shifts in locale and intensity of human power, vigor, lethargy, purpose, and resources. Representative government and democracy are based in theory upon the principle of consent of the governed and the accountability of government to society; but consent, accountability, and responsibility are often hard come by, in such times.

The Umbrella of Constitutional Order

We might first ask whether these processes take place under the larger umbrella of some established constitutional order. Today many states in the society of nations are, in a certain sense, *only* processes, so new, provisional, and transitory do their political institutions appear. Nearly a third of the total United Nations membership today consists of nation-states which did not exist ten years ago. But even many "older" state entities today appear equally provisional as far as their basic constitutional order and their claim to statehood is concerned. A governmental process which we see today may, like that of the United Arab

Republic, simply not exist tomorrow. The legitimacy of a particular existing constitutional order may be widely challenged, both at home or abroad. In some states, there is not even a rudimentary popular consciousness of nationality, much less a popular acceptance of the existing constitutional order of things.[1] Such conditions provoke instability and indeterminacy in foreign affairs. Harold Lasswell's generally insufficient description of the state as a "manifold of events"[2] is quite appropriate for many of these valuable and volatile nations, notably those of the new Afro-Asian bloc, where tradition, custom, and a domestic political consensus are too rudimentary to amount to much.

A state or political community must have a stable constitutional order if it is to survive in the sea of events around it. Yet such an order, essential elements of which are popular consent and understanding, is present in the world today only among a few of the more highly integrated and historically deep-rooted political communities of the Western world. Clearly it exists in Great Britain and the United States. Their political orders are regarded as much more than ephemeral processes. They are widely comprehended, authoritative arrangements of political power. The state itself is subordinate to this constitutional order, which, so it is said, both legitimizes the exercise of political power and sets limits upon it. While one might point to some states in the Soviet or Communist world as also possessing rudimentary elements of popular consent and political continuity, it should be pointed out that force and violence play an essential role in their constitutional stability. Marxist theory about the state explicitly proclaims its provisional charter: i.e., the state is an historically contingent entity which shall

---

1. An extreme instance of this political condition may be seen today in the relationship of the West German *Bundesrepublik* and the Soviet *Deutsche Demokratische Republik* of East Germany. No one would deny the existence, in Germany as a whole, of something known as consciousness of nationality, but there is hardly any popular consensus about the desirable territorial or constitutional order of things. West German Foreign Minister von Brentano, when asked whether the *Bundesrepublik* would be willing to negotiate about the relationship of these two regimes, replied, "Yes, but not with the prison guards" (namely, the East German authorities). *Washington Post*, October 15, 1961.

2. See his *Psychopathology and Politics*, rev. ed. (New York: Viking, 1960), chap. XIII. "The time-space abstraction of the 'group,'" Lasswell writes, "is just as 'real' or 'unreal' as the time-space abstraction called the 'individual.' They are both equally real or unreal, and they stand and fall together." This definition would be equally adequate and puzzling to both Queen Elizabeth and Mr. Moise Tshombe as descriptive of their respective states.

pass away when certain objective transformations have taken place in society. Marxist doctrine thus provisionalizes even the institutions of the Soviet world itself. . . .

A supreme constitutional problem of all national political entities is that of arranging both authority and political power so that the state may legitimately, purposively, and effectively act in the realm of world politics, a realm occupied by many other states similarly claiming their sovereign rights. In relatively stable political entities, the foreign policy processes thus possess a certain orderliness and stability. These foreign policy processes are products of a perpetual tension between constitutional forms and unique political contingencies of the moment.

A constitution is not merely a description of transitory allocations of political influence and power in a state; it is also something less than a description of the totality of form and order in the whole society. In Western political thought, a constitutional order signifies a government of laws, not of men. Ultimate authority theoretically resides in supreme law, with which lesser laws, enacted by men, supposedly should harmonize. A constitutional order is ideally an order in which political power is legitimized, allocated, limited, and synchronized. A constitutional order not merely legitimizes the exercise of political power but also serves to ensure its orderly, civil transfer so that there may be continuity of government among men. Two general types of politics might be distinguished here for our purposes: the political system which is constitutional by the above definition and the one which is not. For while all regimes and governments exercise political power by nature and customarily seek to perpetuate themselves, some are essentially formless or even limitless both in the power they seek, and the objects over which they would employ it.

A nonconstitutional political system could be defined as one in which the actual distribution of power differs radically from the proclaimed or specified distribution of power which a written document, basic law, or customary usage may speak of. (Of course a written constitution may actually serve to obscure the essential order of things.) But in the modern totalitarian state, a nonconstitutional order may have a certain formlessness of a political system which defies conceptualization because it contemptuously rejects restraints and forms. This quality has frequently been pointed out in Nazi totalitarianism. Not only did Hitler smash the Weimar Constitution without even bothering to replace it with another "paper document" (something which the Bolsheviks, with their greater reverence for the state, did do quickly after seizing power); the very absence of any constitutional specification of rights and obligations, of distribution of powers, of any enduring perquisites and duties, or functional authorities meant that both in theory and fact the whole system was subject to change at any time. Thus, in a sense, there was no limit to power, since no form persisted. The concentration camps of Auschwitz, Belsen, and elsewhere are memorials to this condition. Attempts by Nazi constitutional apologists to legitimate the regime by proclaiming a direct, unmediated relationship between the Führer and the German volk, whose will he supposedly expressed (just as Castro embodies the Cuban "will"), veiled a fatal constitutional flaw in the system which Hitler's defeat in war only further obscured: the system specified no legitimate procedure by which the charismatic leader's power and authority could be transmitted in orderly constitutional fashion to a successor. H. R. Trevor-Roper describes the Nazi political system as a court, but it was the court of a king, who, like the donkey, had neither pride of parentage nor hope of progeny.

A Juridical Contradiction

A curious juridical contradiction inheres in many Western constitutions, including that of the United States. While the domestic power of the state over its subjects is typically limited by the constitution (which specifies checks upon executive and lawmaking power) still, the power of the state in the larger context of the society of nations is invariably regarded as sovereign and plenary. Seen from the outside, the state is a juridical entity in international law, to be held accountable for its actions in the international society. It is also an entity which, charged with promoting the security and general welfare of its people, should act in a unitary fashion, even though its domestic, constitutional attributes of power may be juridically separated and divided. John Locke, one of the foremost political theorists of the English-speaking world, sought to account for this necessary contradiction between the plenary sovereign power of the state and its executive in foreign affairs and the limited power of the constitutional state and executive power *within* the society. According to Locke:

> There is . . . [a] power in every commonwealth which one may call natural, because it is that which answers to the power every man naturally had before he entered into society. For though in a commonwealth, the members of it are distinct persons, still in reference to one another, and as such are governed by the laws of the society; yet

in reference to the rest of mankind, they make one body, which is, as every member of it before was, still in the state of nature with the rest of mankind, hence it is, that the controversies that happen between any man of the society with those that are out of it, are managed by the public; and an injury done to a member of their body engages the whole in the reparation of it. So that, under this consideration, the whole community is one body in the state of Nature, in respect of all other states or persons out of its community.

This therefore contains the power of war and peace, leagues and alliances, and all the transactions, with all persons and communities without the commonwealth; and may be called federative, if any one pleases. So the thing be understood, I am indifferent as to the name.

These two powers, executive and federative, though they be really distinct in themselves, yet one comprehending the execution of the municipal laws of the society within itself, upon all that are parts of it; the other the management of the security and interest of the public without, with all those that it may receive benefit or damage from; yet they are always almost united. And though this federative power in the well or ill management of it be of great moment to the commonwealth, yet it is much less capable to be directed by antecedent, standing, positive laws than the executive; and so must necessarily be left to the prudence and wisdom of those whose hands it is in, to be managed for the public good. For the laws that concern subjects one amongst another, being to direct their actions, may well enough precede them. But what is to be done in reference to foreigners, depending much upon . . . them, to be managed by the best of their skill, for the advantage of the commonwealth.[3]

Thus the domestic, executive authority of a constitutional commonwealth might be required to obey and to execute the laws made by a legislature and to be subject to many constitutional restraints on his power. But in the realm of foreign affairs these legislative-executive functions became, in a sense, fused. To act swiftly, purposively in world politics to protect or advance the interests of the society itself, the federative power was thus liberated in significant ways from constitutional constraints. Locke sees an executive as a Janus: one head looking inward upon the constitutional society, benign and limited in its power and authority; the other, looking outward to the world, authoritative and powerful, speaking, acting, and legislating with the authority of

---

3. John Locke, *Of Civil Government* (New York: Dutton, 1924), pp. 191–192.

the whole society itself. This Lockean distinction between federative and executive power is embodied in the United States Constitution.

The American Constitution and the Problem of Power

The Constitution and foreign policy can hardly be discussed without first pointing to the remarkable durability and adaptiveness of the American political framework. The Constitution is more than 170 years old, older than the written constitution of any other modern state. The unwritten British constitution may, of course, be regarded as a far older, though a far more elusive judicial order—an amalgam of customs, uses, prerogatives, statutes, and Acts of Parliament. In contrast, the constitution of the French Fifth Republic today is only four years old; and France, since 1789, has had more than seven written constitutions. But equally remarkable, the constitutional entities which the Constitution originally prescribed have persisted vigorously despite the massive changes in American society and culture since the eighteenth century. Most Americans take it for granted as the judicial framework within which political life occurs. All major movements in American political life, even those which have stood on the radical fringes of the political spectrum, have accepted the Constitution as a desirable, enduring framework of political power and discourse. Since the eighteenth century there has been no significant American political movement which explicitly rejected it or posed any constitutional alternative.

By way of contrast, in nineteenth- and twentieth-century European politics, all of the major continental states have had profound disputes about what constitutional order was preferable. Thus, Professor Duverger, in writing of French politics, has made the interesting distinction between the "parties of order" and the "parties of movement," between those for whom a constitutional order was a paramount concern and those for whom political transformation was deemed superior to order itself. No such distinction could possibly be made in American politics, unless the American Communist party were included in the argument. But even American Communists have recently been pressed into doctrinal conformity by denying un-Constitutional purposes! The great debate during the New Deal in the 1930s about the legitimacy of Roosevelt's social reforms was between those who denied their constitutionality and those who defended it. The great debate between North and South, preceding and during the Civil War, was couched also in constitutional terms, both sides stressing the correctness of their own constitutional interpretations. What was originally designed for thirteen states and four million people, chiefly farmers and craftsmen, now applies to a nation of fifty states and 180,000,000 people, living in a highly complex industrial society. Perhaps in no earlier period in history has a constitutional system ever shown such vigorous adaptability and staying power.

The Constitution has been a framework within which a political dialogue about domestic and foreign policy has taken place, but it also has been a powerful agent to "legitimately" organize, diffuse, and separate political power and rights. During international crises, when alternative American courses of action have been subjects of domestic political debate, the meaning of the Constitution has invariably been reexplored, particularly, as we shall see, with respect of the extent of interrelationships and limits of federal, presidential, and congressional powers. The chief purpose of the Constitution was to "establish a more perfect Union," but an ancillary purpose was to subject political power and to distribute it among disparate functional elements of the American body politic. In the *Federalist* papers, Madison justified this latter purpose: "We must not shut our eyes to the nature of man. . . . All power in human hands is liable to be abused. No form of government can be a perfect guard against the abuse of power. The recommendation of the republican [form of government] is that the danger of abuse is less than in any other."

Skepticism about human nature and concern for human liberties and political order and prosperity thus established a continuing tension between the domestic constitutional order of a republican policy (with power distributed and separated) and the international needs of a sovereign state, which require a separate and more trenchant kind of authority. This tension has been enduring and necessary. As a consequence, the federative power necessary to the survival of a state has constantly endangered the organizational principles of a free society at all times.

Fear of possible abuse of centralized power runs like a thread through the history of American political thought. The dangers it poses to contemporary American freedoms were recently stressed by President Eisenhower in his Farewell Address to the American people in January 1961:

> In the councils of Government, we must guard against the acquisition of unwarranted influence, whether sought or unsought by the military-industrial complex. The potential for the disastrous rise of misplaced power exists and will persist.

We must never let the weight of this combination endanger our liberties or democratic processes. We should take nothing for granted. Only an alert and knowledgeable citizenry can compel the proper meshing of the high industrial and military machinery of defense with our peaceful methods and goals, so that security and liberty may prosper together.[4]

This remarkable caveat against possible abuses of military power obscured from public attention at the time a warning by Eisenhower against another possible threat to individual liberties from quite another source: "In holding scientific research and discovery in respect, we must also be alert to the equal and opposite danger that public policy could itself become the captive of a scientific-technological elite."[5]

This fear was anticipated by the framers of the Constitution. Constitutional power was spatially and functionally dispersed: spatially, between a federal government and the governments of individual states; functionally, between executive, legislative, and judicial branches of government. The first ten amendments to the Constitution specify civil rights enjoyed by citizens against both federal and state authority. Within the overarching federal government, power was given in classic, Montesquieu fashion, to the president, the Congress, and the Supreme Court. The Bill of Rights, added to the Constitution as its first major amendment, specifies restraints upon the exercise of power by the state. It denies to authority, to government as a whole, certain powers which could conceivably make it limitless in power over the public and over individuals. Certain specified human rights of thought, expression, and action were juxtaposed to political authority, and the state, in theory, should not erode them. Freedom of speech, due process, free assembly, a free press—these provisions of the first ten amendments made explicit certain implicit characteristics of constitutions in general, i.e., the limitations upon state power vis-à-vis the public. Thus the authority of the American Constitution came in part to consist of its own self-restraint and the restraints which it supposedly should instill in those who were to exercise legitimate authority in its name.

A tension developed between these doctrines of separation and limitation of powers and the exigencies of world politics. Domestic constitutionalism restrained power and established checks upon the modes

4. *New York Times,* January 18, 1961.
5. Ibid.

and objects of its employment. A concern for national political and military security could often recommend exactly the opposite. In foreign affairs, protection of national interests and extension of American power abroad often seemed to require secrecy, authority, and almost authoritarian power. In conflicts of interest, ideology, or purpose among sovereign state entities, any state which was enfeebled by internal constitutional arrangements might be unable to act decisively. Such a state could not long endure and would inevitably fall victim, perhaps to its own domestic political virtues. Not without good reason did Tocqueville, in the early nineteenth century, write that democracies such as the United States seemed institutionally deficient in the realm of foreign affairs, incapable of pursuing any fixed design and perpetually inhibited by domestic political processes and whimsical wills of the public. What in a domestic context was virtue was in an international context a vice. Democracy, incapable of the purposefulness of authoritarian states, could be destroyed (or transformed into authoritarian form) by engaging in the necessary acts in which it was by nature least skillful.

Logic, wisdom, and reason cannot dissipate insoluble political problems. The *realpolitik* tendency was toward sharp centralization of state power for foreign policy purposes. The constitutional tendency was to restore balance in politics and to assert the *separateness* of powers. During grave crises, the matter recurrently rose to the surface of American political discourse.

Some constitutional lawyers thought this tension originated in deficiencies of the Constitution as a written document. Professor E. L. Corwin has described the Constitution as a "standing invitation to struggle for the privilege of directing American foreign policy." But the essential difficulty was not only what the Constitution (as written document) said, but what it did not or could not say, and finally, what the particular problems were which the founding fathers[6] probably preferred to evade by silence. The Constitution clearly specified basic,

---

6. Eisenhower, during his benign reign, sometimes spoke of the Constitution and the Declaration of Independence as the "founding documents," an awkward yet intriguing remark which few Americans noted. It seemed to suggest that the "documents" had simply ordered the "founding fathers" to write them. The innocence of the remark reflects a widespread popular reverence, if not a mystique, which Americans have for these documents: if the Constitution did not exist, God would have had to invent it. On such strange, unfathomable premises do some stable constitutional orders persist.

organizational forms and principles of the domestic polity, but its prescriptions for foreign affairs powers were brief, insufficient, and ambiguous. The difficulty was unavoidable: how to preserve the theory of separation and limitation of powers yet at the same time construct effective agencies of power, and authority, in dealing with other states.

We should not detract too much from the Constitution. It confirmed the supremacy of federal agencies and authorities over individual states in the management of foreign affairs; it vested the supreme and exclusive powers of treaty making, and war making, and diplomacy in the federal government. Treaties were exclusively to be negotiated by the federal government. When ratified, they were to become the "supreme law of the land," thus, presumably, prevailing over both state laws and prior congressional legislation. States were enjoined from concluding treaties with other powers. Command over national armed forces was vested in the president as commander in chief. He could dispose of them as he saw fit. The power to declare a state of war was vested in the Congress, which itself was a creature of the federal government. By inference, so too did Congress come to possess the power to declare a state of war ended. The president, "by and with the advice and consent of the Senate," was empowered to negotiate and to conclude treaties. Finally, the president was empowered to "send and receive Ambassadors," a power subsequently interpreted to imply that he could also "not send," and "not receive," the essential power of recognition and non-recognition of foreign states.

Here ends the catalogue of "enumerated" powers over foreign affairs. Yet even when these scanty specifications were set alongside other constitutional provisions, potential institutional conflicts were obvious. Meager as the specifications were, they bore seeds of dissension. What was not said also proved ultimately more important than what was.

The enduring constitutional issue rested in a single problem. The United States was a sovereign state in a system of sovereign states. If such sovereign power were supreme, how much of it could constitutionally be reposed in a sovereign executive without endangering the limitations, checks, and balances upon which the constitutional system was grounded? Or, to put the question in another way: how much and what kinds of constitutional powers did the executive require to make possible the rational, purposeful, and powerful conduct of foreign affairs? A deep-felt suspicion of power in the American democratic tradition gave rise to another question: how could a democratic political order, reposing upon the "consent of the governed," be reconciled with intrinsic authoritarian necessities of foreign affairs?

The Problem of Inherent Power

An early constitutional question was whether, in fact, the authority and power to conduct foreign relations derived from the Constitution alone. Was the source of authority, as some suggested, possibly meta-constitutional? If so, then what possible restraints, other than political ones, could be imposed upon the exercise of powers derived from some law or authority beyond or above the Constitution itself?

The possibility was that both the power to conduct foreign relations and the supreme attribute of sovereignty itself arose because of the United States sovereignty in the society of nations. This attribute and authority was inherited from its former possessor, the British crown. Whether power had passed directly from the British crown to the federal authorities of the new Republic or whether it came indirectly to those authorities via the individual states themselves (which, in the Constitution, supposedly had bequeathed them to the federal government), was somewhat beside the point. All states in the society of nations had such plenary powers. James Wilson first asserted the theory during the Constitutional Convention of 1787: "When the United States declared their independence, they were bound to receive the Law of Nations in its modern state of purity and refinement."[7]

This notion of inherent power, arising from the fact that the United States of America was a sovereign entity at international law, was elaborated by later American statesmen and jurists. In the hands of statesmen and Supreme Court Justices, the doctrine grew. America's entrance as a sovereign entity under international law implied the existence of a single government with unified and adequate power. Ironically it was Justice Sutherland, one of the willful "old men" of the Court of the 1930s (whose narrow conceptions of presidential and federal power over domestic matters during the New Deal marked him as somewhat of a juridical troglodyte), who carried this meta-constitutional doctrine to its furthest extent. In the now-famous case of Curtiss-Wright in 1936 (a constitutional test of the extent of congressional and executive authority over foreign commerce), Justice Sutherland wrote:

7. Quoted in Edwin S. Corwin, *The Presidency: Office and Powers* (New York: New York University Press, 1957), p. 172.

> A political society cannot endure without a supreme will somewhere.
> Sovereignty is never held in suspense. When, therefore, the external
> sovereignty of Great Britain in respect of the colonies ceased, it
> immediately passed to the union.[8]

This possibility suggested extreme constitutional difficulties. It
suggested that sovereign executive authority in foreign affairs, juridically speaking, drew strength from traditional laws of the universe of
the society of nations. Yet in this universe of states at the time of the
founding of the Republic, the conception of state sovereignty was all
too tightly associated with Continental European conceptions of
Staatsraison and *Machtpolitik*. In the eighteenth-century society of
nations, the dynastic states derived legitimacy from the "grace of God,"
not the "will of the people"; in practice these states assumed that state
interests were fundamental and that their pursuit was the exclusive
task of the sovereign statesman or ruler. The national or dynastic interest could thus be established by the ruler himself, his ministers, and his
bureaucratic associates and translated into policy and action. Acts and
declarations of war, treaties, alliances, peace itself, and the military
and diplomatic maneuvering which all these involved were matters of
Grosse Politik. Normally they were shrouded from public view by the
majestic machinery of the state. They were subject to few constitutional restraints or limitations of the people and their elected representatives. The Continental European tradition thus stressed the
unitary and authoritarian character of sovereign power in foreign relations. The people and their elected representatives, if any, had no
legitimate role to play in the control and conduct of foreign policy. But
then, they had no significant role to play in domestic policy either. The
constitutional dilemma posed for the American Republic was, at the
time, unique.

In the famous pseudonymic debate concerning presidential foreign
policy powers in 1793 between Hamilton and Madison, Madison (reply-
ing as *Helvidius* to Hamilton's *Pacificus*) accused Hamilton of seeking
surreptitiously to invest the presidency with the prerogatives of the
British crown:

> . . . By whatever standard we try this doctrine, it must be condemned
> as no less vicious in theory than it would be dangerous in practice. It
> is countenanced neither by the writers on law; nor by the nature of the

---

8. 299 U.S. 304, 1936, pp. 316–17.

> powers themselves; nor by any general arrangements . . . to be found in the constitution.
>
> Whence then can the writer have borrowed it? There is but one answer to this question. The power of making treaties and the power of declaring war, are royal prerogatives in the British government, and are accordingly treated as executive prerogatives by British commentators. . . .[9]

The particular issue then at stake concerned the constitutional justification of the president's power to proclaim neutrality in the war between France and England.

This constitutional novelty arose not just from the intrinsic tension between the Constitution as written document and the prevailing laws of the society of nations but from a qualitative difference between the American constitutional order and the traditional political orders of Europe out of which the laws of nations themselves had arisen. The American experiment, as its founders readily acknowledged, was unique. Democracy was to come into play. Such fundamental attributes of democracy as participation in law making and popular consent to laws could not fail to flow over into the field of foreign affairs from the domestic realm wherein they were to play. Conversely, constitutional understandings pertaining to powers of the presidency and the federal government in foreign relations could not help but profoundly influence and affect both democracy and republican practice.

No matter what the Hamiltonians, including Sutherland, wrote, there still were severe juridical limitations on federal and presidential authority in foreign affairs which the Constitution made explicit. The society of nations to the contrary, Congress, not the president, had the constitutional power to declare a state of war. President and Senate were *jointly* empowered to use the treaty power for national purposes and objects, and in addition, the Constitution reserved certain powers and rights to the states and to the people. Could the president, perhaps, acting as the "federative power," or acting as commander in chief, or acting under the authority of the treaty-making power, then accomplish things which the Constitution otherwise forbade? The boundaries and frontiers of the individual states, for instance, could not be changed without the consent of the states concerned. Did this mean then that the presidency and the "sovereign" federal authority

---

9. Quoted in Corwin, *The Presidency*, p. 180.

by treaty could *not* do constitutionally what all other sovereigns, under the law of nations could: agree to international treaties and convention affecting internal conditions within them? If a treaty, as the Constitution itself so stated, were to be regarded as the "supreme law of the land," could such law perhaps legitimately do things which ordinary congressional law was constitutionally enjoined from doing? The Supreme Court case of *Missouri* v. *Holland* in 1920 posed the issue: could a congressional law implementing an Anglo-American conservation treaty vest in federal authorities regulatory powers within states for protection of game? Admittedly they had invaded a heretofore sacrosanct province of states' police powers which the Constitution until then protected. But the Court, through Holmes' decision, sustained the treaty, and revealed the possibility that:

> Acts of Congress are the supreme law of the land only when made in pursuance of the Constitution, while treaties are declared to be so when made under the authority of the United States. It is open to question whether the authority of the United States means more than the formal acts prescribed to make the convention. *We do not mean to imply that there are no qualifications to the treaty-making power; but they must be ascertained in a different way.* . . . It is not lightly to be assumed that, in matters requiring national action, "a power which must belong to and somewhere reside in every civilized government" is not to be found. . . . The treaty in question does not contravene any prohibitory words to be found in the Constitution. The only question is whether it is forbidden by some invisible radiation from the general terms of the Tenth Amendment. . . . Here a national interest of very nearly the first magnitude is involved. It can be protected only by national action in concert with that of another power. . . .[10]

Justice Frankfurter once referred to some lawyers' habit in argumentation of displaying a "parade of the horribles." By this he meant that any power or law can be made to appear intolerable if one dwells long enough upon its intrinsic possibility of abuse. A parade of horribles could also be assembled from the motley possibilities of constitutional abuse, stalemate, and paralysis, which this whole matter of constitutional authority raised. Holmes might well have been right: when a

---

10. 252 U.S. 1920, p. 416. Quoted in *The Constitution of the United States of America, Analysis and Interpretation* (Washington, D.C.: Government Printing Office, 1953), pp. 428–429. (Italics mine.)

national interest of the first magnitude was involved, the neat and tidy restraints of the Constitution seemed to give way to overriding necessity. But this did not eradicate the problem. It is always philosophically important to consider even constitutional problems in extremis.

As the Holmes decision points out, the exercise of the treaty power could conceivably be a constitutional battering-ram, possibly demolishing customary constitutional rights of states. But if, as *Missouri* v. *Holland* seemed to suggest, the treaty power was a theoretical skeleton key to doors which even Congress was constitutionally forbidden to unlock, it could do even more. It might (as right-wing Brickerites loudly proclaimed in the 1950s) threaten even individual liberties of American citizens. Treaties might erode guaranteed rights of the due process of law, among others.

It was not only the treaty power itself (and the attendant power which the presidency had long exercised in international relations, that of the executive agreement) which might do this. The executive agreement, a less pretentious but more prolific kind of international agreement than the treaty, is a creature of many forms, yet generally regarded as indispensable to the orderly conduct of foreign policy. One form of executive agreement is the international agreement between the U.S. government acting in executive capacity and some foreign state or international organization, binding upon the United States but not subjected to senatorial consent. There are three particular subspecies: those which, as drafted, require and obtain congressional legislative approval and implementation; those which are made like many American commercial agreements, upon the basis of prior statutory authorization of Congress; and those which, like the Yalta agreement of 1945, are subject neither to prior congressional "authorization," nor approval, nor subsequent consent. In practice as well as in theory, most really substantive international agreements entered into by the United States government are both negotiated and designated by the executive branch as treaties, but the executive has wide, theoretical latitude in deciding what to call them. A cynic would define an executive agreement as any agreement not called a treaty by the president. But even exaggerating the iniquities of the White House, which might be tempted to dodge the difficulties of a senatorial two-thirds by dressing an agreement in shabby clothing and slipping it in through the servants' entrance, there are good reasons why no administration would, except in dire straits, play such tricks. For one thing, senators are notoriously sensitive about prerogatives (including their treaty prerogative). For another, the act of senatorial approval of international agreements endows the latter with more majesty than mere enactment by the president or mere approval by Congress as a whole, as with ordinary legislation. Thus senatorial consent gives the substance of the act more authority by giving it greater repute in the international arena as well as in the minds of the American public. Brickerites and McCarthyites in the 1950s, who sought to curtail use of the executive agreement and the objects which treaties might properly deal with, ignored the administrative chaos which elimination of the executive agreement would bring about. They ignored, too, the real political restraints upon presidential power in international agreements which required no constitutional amendment to come into being. They were amply there already.

The exercise of any one right or power by any branch of the federal government in foreign affairs could conceivably work mischief. Senator Henry Cabot Lodge and his colleagues proved this in 1919 when they killed Wilson's League and the Paris Peace Treaty. Willful, shrewd assassins in the Senate could use their treaty power like a stiletto, to dispose of a hated chief executive, even if the ensuing cost to the nation as a whole might be considerable. Conversely, any tyrant might envy the great powers of the president as commander in chief. . . . Their proper constitutional use depended in large measure on the character and purposes of those who possessed them. If there were possibilities of conflict and abuse of power among governmental institutions and such potential abuses were obvious, then conflict must be anticipated by responsible men, constantly aware of the dangers of national paralysis and disunity entailed in sustained partisan struggle.

But no Constitution could avert what Madison once called the "dangers of factionalism." Factionalism was inherent in political life. While its force and passion sometimes arose from petty interests and ambitions, factionalism might also be a reflection of deep substantive issues at stake in political choices. Political debates over institutional powers, the Constitution, and foreign policy, paralleled profound debates about national policy and purpose. Even honest political men could employ the Constitution to block some political purpose from its realization. What was unique in the American experience was that these passionate debates about constitutionalism and foreign affairs were arguments about what the existing Constitution was, what it said, or what it implied. The argument was not about *alternative* constitutional orders. The American Constitution was thus both the regulating mechanism of debate and conflict and a framework of dialogue which reasonable men welcomed.

Conflict over substantive foreign policy issues might thus appear as conflict or deadlock among constitutional entities. When this was so, substantive conflicts could masquerade as constitutional ones. When the will of one entity (the presidency, for instance) threatened to carry the day on behalf of a particular policy or purpose, one way to inhibit the purpose was to challenge the constitutionality of that entity's behavior. Another was simply to exercise, to the fullest possible extent, the constitutional powers of other entities to block action. The frequency with which constitutional issues arose in periods of foreign policy crisis suggests that the debate over forms was one aspect of a debate over essentially nonconstitutional matters (whether, as in 1793, to intervene against England in the Anglo-French war; whether, as in 1940, to intervene on behalf of England in the war between Hitler and the West). This suggested that the Constitution itself might at any time become the hapless prey of the institutions which it prescribed, or even worse, that the institutions themselves were prey of larger forces in the nation which the Constitution neither prescribed nor foresaw.

But before we turn to particular instances where this difficulty of interpretation was most dramatically revealed, we might point out a mitigating fact: the unity of the framework around which dispute took place—the Constitution itself. At no time in American history, not even during the Civil War, was the constitutional framework itself attacked. In foreign affairs, particularly when great issues of the moment are at stake, the vigor of the constitutional debate over powers as such cannot be attributed to the substantive policy debate alone. Much more, it points to the desperate need in crisis to legitimize action and to link action and purpose to enduring forms and public values. The matter of constitutional legitimacy itself is no idle thing. Without it, power itself could easily dissolve in the hands of those who wield it. Worse still, the power might be wholly severed from constitutional authority and become despotic. Thus, in a sense, we can say that such recurrent constitutional debates were, in fact *supremely* constitutional.

Questions

1. "The federative power necessary to the survival of a state has constantly endangered the organizational principles of a free society at

all times." Discuss this statement in terms of the problem of dissent in the United States.

2. Is it true that democracy is not the best form of government to deal with foreign affairs? As a decision maker, would you recommend subordinating domestic norms to international needs? As a politician running for Congress, could you, with impunity, advocate such subordination? Do you know any politicians who have done so? If so, what was their rationale?

3. Do you think the realities of world politics have made the separation of powers in the Constitution unworkable?

4. There are some interesting problems surrounding the issue of the powers of the several states versus the treaty-making power of the United States. Discuss them.

5. You are playing tennis; it is game, set, and match point. You meet the next volley from your opponent, but a sudden downdraft causes the ball to slam into the net and you lose the match. President Wilson may very well have felt similar frustrations after the Senate refused to accept the League of Nations. Must there be such obstacles to the treaty-making power? Is it useful to have internal structures, such as Senate approval of treaties, if most other nations have survived without such a structure? Is it practical? Should the president have unrestricted treaty power?

Chapter Two

The Executive and Foreign Policy

The foreign policy process in the United States is centered in the office, if not in the person, of the president. President Truman stated the case bluntly, albeit accurately: "I make foreign policy," he told a group of visitors. The simplicity of this truth obscures the complex nature of the American presidency, a fact often ignored by Americans, but readily apparent to foreign observers. One of the most perceptive of the latter, Dennis Brogan, writing in *Encounter* soon after the assassination of President Kennedy, described the American president as a monarch—an elected monarch to be sure, but a monarch nonetheless. He was not, of course, thinking of the British crown as it exists today, shorn of all but its ceremonial powers, but of English monarchs in the sixteenth and seventeenth centuries who held, controlled, and exercised a full measure of political power.

This analogy between the roles of an American president and of a monarch who rules as well as reigns is persuasive precisely because the president is, just as British monarchs once were, simultaneously head of state, chief executive, and leader of a political party. He thus combines, in his person, powers that English kings have long since lost and that many republics have been reluctant to entrust to their elected leaders. Seen through the lens of British constitutional development, it is little wonder that Brogan should find it meaningful to characterize the American president as a monarch with the implication of regal power and authority.

The comparison of the president with a monarch emphasizes the truth that the president is at the center of the foreign policy process. He is there precisely because he combines in his person three roles that are normally separated in constitutional governments: head of state, chief executive, and head of a political party. Since the founding of the Republic, these three presidential roles have had within them the seeds of a vast expansion of presidential power, which within the last half century has become fully manifest. This increase of presidential power has taken place simultaneously with the entrance of the United States into the world arena as a world power, a role totally unknown to it during the period of its splendid nineteenth-century isolationism. The emergence of the United States as a great power was accompanied by the assumption that the president should play the dominant role in the making of foreign policy. It was generally believed and vigorously argued that the very nature of the foreign policy process required executive leadership. Furthermore, the American constitutional system with its separation of powers between the legislative and the executive bodies was believed to impose unnecessary restraints on presidential leadership. One of the foremost students of the presidential role in foreign affairs, Professor Warren, concluded that "probably nowhere in the world is executive leadership more hemmed in, more limited by political considerations, more vulnerable to pressure from within and from without than in the United States."

During the two decades following World War II, the belief in presidential dominance in foreign affairs became part of the "conventional wisdom" that was accepted uncritically by the majority of the experts, congressmen, and the public. The series of crises that followed on the heels of World War II—the disintegration of the economic conditions of Europe that called forth the Marshall Plan, the struggle in Korea, the rise of the Soviet Union as a nuclear military power, and the Cuban missile crisis—all seemed to hold one lesson: the need for the president to have as free a hand as possible in the conduct and formulation of American foreign policy.

The view that the president might utilize any or all of the resources including the armed forces available to the nation in pursuit of foreign policy goals was called into question by the Vietnamese conflict, which after 1965 became a more and more explosive political issue in the United States. The opponents of the Vietnam War began to reexamine the past in search of precedents that could be used to restrict presidential initiative in foreign affairs, particularly the president's right to use the armed forces of the United States without a declaration of war. The bombing of Cambodia intensified the search for limits on presidential leadership. The Vietnamese conflict became then a crucial turning point in American history, not only because it challenged the assumptions on which the substance of foreign policy had been based since 1945, but also because it raised important issues about the way in which foreign policy was made and particularly about the wisdom of giving the president complete latitude in the conduct of American foreign policy.

Simultaneously with the rise of presidential power over foreign policy, a search was begun for a more effective way to organize the federal government to formulate and carry out American foreign policy. The result of that search was the National Security Act of 1947, which was enacted primarily to assure the integration of diplomatic and military policy into a single unified national security policy. This act created the National Security Council (NSC), which was originally expected to be a decision-making body and not just a group of presidential advisers, but the nature of the presidential system of government dictated that no president would be willing to surrender his constitutional power over foreign affairs. Thus, it is fair to say that our experience with the NSC shows that under our constitutional system it is impossible for Congress to provide by statute for advisory machinery that the president must use; that presidents have only a limited power to institutionalize decision-making processes and to impose those institutional forms upon their successors; and that the NSC did not provide an independent forum where the president could test the advice that his principal military and diplomatic advisers gave him. This last point must be stressed, for the NSC was composed of the very advisers who saw the president in their roles as heads of departments, and therefore it is apparent that organizational reform has not been a significant factor in assuring the coordination of military and diplomatic elements of national security policy. This coordination occurred not because the NSC was created but because in a world of nuclear weapons there was no way that the military and diplomatic elements could be separated.

Although the framers of the National Security Act of 1947 expected that the National Security Council would be a major contribution to the formulation of American foreign policy, they did not foresee that the office of the presidential assistant for national security affairs, which was also created by the act, would become the powerful office that it did under McGeorge Bundy, Walt Rostow, and Henry Kissinger. The crucial turning point in the emergence of that office came in the Kennedy administration when the presidential assistant, who prior to that time had served as an administrative officer, became simultaneously a presidential adviser. He was, after that point, not only responsible for seeing that the system worked properly, but also a major participant in the system itself. The result was that the presidential assistant for national security affairs became closer and closer to the president until, in the Nixon-Kissinger relationship, the secretary of state was all but eclipsed. One must note that the last chapter in this development of the presidential machinery for making foreign policy has not yet been written, because the appointment of Henry Kissinger as secretary of state while retaining the office of presidential assistant for national security affairs created a precedent out of which may grow an office that will finally be able to coordinate all aspects of American foreign policy more completely than either the secretary of state or the presidential assistant for national security affairs was able to do in the past.

Simultaneously with the emergence of the questions about the nature of presidential power and the search for limits on presidential initiative in foreign affairs, analysts began to turn their attention to the foreign policy process to ask searching questions about the way in which the process itself operated. One of the concepts that has come under ever closer scrutiny is the image of the president as a decision maker. Drawing on the vast amount of research into organizational behavior that has been done by sociologists and others, Graham Allison in his book, *The Essence of Decision,* has challenged the image of the president as a rational decision maker. He suggests that it is more realistic to view the foreign policy process as the outcomes that are produced by bureaucracies as they carry out their assigned tasks. Foreign policy thus becomes the result of standard operating procedures that not only determine how organizations will respond to policy issues but also define the issues that they are capable of solving. An alternate view, which Allison also proposes, is what he calls the bureaucratic politics model in which foreign policy is seen as the result of the bargaining process that occurs between the important players in the foreign policy game. These views are determined by the positions the players occupy in or outside of government, and by the way they perceive the president as well as the issues involved. The president is therefore seen in this context not so much as a rational decision maker as a validator of the winning side in the bureaucratic politics struggle.

While this latter perception of the foreign policy process frequently results in down-playing the role of the president in the foreign policy process and perhaps underestimating his influence, it does provide valuable insights into the complexity of the process. Students of the foreign policy process who wish to gain a full understanding of that process must be aware of its dynamic nature. They must look beyond the textbook image of the completely rational foreign policy maker who chooses between foreign policy options by measuring them against some predetermined value such as the national interest, and they must see that foreign policy results from the hauling and pulling of a variety of political and bureaucratic interests.

The readings in this section have been chosen to underline the most recent research into the foreign policy making. The reading by Richard Neustadt contrasts the clerkship and the leadership possibilities inherent in the constitutional political powers of the president. He makes the telling point that relying solely on the formal powers of the office necessarily limits the leadership potential of the president. Rather, the combination of these powers with the power to persuade confers the mantle of leadership upon the president. The selection from an important article by Alexander George emphasizes and describes conditions under which the president is likely to make bad policy decisions. The long selection of I. M. Destler describes the way in which the presidents have used the machinery created by the National Security Act of 1947 to assist them in making foreign policy. And finally, the discussion of presidential wars by Francis Wormuth is a search for limitations on the president's right to commit the United States to military action without making a declaration of war.

Sources of Presidential Power*

Richard E. Neustadt

Richard E. Neustadt was named special consultant to President Kennedy in 1961. Before that year, he had been consultant to the United States Senate Subcommittee on National Policy Machinery and special assistant to the White House (1950–53) under President Truman. He is Dean of the John F. Kennedy School of Government at Harvard University, and has taught at Columbia and Oxford universities.

In the United States we like to "rate" a president. We measure him as "weak" or "strong" and call what we are measuring his "leadership." We do not wait until a man is dead; we rate him from the moment he takes office. We are quite right to do so. His office has become the focal point of politics and policy in our political system. Our commen-

Presidential Power, Richard E. Neustadt. Copyright © 1960 by Wiley. Reprinted by permission of John Wiley & Sons, Inc.

tators and our politicians make a specialty of taking the man's measurements. The rest of us join in when we feel "government" impinging on our private lives. In the third quarter of the twentieth century millions of us have that feeling often.

. . . Although we all make judgments about presidential leadership, we often base our judgments upon images of office that are far removed from the reality. We also use those images when we tell one another whom to choose as president. But it is risky to appraise a man in office or to choose a man for office on false premises about the nature of his job. When the job is the presidency of the United States the risk becomes excessive. . . .

We deal here with the president himself and with his influence on governmental action. In institutional terms the presidency now includes 2,000 men and women. The president is only one of them. But *his* performance scarcely can be measured without focusing on *him*. In terms of party, or of country, or the West, so-called, his leadership involves far more than governmental action. But the sharpening of spirit and of values and of purposes is not done in a vacuum. Although governmental action may not be the whole of leadership, all else is nurtured by it and gains meaning from it. Yet if we treat the presidency as the president, we cannot measure him as though he were the government. Not action as an outcome but his impact on the outcome is the measure of the man. His strength or weakness, then, turns on his personal capacity to influence the conduct of the men who make up government. His influence becomes the mark of leadership. To rate a president according to these rules, one looks into the man's own capabilities as seeker and as wielder of effective influence upon the other men involved in governing the country. . . .

. . . .

There are two ways to study "presidential power." One way is to focus on the tactics, so to speak, of influencing certain men in given situations: how to get a bill through Congress, how to settle strikes, how to quiet cabinet feuds, or how to stop a Suez. The other way is to step back from tactics on those "givens" and to deal with influence in more strategic terms: what is its nature and what are its sources? What can *this* man accomplish to improve the prospect that he will have influence when he wants it? Strategically, the question is not how he masters Congress in a peculiar instance, but what he does to boost his chance for mastery in any instance, looking toward tomorrow from today. The second of these two ways has been chosen for this book.

To look into the strategy of presidential influence one must decide at whom to look. Power problems vary with the scope and scale of government, the state of politics, the progress of technology, the pace of world relationships. Power in the nineteen-sixties cannot be acquired or employed on the same terms as those befitting Calvin Coolidge, or Theodore Roosevelt, or Grover Cleveland, or James K. Polk. But there is a real likelihood that in the next decade a president will have to reach for influence and use it under much the same conditions we have known since the Second World War. If so, the men whose problems shed most light on White House prospects are Dwight David Eisenhower and Harry S Truman. . . . To do so is to see the shadow of another, Franklin D. Roosevelt. They worked amidst the remnants of his voter coalition, and they filled an office that his practice had enlarged.

. . . .

In form all presidents are leaders, nowadays. In fact this guarantees no more than that they will be clerks. Everybody now expects the man inside the White House to do something about everything. Laws and customs now reflect acceptance of him as the Great Initiator, an acceptance quite as widespread at the Capitol as at his end of Pennsylvania Avenue. But such acceptance does not signify that all the rest of government is at his feet. It merely signifies that other men have found it practically impossible to do *their* jobs without assurance of initiatives from him. Service for themselves, not power for the president, has brought them to accept his leadership in form. They find his actions useful in their business. The transformation of his routine obligations testifies to their dependence on an active White House. A president, these days, is an invaluable clerk. His services are in demand all over Washington. His influence, however, is a very different matter. Laws and customs tell us little about leadership in fact.

Why have our presidents been honored with this clerkship? The answer is that no one else's services suffice. Our Constitution, our traditions, and our politics provide no better source for the initiatives a president can take. Executive officials need decisions, and political protection, and a referee for fights. Where are these to come from but the White House? Congressmen need an agenda from outside, something with high status to respond to or react against. What provides it better than the program of the president? Party politicians need a record to defend in the next national campaign. How can it be made except by "their" administration? Private persons with a public axe to grind may need a helping hand or they may need a grinding stone. In either case who gives more satisfaction than a president? And outside the United States, in every country where our policies and postures influence home politics, there will be people needing just the "right" thing said and done or just the "wrong" thing stopped *in Washington*. What symbolizes Washington more nearly than the White House?

A modern president is bound to face demands for aid and service from five more or less distinguishable sources: from executive officialdom, from Congress, from his partisans, from citizens at large, and from abroad. The presidency's clerkship is expressive of these pressures. In effect they are constituency pressures and each president has five sets of constituents. The five are not distinguished by their membership; membership is obviously an overlapping matter. And taken one by one they do not match the man's electorate; one of them, indeed, is outside his electorate. They are distinguished, rather, by their different claims upon him. Initiatives are what they want, for five distinctive reasons. Since government and politics have offered no alternative, our laws and customs turn those wants into his obligations.

Why, then, is the president not guaranteed an influence commensurate with services performed? Constituent relations are relations of dependence. Everyone with any share in governing this country will belong to one (or two, or three) of his "constituencies." Since everyone depends on him why is he not assured of everyone's support? The answer is that no one else sits where he sits, or sees quite as he sees; no one else feels the full weight of his obligations. Those obligations are a tribute to his unique place in our political system. But just because it is unique they fall on him alone. *The same conditions that promote his leadership in form preclude a guarantee of leadership in fact.* No man or group at either end of Pennsylvania Avenue shares his peculiar status in our government and politics. That is why his services are in demand. By the same token, though, the obligations of all other men are different from his own. His cabinet officers have departmental duties and constituents. His legislative leaders head *congressional* parties, one in either House. His national party organization stands apart from his official family. His political allies in the states need not face Washington, or one another. The private groups that seek him out are not compelled to govern. And friends abroad are not compelled to run in our elections. Lacking his position and prerogatives, these men cannot regard his obligations as their own. They have their jobs to do; none is the same as his. As they perceive their duty they may find it right to follow him, in fact, or they may not. Whether they will feel obliged *on their responsibility* to do what he wants done remains an open question. . . .

In the early summer of 1952, before the heat of the campaign, President Truman used to contemplate the problems of the general-become-president should Eisenhower win the forthcoming election. "He'll sit here," Truman would remark (tapping his desk for emphasis), "and he'll say, 'Do this! Do that!' *And nothing will happen.* Poor Ike— it won't be a bit like the Army. He'll find it very frustrating."

Eisenhower evidently found it so. "In the face of the continuing dissidence and disunity, the president sometimes simply exploded with exasperation," wrote Robert Donovan in comment on the early months of Eisenhower's first term. "What was the use, he demanded to know, of his trying to lead the Republican party. . . ." And this reaction was not limited to early months alone, or to his party only. "The president still feels," an Eisenhower aide remarked to me in 1958, "that when he's decided something, that *ought* to be the end of it . . . and when it bounces back undone or done wrong, he tends to react with shocked surprise."

Truman knew whereof he spoke. With "resignation" in the place of "shocked surprise" the aide's description would have fitted Truman. The former senator may have been less shocked than the former general, but he was no less subjected to that painful and repetitive experience: "Do this, do that, and nothing will happen." Long before he came to talk of Eisenhower he had put his own experience in other words: "I sit here all day trying to persuade people to do the things they ought to have sense enough to do without my persuading them. . . . That's all the powers of the president amount to."

In these words of a president, spoken on the job, one finds the essence of the problem now before us: "powers" are no guarantee of power; clerkship is no guarantee of leadership. The limits on command suggest the structure of our government. The constitutional convention of 1787 is supposed to have created a government of "separated powers." It did nothing of the sort. Rather, it created a government of separated institutions *sharing* powers. "I am part of the legislative process," Eisenhower often said in 1959 as a reminder of his veto. Congress, the dispenser of authority and funds, is no less part of the administrative process. Federalism adds another set of separated institutions. The Bill of Rights adds others. Many public purposes can only be achieved by voluntary acts of private institutions; the press, for one, in Douglass Cater's phrase, is a "fourth branch of government." And with the coming of alliances abroad, the separate institutions of a London, or a Bonn, share in the making of American public policy.

What the Constitution separates our political parties do not combine. The parties are themselves composed of separated organizations sharing public authority. The authority consists of nominating powers. Our national parties are confederations of state and local party institutions, with a headquarters that represents the White House, more or less, if the party has a president in office. These confederacies manage presidential nominations. All other public offices depend upon electorates confined within the states. All other nominations are controlled within the states. The president and congressmen who bear one party's label are divided by dependence upon different sets of voters. The differences are sharpest at the stage of nomination. The White House has too small a share in nominating congressmen, and Congress has too little weight in nominating presidents for party to erase their constitutional separation. Party links are stronger than are frequently supposed, but nominating processes assure the separation.

The separateness of institutions and the sharing of authority prescribe the terms on which a president persuades. When one man shares authority with another, but does not gain or lose his job upon the other's whim, his willingness to act upon the urging of the other turns on whether he conceives the action right for him. The essence of a president's persuasive task is to convince such men that what the White House wants of them is what they ought to do for their sake and on their authority.

Persuasive power, thus defined, amounts to more than charm or reasoned argument. These have their uses for a president, but these are not the whole of his resources. For the men he would induce to do what he wants done on their own responsibility will need or fear some acts by him on his responsibility. If they share his authority, he has some share in theirs. Presidential "powers" may be inconclusive when a president commands, but always remain relevant as he persuades. The status and authority inherent in his office reinforce his logic and his charm.

Status adds something to persuasiveness; authority adds still more. . . . In Walter Bagehot's charming phrase, "no man can *argue*

on his knees." Although there is no kneeling in this country, few men
—and exceedingly few cabinet officers—are immune to the impulse
to say "yes" to the president of the United States. It grows harder to
say "no" when they are seated in his oval office at the White House,
or in his study on the second floor, where almost tangibly he partakes
of the aura of his physical surroundings. . . .

A president's authority and status give him great advantages in
dealing with the men he would persuade. Each "power" is a vantage
point for him in the degree that other men have use for his authority.
From the veto to appointments, from publicity to budgeting, and so
down a long list, the White House now controls the most encompassing
array of vantage points in the American political system. With hardly
an exception, the men who share in governing this country are aware
that at some time, in some degree, the doing of *their* jobs, the furthering
of *their* ambitions, may depend upon the president of the United States.
Their need for presidential action, or their fear of it, is bound to be
recurrent if not actually continuous. Their need or fear is his advantage.

A president's advantages are greater than mere listing of his
"powers" might suggest. The men with whom he deals must deal with
him until the last day of his term. Because they have continuing relationships with him, his future, while it lasts, supports his present influence.
Even though there is no need or fear of him today, what he could do
tomorrow may supply today's advantage. Continuing relationships
may convert any "power," any aspect of his status, into vantage points
in almost any case. When he induces other men to do what he wants
done, a president can trade on their dependence now *and* later.

The president's advantages are checked by the advantages of
others. Continuing relationships will pull in both directions. These
are relationships of mutual dependence. A president depends upon
the men he would persuade; he has to reckon with his need or fear of
them. They too will possess status, or authority, or both, else they
would be of little use to him. Their vantage points confront his own;
their power tempers his.

• • • • • • • • • • • • • • • •

The power to persuade is the power to bargain. Status and authority yield bargaining advantages. But in a government of "separated
institutions sharing powers," they yield them to all sides. With the
array of vantage points at his disposal, a president may be far more
persuasive than his logic or his charm could make him. But outcomes

are not guaranteed by his advantages. There remain the counter pressures those whom he would influence can bring to bear on him from vantage points at their disposal. Command has limited utility; persuasion becomes give-and-take. It is well that the White House holds the vantage points it does. In such a business any president may need them all—and more.

This view of power as akin to bargaining is one we commonly accept in the sphere of congressional relations. Every textbook states and every legislative session demonstrates that save in times like the extraordinary Hundred Days of 1933—times virtually ruled out by definition at mid-century—a president will often be unable to obtain congressional action on his terms or even to halt action he opposes. The reverse is equally accepted: Congress often is frustrated by the president. Their formal powers are so intertwined that neither will accomplish very much, for very long, without the acquiescence of the other. By the same token, though, what one demands the other can resist. The stage is set for that great game, much like collective bargaining, in which each seeks to profit from the other's needs and fears. It is a game played catch-as-catch-can, case by case. And everybody knows the game, observers and participants alike.

·   ·   ·   ·   ·   ·   ·   ·   ·   ·   ·   ·   ·   ·   ·   ·   ·   ·   ·

Influence becomes still more a matter of give-and-take when presidents attempt to deal with allied governments. A classic illustration is the long unhappy wrangle over Suez policy in 1956. In dealing with the British and the French before their military intervention, Eisenhower had his share of bargaining advantages but no effective power of command. His allies had their share of counter pressures, and they finally tried the most extreme of all: action despite him. His pressure then was instrumental in reversing them. But had the British government been on safe ground *at home*, Eisenhower's wishes might have made as little difference after intervention as before. Behind the decorum of diplomacy—which was not very decorous in the Suez affair—relationships among allies are not unlike relationships among state delegations at a national convention. Power is persuasion and persuasion becomes bargaining. The concept is familiar to everyone who watches foreign policy.

In only one sphere is the concept unfamiliar: the sphere of executive relations. Perhaps because of civics textbooks and teaching in our schools, Americans instinctively resist the view that power in this sphere resembles power in all others. Even Washington reporters,

White House aides, and congressmen are not immune to the illusion that administrative agencies comprise a single structure, "the" executive branch, where presidential word is law, or ought to be. Yet we have seen . . . that when a president seeks something from executive officials his persuasiveness is subject to the same sort of limitations as in the case of congressmen, or governors, or national committeemen, or private citizens, or foreign governments. There are no generic differences, no differences in kind and only sometimes in degree. . . .

Like our governmental structure as a whole, the executive establishment consists of separated institutions sharing powers. The president heads one of these; cabinet officers, agency administrators, and military commanders head others. Below the departmental level, virtually independent bureau chiefs head many more. Under mid-century conditions, federal operations spill across dividing lines on organization charts; almost every policy entangles many agencies; almost every program calls for interagency collaboration. Everything somehow involves the president. But operating agencies owe their existence least of all to one another—and only in some part to him. Each has a separate statutory base; each has its statutes to administer; each deals with a different set of subcommittees at the Capitol. Each has its own peculiar set of clients, friends, and enemies outside the formal government. Each has a different set of specialized careerists inside its own bailiwick. Our Constitution gives the president the "take-care" clause and the appointive power. Our statutes give him central budgeting and a degree of personnel control. All agency administrators are responsible to him. But they *also* are responsible to Congress, to their clients, to their staffs, and to themselves. In short, they have five masters. Only after all of those do they owe any loyalty to each other.

"The members of the cabinet," Charles G. Dawes used to remark, "are a president's natural enemies." Dawes had been Harding's budget director, Coolidge's vice-president, and Hoover's ambassador to London; he also had been General Pershing's chief assistant for supply in the First World War. The words are highly colored, but Dawes knew whereof he spoke. The men who have to serve so many masters cannot help but be somewhat the "enemy" of any one of them. By the same token, any master wanting service is in some degree the "enemy" of such a servant. A president is likely to want loyal support but not to relish trouble on his doorstep. Yet the more his cabinet members cleave to him, the more they may need help from him in fending off the wrath of rival masters. Help, though, is synonymous with trouble. Many a cabinet officer, with loyalty ill-rewarded by his lights and help withheld, has come to view the White House as innately hostile to department heads. Dawes's dictum can be turned around.

A senior presidential aide remarked to me in Eisenhower's time: "If some of these cabinet members would just take time out to stop and ask themselves 'What would I want if I were president?' they wouldn't give him all the trouble he's been having." But even if they asked themselves the question, such officials often could not act upon the answer. Their personal attachment to the president is all too often overwhelmed by duty to their other masters.

. . . .

Granting that persuasion has no guarantee attached, how can a president reduce the risks of failing to persuade? How can he maximize his prospects for effectiveness by minimizing chances that his power will elude him? The Marshall Plan suggests an answer: he guards his power prospects in the course of making choices. Marshall himself, and Forrestal, and Harriman, and others of the sort held office on the president's appointment. Vandenberg had vast symbolic value partly because F.D.R. and Truman had done everything they could, since 1944, to build him up. The Treasury Department and the Budget Bureau—which together might have jeopardized the plans these others made—were headed by officials whose prestige depended wholly on their jobs. What Truman needed for those "givers" he received, in part, because of his past choice of men and measures. What they received in turn were actions taken or withheld by him, himself. The things they needed from him mostly involved his own conduct where his current choices ruled. The president's own actions in the past had cleared the way for current bargaining. His actions in the present were his trading stock. Behind each action lay a personal choice, and these together comprised *his* control over the give-and-take that gained him what he wanted. In the degree that Truman, personally, affected the advantages he drew from his relationships with other men in government, *his power was protected by his choices*.

By "choice" I mean no more than what is commonly referred to as "decision": a president's own act of doing or not doing. Decision is so often indecisive and indecision is so frequently conclusive, that choice becomes the preferable term. "Choice" has its share of undesired connotations. In common usage it implies a black-and-white alternative. Presidential choices are rarely of that character. It also may imply that the alternatives are set before the choice maker by someone else. A president is often left to figure out his options for himself. Neither implication holds in any of the references to "choice" throughout this [selection].

If presidents could count upon past choices to enhance their current influence, as Truman's choice of men had done for him, persuasion would pose fewer difficulties than it does. But presidents can count on no such thing. Depending on the circumstances, prior choices can be as embarrassing as they were helpful in the instance of the Marshall Plan. The incidents described [earlier] . . . include some sharp examples of embarrassment. Among others: Eisenhower's influence with Faubus was diminished by his earlier statements to the press and by his unconditional agreement to converse in friendly style at Newport. Truman's hold upon MacArthur was weakened by his deference toward him in the past.

Assuming that past choices have protected influence, not harmed it, present choices still may be inadequate. If presidents could count on their own conduct to provide them *enough* bargaining advantages, as Truman's conduct did where Vandenberg and Marshall were concerned, effective bargaining might be much easier to manage than it often is. In the steel crisis, for instance, Truman's own persuasiveness with companies and union, both, was burdened by the conduct of an independent Wage Board and of government attorneys in the courts, to say nothing of Wilson, Arnall, Sawyer, and the like. Yet in practice, if not theory, many of *their* crucial choices never were the president's to make. Decisions that are legally in others' hands, or delegated past recall, have an unhappy way of proving just the trading stock most needed when the White House wants to trade. One reason why Truman was consistently more influential in the instance of the Marshall Plan than in the steel case, or the MacArthur case, is that the Marshall Plan directly involved Congress. In congressional relations there are some things that no one but the president can do. His chance to choose is higher when a message must be sent, or a nomination submitted, or a bill signed into law, than when the sphere of action is confined to the executive, where all decisive tasks may have been delegated past recall.

But adequate or not, a president's own choices are the only means *in his own hands* of guarding his own prospects for effective influence. He can draw power from continuing relationships in the degree that he can capitalize upon the needs of others for the presidency's status and authority. He helps himself to do so, though, by nothing save ability

to recognize the pre-conditions and the chance advantages and to proceed accordingly in the course of the choice making that comes his way.
To ask how he can guard prospective influence is thus to raise a further
question: what helps him guard his power stakes in his own acts of
choice?

Questions

1. Richard E. Neustadt says that presidential power is the power to persuade. Comment and give instances when this has occurred.
2. The president creates his own role as leader but he cannot avoid being
   clerk at the same time. What factors determine his role as clerk, and
   is it possible for him to reject this role? If so, at what cost?
3. Many people on both sides of the political fence have charged that
   President Eisenhower was less effective than he could have been
   because he was too nonpolitical. Whether this is true or not, it is obvious that many people expect partisanship from the president. Can a
   president remain aloof from partisan politics in his foreign policy
   decisions? Should he?

Bureaucratic Strategy and Presidential Choices*

Alexander George

Alexander George is professor of political science at Stanford University and is past president of the International Studies Association. He is
the author, with Juliette George, of *Woodrow Wilson and Colonel House*
(New York: The John Day Company, 1966).

Nine possible malfunctions of the policy-making process have been
identified. These malfunctions can occur whether the policy-making
system is modeled on one prescriptive theory or another, or even when
it lacks any well-defined modus operandi. "Preventive interventions"
by the custodian-manager of the policy-making system, therefore, are
required to deal with emerging malfunctions of this kind of a system.

*Reprinted from *The American Political Science Review*, September 1972, pp. 769–781,
 by permission of the publisher.

such as the present Nixon-Kissinger National Security Council as well as in a system of multiple advocacy. The nine malfunctions thus far identified are listed separately, although they may be interrelated in a particular historical case such as the Bay of Pigs.

1. *When the president and his advisers agree too readily on the nature of the problem facing them and on a response to it.*

Paradoxically, while it is often difficult for an executive to achieve sufficient consensus within the decision-making group on behalf of a wise policy without diluting its ingredients, to achieve consensus too quickly and too easily is also likely to degrade the quality of the decision. An experienced executive will regard a readily achieved consensus within the policy-making group as a reason for *postponing* rather than taking action. Alfred P. Sloan, former chairman of General Motors, is reported to have said at a meeting of one of his top policy committees:

> Gentlemen, I take it we are all in complete agreement on the decision here. . . . Then I propose we postpone further discussion of this matter until our next meeting to give ourselves time to develop disagreement and perhaps gain some understanding of what the decision is all about.

Deferring action is more difficult, of course, when the situation seems to require it or when the chief executive himself is disposed to take immediate action. In certain types of international crisis a kind of spontaneous consensus may quickly emerge among members of the policy-making group on behalf of the "need for action" to prevent damage to U.S. interests—a consensus which may prevent adequate consideration of the magnitude of the expected damage and how much cost and risk one should undertake in order to prevent it. It is particularly when everyone seems to agree on the need for some action to prevent expected damage that the most dangerous mistakes in the calculation of risk and utility are likely to be committed. The typical error under these circumstances is a gross underestimation of the costs and risks of the action taken. Conversely, *disagreement* within the decision-making group on the proper objectives, the proper means, the kinds and level of risk present in the situation, is more likely to improve the analytical process and the advice that precedes the final choice of policy the president makes.

This type of malfunction of the policy-making process can be vividly seen in the events leading to President Johnson's decision to send U.S. military forces into the Dominican Republic in the spring of 1965. As Philip Geyelin (a reporter for the *Wall Street Journal* at the time) put it in his excellent review of this crisis: "If Lyndon Johnson had acted much differently than he did in the early, decisive days of the Dominican crisis, he would have had to invent his own alternatives and ignore the counsel of his principal advisers. . . . " There is nothing in the available record to indicate that the Special Assistant for National Security Affairs, McGeorge Bundy attempted to preserve the president's options in this case.

Indeed, all available accounts of the crisis indicate that consensus on the need for U.S. military intervention developed quickly, easily, and without challenge within the decision-making group. Geyelin notes that Johnson "was remarkably at the mercy of the advice and activities of his subordinates on the scene—who speedily concluded that a rebel victory carried with it the risk of an eventual communist regime. This definition of the situation emerged almost at once in the field and was immediately accepted without question in Washington because everyone's perception of the crisis in the Dominican Republic was shaped by a strong policy predisposition that antedated the crisis. This was the belief that the Dominican Republic should not be allowed to become another Cuba. A distorted, exaggerated perception of the threat in Santo Domingo emerged when available information on the rebels was viewed through the prism of the "Cuban syndrome." No attempt was made until well after the United States was committed to intervention to check the U.S. Embassy's definition of the situation and of the policies most appropriate for meeting it.

But decisional premises of this kind do not always paralyze the ability of decision makers to make a reasoned calculation of the utility of intervention. Vigorous multiple advocacy within the Eisenhower administration in the Indochina crisis of 1954 helped to control the effect that ideologically reinforced decisional premises were allowed to have on the final decision. The policy-making process worked much better in the 1954 crisis than in the Dominican crisis. In the spring of 1954 the Eisenhower administration was suddenly faced with having to decide whether to intervene in Indochina. Intervention on behalf of the beleaguered French forces at Dienbienphu was strongly favored by Chairman of the Joint Chiefs of Staff Admiral Radford and apparently also by Secretary of State John Foster Dulles, and it was supported by other members of the administration. The psychological momentum for intervention took hold quickly. Advocates of intervention within the administration attempted to develop a wider consensus by emphasizing the expected damage to U.S. interests if Indochina were lost. These efforts were crowned by Eisenhower's invocation of the "row-of-dominoes" analogy.

The president was ambivalent about intervention, however, and had second thoughts about its costs and risks. He was unwilling in any case to act without consultation with congressional leaders. Some observers feel that the president deliberately slowed up the momentum for intervention within his administration and indirectly strengthened the hand of those advisers who were opposed to it by directing Dulles and Radford to take their case to congressional leaders. In Congress it soon became apparent that the air strike advocated by Radford to relieve pressure on French forces at Dienbienphu did not have the backing of all members of the JCS. Moreover, it seemed highly probable that the air strike would fail to achieve its purpose and become instead the first step on an exceedingly slippery slope that could lead the United States into another major ground war on the Asian mainland.

As a result, a wholesome sobriety was introduced into policy calculations. The momentum for intervention was slowed down and eventually reversed, even *despite* the fact that the cold war image of communism and a perception of threatened damage to U.S. interests were widely shared by policy makers and congressional leaders. Given the strength of this decisional premise and the initial definition of the situation, intervention could be avoided only because the *process* of policy making worked in such a way as to force decision makers to face up to the sobering question of the costs and risks of intervention. With the memory of the recent Korean War still fresh, some policy advisers insisted that the administration face up realistically to the level of effort that would be required to win in Indochina before taking the first step.

General Matthew Ridgway, then chief of staff of the army, played the leading role in this respect. At the first indication that advocates of intervention were considering the use of air and naval forces in Indochina, Ridgway labeled the proposed action "ominous." He warned that a commitment of air and naval forces would inevitably lead to use of ground forces. It was "incredible" to him that Washington should forget the bitter lesson of Korea so soon. Determined that the administration should face up to the costs of intervention, Ridgway quickly dispatched a group of army specialists under General Gavin to Indochina to determine at first hand the difficulties and requirements of a U.S. intervention. On the basis of this study, Ridgway reported to Eisenhower that the cost in men and money of successful intervention in Indochina would be greater than in Korea.

While it is difficult to ascertain the precise impact of Ridgway's advice on Eisenhower's decision, Ridgway himself believed that his report, brought before the National Security Council, played a considerable, perhaps decisive role in persuading the administration against intervention.

2. *When advisers and advocates take different positions and debate them before the president but their disagreements do not cover the full range of relevant hypotheses and alternative options.*

There is no assurance that on any given policy problem each of the relevant options will find an advocate within the policy-making group. Some options may fail to get serious consideration because it is felt that the president has excluded them or would reject them, or because they are not in the interest of any agency and no one wants to pay the bureaucratic cost of asking the president to adopt them. Thus, the option of not giving direct military assistance to South Korea when it was attacked by North Korea in June 1950 was never really considered by Truman's advisers, in part because the president had made it clear at the outset that the United States would not allow the attack to succeed. (A fuller account of this case is given below.)

Other options may fail to get consideration because policy-making officials serving under the chief executive are disinterested in them. There are various ways of reducing the executive's freedom of action even while seemingly providing him with multiple options. As Robert H. Johnson notes: "One of the chief problems with attempts to lay out major policy alternatives is the strong temptation to load the dice. A typical procedure is to set up a straw man alternative on either side of a middle course of action which quickly becomes the logical choice over the more 'extremist' options." Whether or not this type of malfunction took place during the planning of the Vietnam escalation is uncertain. Possibly it did occur to some extent and for a combination of the two reasons indicated. President Johnson's advisers may have felt that he had already excluded the withdrawal option and, besides, many of them were against withdrawal and were not motivated therefore to provide a well-considered, persuasive version of this option. The Pentagon Papers give the impression that most of the principals in the policy-making system had for some time come to feel that the United States could not withdraw from South Vietnam but would have to engage in some degree of military escalation, if necessary. During 1964 President Johnson himself was largely preoccupied with the forthcoming presidential election and with domestic policy; he did not participate actively in the extensive planning activities that went on during the first ten months of the year. While Johnson apparently indicated that he wanted all options considered, there is no indication that the option of U.S. withdrawal became the subject of major study before the election.

After Johnson's election in early November, his advisers succeeded in drawing him into serious discussion of the situation in Vietnam and consideration of additional U.S. assistance. The internal political situation in Vietnam was now so unstable, however, that in the policy review of late November it was agreed that no increase in assistance by the United States was to be contemplated until a more stable government and political climate emerged in Saigon. Given little attention in the deliberations of American policy makers was the sound (and not unfamiliar) proposition that the United States should not lend military and economic aid to regimes which lack the will to help themselves, the capacity to govern, and sufficient popular support. In the important policy review of late November which, as it turned out, afforded the last opportunity for calm, unhurried deliberation on the situation, there was little disposition to consider whether or not the United States should now face up to the necessity or desirability of withdrawing from South Vietnam on the grounds that the prerequisites for continued, let alone increased, U.S. involvement were totally lacking.

Noteworthy is the attenuated, ineffectual role of a heretofore important decisional premise. Ever since the Chinese civil war, American policy towards Asian countries subjected to the threat of communism had been constrained by the proposition that the United States should not become inextricably committed via economic and military aid to regimes which lacked the will to help themselves, the capacity to govern, and sufficient popular support. The logical implication of this decisional premise, given the internal political situation in South Vietnam, was that further involvement should be avoided and that, instead, preparations be made for a face-saving exit from South Vietnam. No one in the top-level group of policy makers, attempted to make a case for this option, however; and neither the president nor, apparently, his special assistant for national security affairs, McGeorge

Bundy, requested that this option, too, should be given careful consideration.

To be sure, elements of this point of view were clearly articulated in November by George Ball, undersecretary of state, who emerged as the focal point of a weak "dovish" coalition at lower levels in the policy-making system. But Ball's viewpoint was late in emerging and indeed it never entered the mainstream of policy planning on Vietnam. He was "heard" in November, but not "listened to" in part because he was regarded as a "Europe man" who did not share the top policy makers' premise that Southeast Asia had become strategically important to the United States. The importance of this new decisional premise cannot be minimized. The Pentagon Papers indicate that it had gradually emerged in the preceding years and had come to be accepted by most, if not all, of the principal policy makers. Certainly it succeeded in neutralizing the earlier decisional premise to which we have referred, evidently without the conflict between the two premises being clearly identified and subjected to a major policy debate. In the end, this new decisional premise restricted the scope of multiple advocacy; it dominated policy planning and the decision for escalation.

3. *When there is no advocate for an unpopular policy option.*

In the Vietnam escalation case we have just reviewed there was, at least, an advocate for the unpopular option of withdrawal in the person of George Ball. In the Korean case, by contrast, the policy-making group assembled by President Truman on the first day of the North Korean invasion quickly developed a consensus on the need for action to prevent the expected damage to U.S. interests. While members of the group were by no means uniformly enthusiastic at the prospect of U.S. military involvement, the consensus to act was at no time subjected to challenge. This was not because of any previously agreed-upon contingency plans which had only to be put into operation. Indeed no such plans existed. The North Korean attack came as an unexpected shock. It was this rude reality, not the availability of pre-existing plans, that helped produce consensus within the policy-making group. Critical in this respect, too, was the president's initial definition of the situation as one in which too much was at stake to permit the United States to acquiesce. The ingredients for bureaucratic politics and multiple advocacy were present in the long-standing policy and personal conflicts between Secretary of State Dean

Acheson and Secretary of Defense Louis Johnson, but their expression was muted by the president's attitude, the atmosphere of crisis, and Acheson's reversal of administration policy on Formosa in the direction that Johnson had advocated.

As a result, the military pressures of the quickly deteriorating situation in Korea determined the choices made. The participants in these decisions believed they had few alternatives to the actions they took. Indeed, in one sense of the word no "decision" about intervention was made; that is, the president and his advisers did not at any point sit down to weigh the political and military factors for and against direct U.S. military intervention. There was no search for options, for alternative ways of limiting the expected damage to U.S. national interests. Decisional premises and assumptions that shaped the definition of the situation in such a way as to make U.S. intervention a necessary response—such as the belief that the aggression in Korea was like Nazi aggression in the thirties and, if unopposed, would also encourage communists to undertake new aggressions—were not singled out for any kind of critical examination.

During the first few days of the conflict, at a time when U.S. assistance was still limited to air and naval support, several of Truman's advisers expressed their reluctance to see U.S. ground troops committed to combat in South Korea. Indeed, the president's own hesitation in the matter was also noticeable. There was some discussion of the disadvantages and hazards of this course of action before the need for U.S. combat troops became evident. Once the deteriorating battlefield situation made it imperative, however, no adviser questioned the introduction of American combat forces except George Kennan, who hesitated on the grounds that it would increase the likelihood of Soviet counterintervention. Neither Kennan nor military advisers who were unenthusiastic about being drawn into a land war on the Asian continent were given any encouragement to play a more vigorous advocate's role in the policy discussions.

Nor was an effort made to calculate soberly the level of military effort that would be required and the full costs of attempting to defend South Korea. General MacArthur's recommendation of introducing U.S. ground combat forces was accepted unquestionably on the basis of his quickly improvised estimate that two divisions under his command from Japan would enable "early offensive action" to save South Korea. The seemingly high value that policy makers attached to the objective of resisting the North Korean aggression was not tested by calculating realistically what the price tag might turn out to be.

Later in the Korean War, when the decision was being made to send U.S. and U.N. forces across the 38th parallel to pursue the defeated North Korean army and to unite the two parts of the country, the threat of Chinese Communist intervention became a factor. Important officials in Truman's circle of policy advisers (Secretary of the Air Force Thomas Finletter and Chief of Naval Operations Admiral Forrest Sherman, as well as George Kennan) were disturbed by the risks of Chinese intervention. Once again, however, Truman's structuring and management of the policy-making process discouraged those with reservations about the drift of policy from playing the role of more articulate devil's advocates. Indeed, such a role was not generally congenial to President Truman. He preferred to structure the policy-forming process in terms of functional expertise. Each agency head was expected to provide his considered view of that aspect of the problem for which he was responsible. Within each department second- and third-level officials contributed their advice to their department head, and deviations from this hierarchically organized flow of advice within each department were discouraged. Kennan's advice on this and other occasions when it differed from Acheson's was overshadowed and controlled by the advice of the secretary of state.

4. *When advisers to the president thrash out their own disagreements over policy without the president's knowledge and confront him with a unanimous recommendation.*

In this variant of the workings of bureaucratic politics the other actors in effect "gang up" on the chief executive and try to sell him the policy they have worked out among themselves. Clark Clifford gives a succinct, authoritative account of this practice in an interview describing his role as assistant to President Truman on domestic affairs:

> The idea was that the six or eight of us would try to come to an understanding among ourselves on what directions we would like the president to take on any given issue. And then, quietly and unobtrusively, each in his own way, we would try to steer the president in that direction. . . . Well, it was two forces fighting for the mind of the president, that's really what it was. It was completely unpublicized, and I don't think Mr. Truman ever realized it was going on. . . .

In this case, as Clifford's account makes clear, two coalitions of advisers were competing for influence over policy. A more dangerous situation arises when all major advisers on a policy issue reach an agreement among themselves before going to the executive. This type of malfunction of the process almost occurred in the late autumn of 1964 when President Johnson was confronted with a solid line-up of advisers recommending that he proceed with the Multilateral Force for NATO. The M.L.F. was a strategic force to be composed of surface ships manned by mixed crews drawn from a number of NATO countries. For several years a small but strong group of M.L.F. partisans within the administration had pushed this idea as a way of knitting the alliance together. An opportunity for final U.S. approval of the plan and its implementation arose in connection with Prime Minister Harold Wilson's visit to Washington for discussions with the president. The advocates of the M.L.F. within the administration succeeded in coordinating with all of the president's chief advisers a position paper that would finally have committed the United States firmly to the M.L.F. Hence, on the eve of his critical meeting with the British prime minister, Johnson "was confronted with a spirited, consecrated, nearly united bureaucracy. . . ."

Now, it is extremely difficult for a president to act contrary to the unanimous advice of all his national security advisers. It is well to regard this variant of the bureaucratic politics process as a possible malfunction, for its occurrence threatens to deprive the chief executive of an adequate evaluation of available options. The president does not benefit adequately from multiple advocacy when the actors thrash out or compromise their differences *privately* and confront him with a unified recommendation. It is for this reason one of the conditions for effective multiple advocacy stressed earlier is presidential-level participation in or, at least, sensitivity to the day-to-day workings of the bureaucratic political aspects of policy making. Since the chief executive himself cannot be expected to participate directly in this process on every occasion or even to monitor it closely, clearly this participation becomes a critical task for his personal assistants. It is only through alter egos who clearly understand the president's responsibilities and needs in this respect that the chief executive can monitor the workings of the policy-forming system and intervene as necessary to correct malfunctions of process before they have an adverse effect on his policy choices.

As a matter of fact, this critical task was performed ably by one of the president's alter egos in the M.L.F. case just reviewed. Geyelin states that the position of McGeorge Bundy, special assistant for national security affairs, as "guardian of options and protector of the president was perhaps never more effectively displayed than in the episode of the M.L.F. Bundy had sensed trouble building up earlier in the year. With the M.L.F. partisans in full cry, the president's position was uncertain. . . ." Sensing the development of the type of malfunction we have been discussing, Bundy initiated a strategy of preventive intervention to restore some semblance of multiple advocacy to the system. He quietly called upon Richard Neustadt, a part-time consultant to the White House, to make an independent appraisal, for the president's benefit, of the M.L.F. issue in Europe as well as in Washington. Armed with this and other information which Bundy assembled, the president entered the final briefing conferences with his foreign policy advisers prepared to challenge the decisional premises, information, and recommendation of their position paper on the M.L.F. "In the course of the protracted conferences in preparation for the Wilson visit," Geyelin reports, "Johnson assailed the men around him, questioning their competence as well as their counsel. . . ."

In emphasizing the importance of Bundy's intervention in this case, we do not ignore that other factors also worked against Johnson's adherence to the M.L.F. There was by no means a clear consensus on its behalf, let alone enthusiasm, within NATO: and senior members of Congress as well as many officials in the executive branch were not enthusiastic supporters of the M.L.F. What Bundy's timely intervention accomplished was to bring these factors into greater prominence for the president's benefit.

5. *When advisers agree privately among themselves that the president should face up to a difficult decision, but no one is willing to alert him to the need for doing so.*

In direct contrast to the malfunction just discussed, in which his advisers privately agree upon a policy which they then attempt to get the president to adopt, this malfunction refers to the unusual and dangerous situation in which a private consensus on the need for presidential action emerges among his advisers but is not communicated to the president. This highlights once again the critical importance of presidential-level participation and sensitivity to policy-making discussions within the system.

In the M.L.F. case, we have seen, monitoring of these discussions by the special assistant for national security affairs alerted the president in time. But in a different crisis under Truman in November 1950, failure to alert the president resulted in a classic example of this kind of breakdown in the advisory system. By early November, large

numbers of Chinese Communist forces had already intervened in the
Korean War and had subjected U.S. and South Korean forces to sharp
tactical combat; but they had not yet launched an all-out offensive
against U.S. and U.N. forces. Nonetheless, Truman's chief civilian
and military advisers in Washington were acutely concerned over the
risks associated with the maldeployment of MacArthur's forces in
North Korea in the presence of large numbers of Chinese Communist
forces. The president's advisers seemingly agreed among themselves
that MacArthur's directives should be changed in order to reduce the
vulnerability of his forces, but this consensus was not translated into
action. According to Richard Neustadt's account, each adviser had his
own reasons for not taking the problem to Truman. And each adviser
interpreted his official role quite narrowly in order to relieve himself
of the obligation to take the initiative.

"No one went to Truman," Neustadt writes, "because everyone
thought someone else should go." He continues:

> The military chiefs deferred to State; let Acheson, as guardian of
> "policy," ask Truman to reverse MacArthur. But Acheson, already
> under fire from the Capitol, was treading warily between the Pen-
> tagon and that inveterate idealist about generals, Harry Truman.
> In immediate terms the risk was "military"; if it justified reversing
> the commander in the field, then the joint chiefs must make the
> judgment and tell Truman. So Acheson is said to have insisted,
> understandably enough, and there the matter rested.

As for Secretary of Defense George Marshall, who had preceded
Acheson at State and had himself been army chief of staff when Bradley
(now chairman of the joint chiefs of staff) was subordinate commander,
he had "leaned over backwards" since returning to the government
as secretary of defense shortly before these events took place, so as

> not to meddle with the work of his successors in *their* jobs. He had
> also leaned over backwards not to revive the old Army feud between
> him and MacArthur. What Acheson and Bradley were not ready to
> initiate, Marshall evidently felt he could not take upon himself. . . .
> The president, meanwhile, had little thought of over-riding, on his
> own, the tactical decisions of a qualified commander.

This was a sorry example, indeed, of narrow bureaucratic role
playing at the highest advisory level. One can only speculate what
Truman's response would have been had his advisers shared their

concern with him and recommended that MacArthur's directives be changed. If Truman had acted promptly, there would have been time to pull back MacArthur's forces before the Chinese launched their major offensive on November 28th. The catastrophe that followed might have been avoided altogether or greatly reduced.

6. *When the president, faced with an important problem to decide, is dependent upon a single channel of information.*

A seldom-noted aspect of Khrushchev's behavior during the Cuban missile crisis was that he quickly established multiple channels for securing information on Kennedy's intentions. Too much was at stake for the Soviet government for it to wait passively for Washington to provide deliberate or inadvertent signals regarding the president's intentions. Instead, the Soviet government initiated attempts of its own through several channels to secure such information—for example at the U.N.; through the Soviet ambassador's conversations with Robert Kennedy and other members of the administration; through the special contacts that Alexander Fomin, the top intelligence specialist in the Soviet Embassy in Washington, established with John Scali, an American journalist known to have high-level contacts in the State Department.

Faced with the need to make important decisions momentarily, the Soviet premier grasped the value of redundancy in information coverage of critical aspects of his opponent's behavior. In striking contrast, U.S. leaders have allowed themselves in several crises to remain dependent on a single channel of information about critical aspects of the situation. Among the many malfunctions of the policy-making process evident in planning the Bay of Pigs in 1961 was the fact that Kennedy and his advisers, including the JCS, depended on CIA's estimates of Castro's military and political strength. Both were miscalculated and underestimated by CIA. It was incorrectly estimated that there was a substantial anti-Castro underground, which would lead to an uprising when the invasion by Cuban exiles took place. It was erroneously believed that Castro's air force was weak and vulnerable and that he did not have the air power to defeat the invading force. CIA argued that the invasion should not be delayed since Cuba would soon receive modern air power from the Soviets. As a matter of fact Castro had already received these modern aircraft.

Although the single channel of information on these and other inputs to policy planning was controlled by CIA, where the chief advocates and planners of the invasion resided, Kennedy's suspicions were not aroused. There was ample time to set up independent channels of information and intelligence evaluation, but the president and his alter egos did not move in this direction. Rather they allowed CIA to maintain unchallenged its position as dominant advocate, a position which rested partly on its exclusive custodianship of critical information and intelligence inputs.

The Bay of Pigs disaster made the White House reluctant to rely on established procedures existing in other departments and agencies for the selection and analysis of information. Shortly thereafter a "situation room" was set up in the White House basement adjoining the offices of the NSC staff. Teletype machines were installed to receive all important messages from military, diplomatic, and intelligence centers around the world simultaneously with their arrival at the State Department, the Department of Defense, and CIA. While the purpose of the "situation room" was ostensibly to improve the president's ability to manage crises and to stay on top of fast-breaking events, by equalizing the White House's access to critical information, it also improved its ability to deal with other actors in the bureaucratic politics system. Thereby the position of the special assistant for national security affairs was appreciably strengthened. "Immediate access to routine cables made it possible for Bundy and his staff to deal with the bureaucracy on an informed basis."

Timely access to *available* information, however, does not in itself assure that multiple channels will exist when they are most needed. The type of malfunction we have been discussing occurred again in the Dominican intervention of April 1965. For its picture of developments in the complex internal political situation in the Dominican Republic, Washington was dependent on a single channel of information—this time the U.S. Embassy in Santo Domingo. There was no independent source of information on these events. Accordingly, had Johnson (or any of his advisers) wished to act differently in this crisis, as Geyelin puts it, "he would have had to discount the overwhelming weight of intelligence he received from the scene. . . ."

Washington's dependence on a single channel of intelligence cannot be explained on the ground that the crisis developed too swiftly to initiate additional channels. Warning was available that the internal political conflict in the Dominican Republic might get out of hand. But neither the president nor his special assistant for national security affairs, "the guardian of presidential options," utilized the available warning to establish quickly the necessary additional independent sources of information on what was going on in the Dominican Republic.

7. *When the key assumptions and premises of a plan have been evaluated only by the advocates of that option.*

A striking example of this type of malfunction occurred in the Bay of Pigs case. Because Kennedy persistently entertained grave doubts about the CIA invasion plan and, moreover, did *not* regard Castro as a direct threat to the United States, it is puzzling that the key premises of the CIA plan were not subjected to thoroughgoing scrutiny. As Irving Janis emphasizes in his forthcoming study, *Victims of Groupthink*, the answer lies partly in the considerable respect and prestige enjoyed in the new administration by CIA Chief Allen Dulles and Richard Bissell, both carry-overs from the Eisenhower administration, and partly also in Kennedy's wish to have them join his team.

Kennedy's reservations about the invasion plan were never translated into an effective search for an alternative. Instead, a number of partial constraints were imposed on the plan to make it more acceptable to the president. Questions that the president and other policy makers raised from time to time were answered only by those who were preparing the plan and supporting it. As Irving Janis notes, the president let these meetings degenerate into question-and-answer periods. When an occasional skeptic, like Senator Fulbright, who was invited by the president to attend one of the policy meetings, raised questions about the plan, Kennedy was satisfied to allow the CIA representatives to respond. In the last analysis, the key assumptions and premises of the invasion plan were not subjected to thorough independent analysis because the president allowed the CIA to dominate and weaken the multiple advocacy system. The JCS, it is true, was asked to evaluate the CIA plan, but there was no disposition on the part of Kennedy or his leading advisers to ensure that the JCS was sufficiently motivated to give it a properly critical scrutiny, or to look closely at the qualified endorsement the JCS came up with.

In providing consistently reassuring answers, the CIA representatives were not necessarily engaged in conscious deception, though wishful thinking may have been at work in their assessment of uncertainties. This reassurance is not surprising if we keep in mind that the CIA leaders firmly believed that action against Castro was necessary. They had created and trained a Cuban exile force to carry out the invasion; the preparations had already achieved a certain bureaucratic momentum by the time the new president established himself in office and turned some of his attention to reviewing the plan.

8. *When the president asks advisers for their opnions on a pre-ferred course of action but does not request a qualified group to examine more carefully the negative judgment offered by one or more advisers.*

It is by no means certain, we have seen, that multiple advocacy will come into play on any given policy issue or function effectively to illuminate all sides of the issue. We have noted the danger that may arise when no actor in the system is willing to speak up for an un-popular option or to oppose the group's preferred course of action. A different kind of malfunction occurs when advisers who give counsel that runs against the grain suffer from inadequate resources for advocacy in the competitive marketplace of bureaucratic politics. Maldistribution among the actors of informational and analytical resources, of formal status, of informal prestige and reputation, or access to presidential confidence, and so on, can severely weaken the actual workings of multiple advocacy and give lopsided advantages to some actors within the bureaucratic politics system.

As a result, the president may "hear" the negative opinion of an adviser but not really "listen." Or he may be satisfied all too easily with the seemingly impressive rebuttal of a more powerful and prestigious advocate. This type of malfunction of the policy process was evident in the deliberations leading up to the Bay of Pigs fiasco. On various occa-sions the CIA plan to invade Cuba was strongly opposed by individual advisers—Chester Bowles, Arthur Schlesinger, Senator Fulbright. All accounts of Kennedy's management of the policy-making process in this case make clear that far from seeking opportunities to encourage vigorous multiple advocacy, he was reluctant to see it develop and hoped to satisfy his own doubts about the plan by procedures which did not so directly challenge its advocates and supporters.

Following the president's cue, neither did McGeorge Bundy, his alter ego for national security affairs in the White House, nor Robert Kennedy, nor Secretary of State Rusk, attempt to initiate or encourage an independent evaluation of the plan. When Hilsman suggested that his office do so, Rusk refused on the grounds of secrecy. And at one point, Arthur Schlesinger, who had written two memos opposing the plan, was taken aside by Robert Kennedy and told to "lay-off." Those who opposed the invasion were "heard" but given no encouragement to develop the case against it or to form themselves into a group that would look into the issues more thoroughly.

What this case shows, therefore, is that the advice of policy dissidents which remains the mere opinion of the individuals concerned will not suffice to check the momentum of a dominant policy faction that is attempting to control the president's decision. In the Bay of Pigs case the futility of the dissidents' efforts cannot be explained on the grounds that the president enthusiastically supported the policy option in question. In fact, he disagreed with the major premise on which the CIA plan was based—namely, that Castro constituted a threat to vital U.S. interests—and had various reservations about the plan itself. Rather the explanation must be sought in part, as Kennedy recognized later, in his failure to manage the policy-shaping process more effectively.

It is less certain whether this type of malfunction also occurred in the policy discussions that led to the increase in the number of U.S. military advisers in South Vietnam in late 1961. Doubts and hesitations over this course of action were shared by important policy advisers as well as by President Kennedy himself. The Pentagon Papers disclose that at one point in the policy debate Secretary of State Rusk himself warned the president that to send 8,000 additional military advisers to Vietnam would mean that the United States would be irretrievably committed. On another occasion Under Secretary of State George Ball argued against more military assistance to Saigon because he feared it might lead eventually to a deployment of as many as 300,000 troops.

It must also be noted that advisers who favored additional escalation at this time did not disguise their belief that this decision was linked to the more fundamental question of whether the United States should now make a commitment to preserve South Vietnam, and that additional escalation might well be required later on. Nevertheless, despite these efforts of advisers on both sides of the issue to structure the president's choice in a clear-cut fashion, Kennedy approved some of the recommendations for additional U.S. assistance without clarifying the fundamental question of the extent of the U.S. commitment.

Although the president was aware that the real problem in South Vietnam was Diem's lack of political strength, he felt he had to do something to bolster the resistance of the Saigon regime for global cold war reasons, to protect his attempt to neutralize Laos, and perhaps as a gesture to propitiate hawks in his administration. Kennedy did not feel himself obliged to make a clear-cut decision; he very definitely preferred to equivocate and buy time. He did not share fully the urgency of the doubts and hesitations expressed by some of his advisers, and was not receptive to their warnings that sending additional military advisers would harden the U.S. commitment. As a result, the option of the U.S. withdrawal did not attract the kind of vigorous policy advocacy for which some sentiment existed within the advisory group. The lesser possibility of working toward a neutral South Vietnam was advanced by Chester Bowles. Although this position was vigorously debated, and although the president did not reject it out of hand, he regarded it at best as a fall-back position in case the South Vietnamese proved unable to cope.

Indeed, despite much sentiment to the contrary within the administration, it now began to view the deteriorating situation in South Vietnam as a military problem requiring military measures. This decisional premise was rejected by important State Department advisers, who held the crisis in South Vietnam was a political one and deplored the tendency to rely on increased military assistance. They lacked, however, a strong bureaucratic power base from which to press their advice particularly as Secretary of State Rusk, overcoming his earlier hesitation, began increasing to support prosecution of the war by military means.

9. *When the president is impressed by the concensus among his advisers on behalf of a particular policy but fails to ascertain how firm the consensus is, how it was achieved, and whether it is justified.*

We spoke earlier of a malfunction (number 4) similar to this one in some respects, in which the other participants in bureaucratic politics thrash out their disagreements on a policy issue privately, without the president's knowledge, and then confront him with a unanimous recommendation. But the chief executive may also be the victim of what Irving Janis calls an "illusory" consensus among his advisers that reflects a rather different working of the policy-forming system. Thus, at the important April 4, 1961, meeting it appeared to President Kennedy that there was no longer any opposition to the Bay of Pigs plan. Evidently he did not realize that the way in which the policy-forming process had been managed had discouraged the emergence of opposition. As Schlesinger recalled it, "Our meetings were taking place in a curious atmosphere of assumed consensus." And, as Sorensen puts it, the advice offered Kennedy "was not so unanimous or so well considered as it seemed."

What this suggests, then, is that a chief executive and his alter egos must not take the consensus among policy advisers at face value. Particularly when the consensus is agreeable to him, the president must force himself to test it in order to establish whether it is complete or obscures important differences and unresolved issues. Similarly, he should ascertain what the consensus is based on and how it was achieved. Is it a well-considered consensus in which all actors have done their homework properly and interacted with each other in a joint problem-solving exercise? Or is it a manufactured or synthetic consensus obtained through the dominance of one policy clique, or through bargaining among the actors that resulted in a compromise that papers over difficult problems and shirks the task of identifying and evaluating relevant options?

Questions

1. How might a president ensure that his advisers do not reach a consensus too readily?
2. In what ways are malfunctions numbers three and six similar? How might they be avoided?
3. Why is it possible for advisers to "gang up" on a president and sell him on a policy they have agreed upon?
4. Do all of these causes of malfunctions in the foreign policy process have some common characteristics? Is the cure for all of them the same?
5. Which of the nine malfunctions do you think might occur most frequently?

The Strategies of Presidents*

I. M. Destler

I. M. Destler is now associated with the Foreign Policy Studies Program at the Brookings Institution. He has been a visiting lecturer at

---

*Selections from "The Strategies of Presidents: Foreign Policy-Making under Kennedy, Johnson, and Nixon," and the Epilogue: "The Nixon System—A Further Look," from I. M. Destler, *Presidents, Bureaucrats, and Foreign Policy: The Politics of Organizational Reform* (Copyright © 1972, enlarged edition © 1974 by Princeton University Press), pages 95–123 and 298–308. Reprinted by permission of Princeton University Press. Footnotes have been omitted.

the Woodrow Wilson School, Princeton University, and has served on a presidential task force on government organization.

If coherence in foreign policy must be built around the president, a realistic approach to the problem requires a look at what specific presidents have done. On what officials have they relied to control the executive branch foreign affairs agencies? Have they sought to build coherence around one subordinate or several? To what extent have they sought enhanced influence through formal policy-making processes? Through informal personal relationships? To what extent did they pursue explicit foreign affairs organizational strategies at all?

The decade ending in 1970 is a particularly fruitful period for seeking answers to these questions. It featured three very different presidents, who handled foreign policy in three very different ways. It was also the period when the National Security Council staff became a strong presidential instrument for foreign affairs management and control.

Two of the presidents of this period saw foreign policy as their field of primary competence and interest. While Lyndon Johnson emphasized domestic matters in his brilliantly improvised early months, John F. Kennedy and Richard M. Nixon gave top priority to foreign affairs from the moment they entered office. And while Johnson's methods of handling foreign policy developed mainly from his personality and his experience in office, Kennedy and Nixon entered the presidency with rather strong ideas of how they wanted to run the show. Their ideas were quite different. Kennedy was attracted to informality and a loose, highly personal style of operating; Nixon has emphasized thoroughness, regular channels, relatively formal procedures. Kennedy sought to develop productive communications and relationships with as many high officials as seemed possible and fruitful. Nixon has preferred to deal with and through a very small number of intermediaries. Yet each seems to have tried quite consciously to develop an approach which maximized his own influence over the foreign affairs government. Those concerned with foreign affairs organization in the future must seek lessons from both their successes and their failures.

The Kennedy Approach

Kennedy inherited a highly structured formal system of national security policy making and coordination which had come under increasing attack as Eisenhower's term drew to a close. The Jackson subcommittee reflected both its own investigation and a broader consensus among experts when it urged the new president to "deinstitutionalize" and "humanize" the NSC process, and to rely more on the secretary of state for policy leadership. More important, its approach to policy-making problems was highly consistent with Kennedy's predispositions, and in his first months the new president acted toward both of these ends.

The negative organizational effort, dismantling the Eisenhower machinery, was the more successful. Less than a month after his inauguration Kennedy abolished the Eisenhower-created Operations Coordinating Board, with the announced aim of "strengthening the responsibility of the individual departments" for operational coordination. Other interdepartmental committees were also abolished in an effort to center responsibility in individuals rather than leaderless groups. National Security Council meetings became less frequent. And, as noted by Special Assistant for National Security Affairs McGeorge Bundy, the administration ". . . deliberately rubbed out the distinction between planning and operation which governed the administrative structure of the NSC staff in the last administration. This distinction, real enough at the extremes of the daily cable traffic and long-range assessment of future possibilities, breaks down in most of the business of decision and action . . . especially . . . presidential action."

Bundy also stressed "increased reliance on the leadership of the Department of State." . . .

> . . . the president has made it very clear that he does not want a large separate organization between him and his secretary of state. Neither does he wish any question to arise as to the clear authority and responsibility of the secretary of state, not only in his own department, and not only in such large-scale related areas as foreign aid and information policy, but also as the agent of coordination in all our major policies toward other nations.

But there is room for question about the extent to which primary reliance on the State Department was a serious Kennedy objective. Many, such as Hilsman and Schlesinger, have argued that it was, and without doubt State was handed a ball it could have carried much farther than it did. But if Kennedy no doubt wished he had a stronger State Department, he does not seem to have been all that serious about it, in the sense of carrying out a deliberate, systematic strategy designed to make it so. His initial appointments to key State posts were aimed at getting good people, recognizing political prominence and service, and cultivating the foreign policy establishment. They certainly were not designed to produce a team of men responsive to the lead of a strong secretary. McNamara accepted his post on condition he would have a free hand in naming subordinates. Rusk was offered his after Under Secretary Chester Bowles, U.N. Ambassador Adlai Stevenson, and Assistant Secretary for African Affairs Mennen Williams had already been selected.

Kennedy did exhort State to try harder. He told the American Foreign Service Association on May 31, 1962, "This is the great period of the Foreign Service"; echoing Harry Truman, he asserted that "the place to be is in the kitchen, and I am sure the Foreign Service officers of the United States feel the same way." But the first two foreign affairs task forces he appointed had Defense Department chairmen, though their subject matters (Laos and Cuba) would have naturally called for State leadership were the department seriously expected to "take charge." Kennedy's May 1961 letter to ambassadors was a milestone in strengthening their authority; ironically, the initial draft was reportedly written by White House aide Ralph Dungan. His November 1961 reshuffling of State personnel (the "Thanksgiving Day Massacre") improved things on balance. Yet even here the aim of strengthening State was not unalloyed. The transfer of Walt Rostow to State's top planning position, for example, seems to have reflected in part a desire to get him out of the White House, since Bundy didn't work well with him and Kennedy was wary of the "dangerous" ideas he tended to produce.

So whatever Kennedy might have liked to see happen, his inauguration did not usher in a golden age of leadership for the State Department. His major organizational contribution lay elsewhere—in the White House basement. It lay in the creation of a strong personal foreign policy staff, and in the way he used that creation.

Central to the Kennedy presidency was a loose, open, dynamic operating style, reflecting a desire to reach out and grab for issues and a sense that overly formal policy machinery might victimize the President it was supposed to serve. In his January 1960 speech to the National Press Club, Kennedy argued that the president must be "the vital center of action in our whole scheme of government," a man "who acts as well as reacts." In the pre-inauguration period he was concerned about "free access" to the idea market, saying, "I simply cannot afford to have just one set of advisers." Kennedy grew to practice what he had preached. Said Sydney Hyman one month before the assassination: "He does not rely merely on the information that reaches his desk through official channels. The president has many auxiliary lines of communication within the government, so that he can get different views on the same subject and allow subsecretaries to reach the ear of the White House by out-flanking their departmental chiefs. And he still seeks information from many independent sources outside the Government. . . ."

Kennedy also disliked formal, fixed committee meetings. Sorensen noted in 1963 that, on important issues, "President Kennedy prefers to invite only those whose official views he requires or whose unofficial judgment he values." As Kennedy himself put it in 1961, "We have averaged three or four meetings a week with the Secretaries of Defense and State, McGeorge Bundy, the head of the CIA and the Vice President. But formal meetings of the Security Council which include a much wider group are not as effective. It is more difficult to decide matters involving high national security if there is a wider group present."

By 1963 the National Security Council had become, in the words of one staff member, "little more than a name." It continued to meet but seldom was the place for serious discussion of serious issues. Still, the name conveyed a legitimacy which was important at times—hence the dubbing of Kennedy's personally chosen Cuban missile crisis group as the NSC "Executive Committee."

The council also served as an umbrella under which Kennedy could create a strong presidential foreign policy staff. His predecessors had had highly valued individual foreign affairs aides. But until 1960 the NSC staff was manned primarily by career officials, with the special assistant to the president for national security affairs (an office created by Eisenhower) supposed to link the career group to the president's needs. Kennedy made the staff a personal staff, with most of its members recruited specifically for his administration. It numbered about ten, and its chief—McGeorge Bundy—was able to bring onto it several exceptionally talented men, who came mainly from outside of government and owed no allegiance to any agency within it.

Kennedy did not want the staff to become a layer separating him from the line departments. It reviewed and commented on papers reaching the president from the departments, and this role gave it an important bargaining advantage. But he kept in close communication

with his key cabinet officers and other agency heads, and dealt periodically with officials at the assistant secretary level. Unlike Franklin
Roosevelt, Kennedy was not inclined to treat his cabinet officers as
"natural enemies." To the extent that he could get personal, staff-type
support from them, he was more than willing to do so.

Inside the White House, relationships were likewise fluid. Kennedy
abolished the hierarchical system of the overall White House staff,
where Sherman Adams had once reigned as *the* assistant to President
Eisenhower. Bundy had a more specific substantive mandate than the
other senior presidential advisers, and his subordinates were organized mainly on regional lines. But access to the president was not
limited to the top man. Personal secretary Evelyn Lincoln guarded a
door to Kennedy's office, armed with a list of staffers permitted to walk
in and talk to the president during his free time. Bundy was one of
them, of course, and he was clearly the major foreign affairs staff official. But also on the list, reportedly, were Carl Kaysen, Robert Komer,
and Michael Forrestal of his staff. And Sorensen, Dungan, Jerome
Wiesner, and Schlesinger from the larger White House also dealt
directly with the president on foreign policy matters, as did of course
his brother Robert.

Because the president sought involvement in so many current
issues, "the [Kennedy] staff concentrated heavily on what was hap-
pening at the moment." There was a corresponding lack of a comprehensive planning process such as the Eisenhower administration had
developed. The Eisenhower system tended to assume that decisions
setting broad objectives or guidelines could and would shape specific
actions. The Kennedy people doubted this, believing that day-to-day
involvement in events brought more results than top-level statements
of purpose and general direction. Rostow tried unsuccessfully to interest Kennedy in a comprehensive policy formulation system, but the
president and his top officials felt they had more important uses for
their time.

The staff was expected, according to Schlesinger, "to become the
president's eyes and ears through the whole area of national security," and "to uncover in the middle levels of government ideas which
deserved a hearing at the top before they had been diluted or choked
off by interbureau or interagency rivalry." Thus the flow of both information and policy ideas received priority. Bundy insisted that the
White House receive the most important cables and intelligence
reports "raw"—before they had been pre-digested by the line agencies.

And a continuing effort was made to avoid the Eisenhower tendency to have "agreed recommendations" subscribed to by all major agencies and officials presented for presidential ratification. Instead, the aim was to discover and illuminate alternative courses of action which would allow real presidential choice among them.

One important Kennedy innovation was the creation of inter-agency task forces to help manage important current issues. They were responsible for both current action and forward planning, and were intended to serve the president rather than the agencies represented. Responsibility was generally centered in the task force chairman to avoid decision making by committee. To relate the various ad hoc groups to one another and to broader administration policy objectives, they usually include one White House staff member.

The Bundy staff tended to concentrate far more on "State" than on "Defense" problems. There were exceptions, notably Kaysen's involvement in arms control issues. But Kennedy and Bundy were more interested in international politics than in weapons management systems. McNamara encouraged this emphasis by demonstrating that he could handle defense matters to the president's satisfaction.

Moreover, as the staff developed in fact into the president's prime "agent of coordination" for foreign affairs, it was inevitable that it would relate most intensively to State, which had the formal coordination mandate and necessarily played a role more central than any other department. And often State was *the problem*, supposed to lead in theory but sluggish in fact. Thus, as Moose has written, "In those instances where the Department of State's response did not measure up to the president's expectations, the NSC staff moved in."

There was serious resentment of White House "interference." Moose suggests, moreover, that Kennedy's staffing procedures purchased "direct responsiveness and immediate feedback" at the cost of diminishing State initiative and disturbing "its already none-too-strong internal organization." This was no doubt true. Yet "moving in" meant anything but taking over exclusive jurisdiction. It meant working with officials of various departments, bringing them together, seeking resolution of issues in directions consistent with presidential wishes, communicating to bureaucrats a sense of presidential priorities and working to make their activities reflect these priorities. As Schlesinger put it, the staff was "helpless without allies throughout the permanent government." And much of the influence of Bundy and the staff came precisely from their ability to connect circuits, to link related individuals and groups and activities with each other. Sorensen reports that Bundy "made certain that no responsible officer or point of view was omitted from meetings on foreign policy," and if major officials did not always cherish being "coordinated" on matters they preferred to handle their own ways, they valued the assurance of "having a shot at" issues which came up for presidential attention.

This does not mean that had the staff not existed line bureaucrats would have found it necessary to invent it. The staff certainly needed bargaining advantages to play a serious substantive coordination role, including personal presidential confidence, independent access to cables and intelligence reports, the right to clear particular messages to the field, and the all-important role of handling the president's daily foreign policy business. But if departmental officials did not originally want the staff, they did learn they could live with it, and they often found it useful. There was a common interest among top officials who had to work closely together whether they would have wished it or not, an interest in an honest broker, a means to get attention paid to issues, and a link to influence to their resolution. One of Bundy's signal achievements is his recognition that service to this widespread interest could bring both power to himself and the president and benefit to the entire system. He proved to be the master at "keeping the game going."

Changes under Johnson

Lyndon Johnson did not plan to be president. Once president, he did not plan to emphasize foreign policy. But Vietnam was a problem he could neither avoid nor resolve. In the course of dealing with this and other challenges, he made the foreign affairs government a far different place from what it had been in the Kennedy era.

There were some strong similarities. Johnson kept Kennedy's three top foreign affairs officials, and two of them served him longer than they did his predecessor. And his penchant for informality and operational flexibility made inconceivable any restoration of a formal policy-making system of the sort Kennedy dismantled. As Bill Moyers noted in 1968, Johnson found the NSC to be "not a live institution, not suited to precise debate for the sake of decision." He found it more useful "to call in a handful of top advisers, confidants, close friends."

Johnson's one important procedural innovation likewise followed the Kennedy pattern: it gave formal emphasis to State Department leadership in a way that had little real effect. In March 1966, at the

urging of General Maxwell Taylor and Deputy Under Secretary of
State U. Alexis Johnson, he established a system of interdepartmental
committees designed to strengthen the secretary's foreign affairs leadership. Interdepartmental Regional Groups (IRGs) chaired by assistant secretaries of state were to coordinate policy at their levels and
report to a Senior Interdepartmental Group (SIG) chaired by State's
under secretary. Included at both levels were representatives of the
secretary of defense, the JCS, CIA, AID, USIA, and the White House.
But neither Johnson nor Rusk gave the committees enough support
to make the system work effectively on important issues.

Yet despite these parallels, Lyndon Johnson was very different
from his predecessor, and his handling of foreign policy reflected the
differences. Kennedy had felt quite at home with both the substance
of foreign policy and the community of men who influenced it. Johnson
was comfortable with neither. His long Capitol Hill experience had
given him confidence about his feel for domestic policy issues and the
people who sought to affect them. But he tended, in the words of one
official of his administration, to view foreign affairs as a sort of "black
art," its substance alien to him and its Eastern establishment practi-
tioners even more so.

Lacking confidence on international matters, feeling that his
strengths and his opportunities lay in the domestic policy arena,
Lyndon Johnson did not seek to duplicate Kennedy's comprehensive
global involvement in international issues. Yet he seems to have seen
foreign policy as an arena that could get him into serious trouble. To
avoid this, he leaned heavily on the men Kennedy had bequeathed him,
above all Rusk and McNamara. If he could be sure of their loyalty to
him and their commitment to his administration's major policy decisions, he apparently thought, their talents and establishment cre-
dentials would make it easier for him to navigate in the dark and
dangerous international waters.

Facilities and procedures developed under his predecessor gave
Johnson access to a broad flow of foreign affairs information, which
he consumed voraciously. He also acted on the considerable number
of issues referred to him for decision. But on only a few matters did
he seek continuing personal control. Some of these were in areas like
foreign aid, where he could press hard for stronger agricultural "self-
help" measures in countries like India without upsetting the East Coast
establishment the way a similarly forceful initiative in European matters would have. Others were problems that he couldn't avoid, like

Vietnam. Once he did move into an area, however, Johnson was likely to insist on very close control over details. He ordered procedures requiring every food aid agreement—and every development loan over $5 million—to come to him personally for approval, and he sometimes held up aid to India for months at a stretch. And his involvement in Vietnam matters, from bombing targets to letters from servicemen, became a legend in his own time.

Johnson kept the personal presidential foreign policy staff. But while it grew somewhat in size—to perhaps sixteen substantive officers in 1967—it diminished in influence. The special assistant continued to have dealings with the president "more frequent than those of any cabinet officer," and his work continued to have a "here and now" orientation. But being less confident than Kennedy had been of his own judgment on foreign policy, Johnson was less inclined to encourage staff questioning of ongoing policies, and less interested in maintaining channels through which subcabinet officials could get their ideas to him without going through their bosses. Bundy had been adept at encouraging a flow of ideas and alternatives to the president. On Vietnam, Bill Moyers had performed a similar function. But after their departures, bureaucrats pressing for policy changes found the White House staff less and less receptive to their efforts.

Particularly important was the appointment of Walt W. Rostow to Bundy's position in early 1966. Johnson emphasized he was not "replacing" Bundy, and while his successor in fact performed many of the same functions—managing the flow of information to the president, communicating presidential wishes to the bureaucracy, providing policy analysis and advice—Rostow seems not to have had as strong a mandate as Bundy under Kennedy. He was also a very different type of person. Bundy was a pragmatist who seldom allowed his personal views on policy to prejudice his presentations of alternative viewpoints and balanced analyses to the president. He was also an exceptional administrator-operator. Rostow, by contrast, was primarily a thinker and more than a bit of an ideologue, who tended to view particular events in terms of the broader theoretical constructs he was most adept at developing.

Rostow proposed the bombing of North Vietnam early in Kennedy's administration and remained a committed "hawk" to the end. And because of this tendency to treat information and issues in terms of strongly held policy convictions that others did not always share, departmental officials were much less likely to trust him to represent their views objectively to the president. This was true even regarding activities like development aid, for which Rostow had long been a determined and influential advocate. On the other hand, his absolute conviction that we were doing the right thing in Vietnam could only reassure a president who felt increasingly under siege, and Rostow's personal relationship with Johnson was apparently much closer than Bundy's had been.

But just as Kennedy's strong trust in McNamara had limited NSC staff involvement on defense issues, Johnson's confidence in Rusk reduced staff influence on those foreign policy problems which were clearly within State's sphere. In areas like aid, where Johnson was personally involved and Rusk was indifferent, or in the international monetary field, where a strong White House role was important to balance Treasury influence, staff members like Edward Hamilton, Francis Bator, and Edward Fried were able to play strong personal roles very much in the Kennedy staff pattern. So also were interdepartmental task forces like the "Deming Group" on monetary problems. But generally the use of task forces with broad mandates declined, and the staff role became more liaison than leadership. Rostow tended to save his influence for Vietnam, and the lack of bureaucratic confidence in him as an "honest broker" made him unable to act as an across-the-board coordinator or circuit-connector in the Bundy manner. Fewer members of his staff had personal relationships with the president, and "fewer memorandums went to the president on the responsibility of individual staff members." Most of the exceptional Bundy group departed well before the end of the Johnson era, and the staff, in Moose's words, "dwindled to a rather small group of officers, most of them detailed from the departments and agencies."

> It was neither a highly structured staff organization like that existing in January 1961, nor the assertive and highly personalized staff inherited by President Johnson. It was, instead, a staff which largely limited itself to monitoring the national-security process from the president's perspective, making sure that the various elements of the process were in touch with each other when other means proved insufficient, and providing the president with whatever in-house advice and support he felt he needed.

To the extent that any institution served as a presidential focal point for foreign policy-making during the Johnson administration, it was the "Tuesday Lunch" held weekly with the secretaries of state and defense and the special assistant for national security affairs. It dealt largely with current Vietnam issues, reflecting top officials' overwhelming preoccupation with the war from 1965 on. It reflected also Johnson's organizational approach to the conduct of the war—what Cooper terms "a mixture of tight personal control and loosely structured organization"—and what James C. Thomson, Jr., has characterized as ". . . the 'closed politics' of policy making as issues become hot: the more sensitive the issue, and the higher it rises in the bureaucracy, the more completely the experts are excluded while the harassed senior generalists take over (that is, the secretaries, undersecretaries, and presidential assistants)."

For the president and his key advisers, the Tuesday Lunch was a highly useful institution. It gave the top officials a chance to discuss Vietnam and other hot issues directly and at length with the president, and provided them a better sense of his and each others' feelings, problems, and priorities. It also made available to their aides a forum where they could seek to have important issues surfaced for top-level consideration.

But it caused their subordinates great difficulties. Staff officials who sought to support the principals and carry out their decisions went to considerable lengths to develop a regular agenda so they could get major issues raised and assure that the top men were adequately briefed. They were not always able to do this, and even when they could they had serious problems finding out whether the issues were actually discussed and what decisions if any were made. Rusk and McNamara were reluctant to discuss the content of Tuesday Lunch discussions with their senior subordinates. Up to a point this was understandable: presidents need to be able to discuss matters in a context where not every word of theirs is taken as law and promulgated. But the secretaries appear to have been much more sensitive to the president's right to confidentiality than to their subordinates' need to know enough to give top-level decisions operational meaning. The top men grew to live in one world, having loyalty primarily to each other, and seeing problems in a context that their subordinates could not understand because they were outside the charmed circle. Not only did the latter find it hard to translate "the policy" into daily action. They also found it difficult to know when a particular issue was being discussed so that they could bring to bear their own information and analysis and advice.

So the problem went beyond the banishment of expertise to a deep communication gap between "that tight little group of desperate men" at the top and the underlings who were supposed to be serving them. It was exacerbated by the president's compulsion about secrecy, and by a personal operating style which sought to maintain tactical flexibility for the president by keeping others in the dark about his intentions. Presidential "options" were kept open, at the cost of not conveying to those below a sufficiently coherent and detailed sense of what the president and his top officials wanted. So the options of those below remained open also, and agencies were able to "interpret" presidential wishes in ways consistent with their own predilections.

Recognizing the weakness of Vietnam coordination at levels below the Tuesday Lunch, Under Secretary of State Nicholas Katzenbach convened a series of interdepartmental meetings at his level. The group he invited was virtually identical to the SIG (which had no mandate to get involved in Vietnam), and its members sought to improve Vietnam operations by sharing information and analyses with one another. But the existence of this ad hoc committee was so closely held that it was dubbed the "non-group." Thus it could hardly provide subordinates with regular policy guidance.

Of course there were reasons for such close handling of the Vietnam issue which went beyond the idiosyncrasies of Lyndon Johnson. In some cases battlefield security may have been at stake. More often, one suspects, it was security against a different enemy. The president's innate tendency to sniff treason within government walls was, by 1967, exacerbated by increasing indications that many subordinate officials who had doubts about the Vietnam policy were regularly unburdening themselves to the press. Such unhappiness below solidified the top group's sense of being embattled, both strengthening their loyalties to one another and their separation from the rest of the government. Apparently, in Johnson's view, McNamara ultimately proved not quite loyal enough. But it was not until Clark Clifford broke into the charmed circle, and until the Tet Offensive shattered the administration's base of national support, that Vietnam policy took a significant shift in course. It is unrealistic to suggest that a different foreign affairs organization or operating style would have averted the unfortunate decisions of early 1965. Establishment of an organizational focal point below the Tuesday Lunch, however, could surely have improved the coordination of government Vietnam operations and the implementations of presidential decisions. And a greater presidential receptiveness to alternative analyses might have encouraged serious reassessment sooner than it finally came.

The Kennedy and Johnson Approaches—
A Broader Assessment

The Kennedy approach to foreign policy had strong virtues. It put the president in daily touch with a wide range of information and opinions, notably reducing the danger of his capture by any one. It gave him the service of a number of exceptionally fine staff aides, and their access to him maximized both their influence with the bureaucracy and their incentive to stay on the team. It recognized the futility of mechanical solutions to the problem of presidentially based policy coherence, such as the Eisenhower NSC system. It recognized that foreign policy making is inherently a political process, and that the president's influence can be stretched through a network of personal relationships which he and those who work on his behalf can use to their mutual advantage.

But it was more effective in recruiting a strong team of bureaucratic players than in placing them in the particular positions where they might do the most good. Kennedy made his major State Department appointments—Rusk, Bowles, Ball—with little if any concern about whether they could work well together as a top-level team. Once he took these actions, his subsequent efforts to improve things had the nature of patchwork. The "Thanksgiving Day Massacre" of 1961, and the elevation of Averell Harriman to the number three State Department position in 1963, raised to higher positions individuals with whom Kennedy could work. But neither did much to strengthen the management of the department as an institution. Instead, Kennedy took the route of Roosevelt before him, creating a new institution (the personal staff) to perform a needed role rather than seeking to reform the existing one (State). As long as he was determined to keep Rusk he had little choice, since the secretary tended not to concern himself very much with how his organization actually operated, and it is unlikely that a president could reorganize a department effectively going around the top man. But by all reports he was not satisfied, and by some he intended to begin his second administration with his cabinet headed by Secretary of State Robert S. McNamara.

The NSC staff did evolve into a good team, its informal operating style suited to the president's preferences. But though Bundy was strong and effective, and probably was more broadly responsive to the president's foreign policy priorities and preferences than anyone else in the government, his job as both he and Kennedy saw it made it necessary for him to defer to cabinet officers, and to avoid making himself too open a rallying point for the Kennedyites in the foreign affairs government. Thus while the system provided a useful locus of coordination and presidentially attuned initiative, it included no primary policy leader short of the president himself.

It did, however, make things very hard on the secretary of state. Rusk resented it when "people like Sorensen and Kaysen with no responsibility were making academic comments," and his regional assistant secretaries had to cope regularly with White House counterparts who were sometimes both more aggressive and on better terms with the source of power. Some of the assistant secretaries, like Hilsman and Harriman, solved this problem by cultivating their own presidential relationships. But this put the secretary a bit more to one side even when amicable relations were maintained. Given Rusk's personality and highly individual approach to his job, no other pattern was likely or even possible if Kennedy was to be president as he saw the meaning of the office. But there is the more general question of whether the type of White House staff that evolved would have been compatible with a strong secretary of state. The excellent relations between Bundy and super-Secretary McNamara, and the frequent productive interchanges and alliances among their subordinates, suggest that it might have been. But the operative word is "might." Given the president's strong interests, such a secretary would have required very, very close attunement to the president's priorities. His staff would probably have had to provide much of the support which Bundy's men ended up giving the president. But even so, he could not generally have been successful with the McNamara technique of providing such thorough staffing and analysis of issues that the president needed no further White House input. The president would have been just too interested, and too likely to have special insights of his own.

The fate of whatever intention Kennedy had to strengthen the State Department provides another insight: that foreign policy-making systems tend to "happen," to evolve as a result of what presidents and other top officials find helpful and necessary as they face daily problems, and to gain whatever viability they have from their role in these processes. It is not necessary to assume that Kennedy secretly planned the central White House staff role which finally evolved. The other explanation is more plausible: State did not provide him what he wanted, while Bundy and Co. were both able and willing to do so in its stead.

If coherence was damaged by State's weakness, the Kennedy regime has also been criticized for its overconcern with the hot issues of the present, resulting in a lack of comprehensiveness of coverage or concern for integrated, longer-term foreign policy planning. Skybolt is the most cited example, where no person or process "coordinated" the systems-management proclivities of the secretary of defense with the urgent if dubious desire of the British to prolong the life-span of their nuclear deterrent. This critique was in fact misleading, since Skybolt resulted not from failure to foresee a potential problem, but rather through mutual miscalculation by American and British officials concerning how their counterparts across the ocean would act. But Joseph Kraft's criticism of the Kennedy staff style was more to the point.

> The staff operation, like many other aspects of the administration, works to put all matters on a pragmatic, case-by-case basis. It does not contribute to the systematic elaboration of coherent programs expressing broad and easily identifiable public policies. A sense of inner purpose may—no doubt does—exist in the White House. But in part because the operation is so casual, so laconic, so frictionless, the purpose and direction of the administration, its intrinsic character, so to speak, have not made themselves felt outside the White House. To that extent at least, the work of the White House staff, excellent as it may be on an ad hoc basis, does not yet serve the president's desire that his administration achieve historic stature.

Kraft was writing mainly of the overall staff operation, and when applied to foreign policy this critique is not entirely fair. Kennedy was able to articulate "the purpose and direction of the administration" on a broad range of issues—the Alliance for Progress, greater general sympathy for new nations and the developing world, a "Declaration of Interdependence" with Western Europe, a policy of toughness and military build-up vis-à-vis Russia in 1961, a policy inviting deténte and re-examining our attitude toward the cold war in 1963. What was harder was to make these general intentions effective. But Kraft's point remains very important. Due to both its ad hoc style and its "multi-polar" power structure, an informal policy-making approach like those of Kennedy and Johnson depends singularly on the president's ability both to conceive in his mind and to convey to the government and the nation a clear sense of direction and priorities. It is not only, as Halberstam rightly emphasizes, that it is dependent "on the President himself to set the guidelines for foreign policy." It also requires exceptional informal lines of communication downward to transmit such "guidelines" from the president to the bureaucrats on the firing line.

The combination of Kennedy's broad world view and the Bundy staff operation met both of these needs in a reasonably effective way, though failure to do much about the State Department meant that the bureaucracy would often be sluggish in responding to presidential wishes. But Johnson's foreign policy-making "system" met neither. He could not convey "the purpose and direction" of his administration because he was not sure of it himself on many issues and because he used secrecy as a tactical tool on others. On Vietnam, where his general objectives were clear from 1965 to 1968, his method of handling day-to-day problems achieved maximum uncertainty in the bureaucracy about what officials were expected to do. Yet while it thus stimulated interagency infighting on day-to-day issues, the Tuesday Lunch phenomenon discouraged consideration of important dissenting viewpoints at the presidential level. Thus the Johnson administration combined the drawbacks of an informal, ad hoc policy-making system—confusion about who is doing what on which issue, lack of a foreign affairs official with a broad mandate short of the president—with a blocking of communications up and down the hierarchy that overreliance on line officials can foster.

Nor did Secretary Rusk exercise the sort of leadership even within his own department that Johnson's confidence in him made possible. He may have progressed, in Halberstam's words, "from being Kennedy's liaison with the Hill to being a secretary of state." Yet he remained, as one of his assistant secretaries put it, "a superb staff officer," one who knew how to serve those above him but not how to lead those below. He neither supported subordinates who sought to exercise strong policy leadership nor communicated his policy preferences to them in areas where the president had not unambiguously spoken. Lacking such leadership and such support, the SIG and IRGs began with two strikes against them.

It was this legacy of non-coherence in policy making which President Nixon inherited from a divided and demoralized administration in January 1969. The Johnson administration had not been without positive achievements in foreign policy. It had stepped down from the unrealistic effort to build a multilateral force, negotiated a nuclear nonproliferation treaty, successfully prodded India to act on her food crisis, and moved forward markedly in the international trade and monetary fields. But its policy-making institutions, formal and informal, had little that would recommend them to its successor.

The Nixon System

Like John F. Kennedy, Richard M. Nixon considered foreign affairs to be his field of special competence. Like Kennedy, he was determined to "call the turn." But if the end was the same, the means he proposed were very different. He promised to "restore the National Security Council to its preeminent role in national security planning," and even attributed "most of our serious reverses abroad since 1960" to its abandonment in favor of "catch-as-catch-can talkfests between the president, his staff assistants, and various others."

Nixon promptly showed that this was more than campaign rhetoric. One month after his election, he named as his assistant for national security affairs the noted Harvard professor of international politics Henry Kissinger, and ordered him to establish an "Eisenhower NSC system," but "without the concurrences." He also sought the advice of General Andrew J. Goodpaster, who had served President Eisenhower as coordinator of day-to-day national security intelligence and operations. Kissinger quickly assembled a staff and developed a set of formal institutions and procedures built around the NSC for coordinated management of foreign policy issues. These were established by the president on the afternoon of Inauguration Day, and announced to the public two-and-one-half weeks later.

The White House statement stressed the role of the council as "the principal forum for the consideration of policy issues" requiring presidential decision. It was to convene "regularly," with "one meeting [to] be held each week for the next few months." To facilitate its work and to "handle more immediate operational problems within the context of the NSC system," "a series of support NSC committees and groups" had been organized. The president had "assigned to the supporting NSC bodies a comprehensive series of studies covering the principal national security issues now confronting the nation."

The White House made it clear that the enhancement of the council was not all that the president was seeking: "As important as the regularity and strengthened structure of the council and its projected policy studies is the approach prescribed by the president for the examination of issues. The guidance to NSC study groups seeks to assure that all pertinent facts are established and all options presented—complete with pros, cons, and costs—so that decisions can be made with a clear understanding of their ramifications."

A year later, in his comprehensive foreign policy message, the president stressed once again his determination to avoid the Eisenhower fate of being confronted with "agreed papers" for his ratification. The aim was what Dean Acheson once called "disagreed papers": "The new NSC system is designed to make certain that clear policy choices reach the top, so that the various positions can be fully debated in the meeting of the council. . . . I refuse to be confronted with a bureaucratic consensus that leaves me no options but acceptance or rejection, and that gives me no way of knowing what alternatives exist."

The "options" sought by the president, moreover, were not supposed to reflect competing agency interests, but rather alternative ways of dealing with a problem which all agencies recognized as reasonable even if they did not support them. As Kissinger explained it in a letter to Senator Jackson, "Formal agency positions are taken only at the level of the council itself, and are argued out in front of the president."

But if the Eisenhower "concurrences" were scorned, the new approach shared with that system the stated belief that broad, careful planning and analysis could lead to wise general presidential decisions which would then shape bureaucratic operations. In fact, the president's justification of his procedures had the ring of older calls for a "rationalized" policy process. "American foreign policy must not be merely the result of a series of piecemeal tactical decisions forced by the pressure of events," he said. "If our policy is to embody a coherent vision of the world and a rational conception of America's interests, our specific actions must be the products of rational and deliberate choice." Thus, he explained, "In central areas of policy, we have arranged our procedure of policy making so as to address the broader questions of long-term objectives first; we define our purposes, and then address the specific operational issues."

In addition to such rational policy making, the system sought thoroughness and dependable relations with the larger government. As Kissinger explained it, "The more ad hoc approach of the 1960s often ran the risk that relevant points of view were not heard, that systematic treatment of issues did not take place at the highest levels, or that the bureaucracies were not fully informed as to what had been decided and why." And the president suggested that a relatively formal system could give officials a sort of administrative due process, a right to their day in court:

The NSC system also insures that all agencies and departments receive a fair hearing before I make my decisions. All departments concerned with a problem participate in the groups that draft and review the policy papers. They know that their positions and arguments will reach the council without dilution, along with the other alternatives.

In several respects the Nixon-Kissinger system restored the planning-operations distinction that the Kennedy-Bundy approach had "rubbed out." Most fundamental have been the apparent assumptions that planning could effectively shape operations in the major policy areas, that operations could wait for planning and not be forced by unanticipated crises (which the system has gone to great effort to avert), and that policy making is something that can basically be directed from one place—the top. But in one important respect a separation of planning and operations was consciously avoided. The new national security studies were not assigned to a special planning staff or staffs, but to committees of officials from the offices that would do the implementing. The goal, as one participant in the system put it, is not just analysis to develop the best possible options, but to get the bureaucracy to endorse the various alternatives as "real" ones capable of implementation, so that the president could make a "real" choice.

To support the NSC and strengthen central management of foreign policy issues, a network of general inter-agency committees was established. The Johnson administration's IRGs were renamed IGs (Interdepartmental Groups), with AID and USIA removed from regular membership but State's assistant secretaries remaining as chairmen. Similarly, the SIG was replaced by the Under Secretaries Committee (USC) headed by the under secretary of state. But unlike under Johnson, these State-chaired groups reported not one to another, but both to the Kissinger-chaired NSC Review Group (on which the same agencies were represented). State officials vociferously protested this breach of their departmental chain of command. But the subordination of the committees to the Review Group and the council did resolve one serious problem in the SIG-IRG system—its lack of any strong link to the presidency. Another change was that the main role of the regional groups was not operational coordination, as it was intended to be under Johnson, but overseeing the preparation of NSC policy papers. These were then examined by the Review Group, "to insure that the issues, options, and views are presented fully and fairly." After appropriate revision, the most important papers were presented to the president and the National Security Council.

The role of the Under Secretaries Committee was to consider policy issues referred to it by the Review Group (presumably of a lesser order of importance than those referred to the NSC), and to provide operational coordination on issues where presidential policy decisions had already been taken. The committee network also provided flexibility by authorizing appointment of "NSC Ad Hoc Groups" to deal with specific problems, and a number of studies have been handled by these rather than in the IG framework.

On balance, the formal policy-making system was a rather sophisticated one, profiting from the experience—and the mistakes—of several administrations. But what most impressed Washington in early 1969 were the people brought to the White House to run it. Nixon might better have expressed his wishes as "an Eisenhower NSC, minus the concurrences, plus the personal staff." For Kissinger and his supporting cast clearly comprised a critical element in Nixon's foreign affairs organizational strategy. And by early February the White House was able to release a list of twenty-eight professionals under the national security assistant's wing, only two of them holdovers from the Rostow group. The staff was quickly labeled "a real powerhouse."

The typical staff members were not too different from the Kennedy period—relatively young, mobile, aggressive men, combining substantial background in the substance of foreign affairs with primary allegiance to the White House. They boasted greater bureaucratic experience than the Kennedy men, however, and a number had formidable reputations for operating effectiveness. And several were known to be critics of Johnson administration policies, particularly on Vietnam.

•   •   •   •   •   •   •   •   •   •   •   •   •   •   •   •   •   •

Has the System Worked?

In the years before 1969, Henry Kissinger frequently expressed the view that only by freeing themselves from bureaucratic encumbrances would foreign policy leaders in modern states be able to accomplish substantial things. The major administration foreign policy achievements are a result of putting this concept into practice. The Nixon NSC system had been partially designed and totally explained as a means of enhancing the quality and responsiveness of the bureaucracy's contribution to foreign policy making. But it became increasingly, in practice, a vehicle for excluding or diverting the bureaucracy while Nixon and Kissinger did the "real" business on their own. The primary targets of attention were China, Russia, and Vietnam. Kissinger handled the most critical negotiations personally, very often secretively, keeping the rest of the U.S. bureaucracy in the dark. His one client was the president, who was intimately involved in planning and directing these efforts, and who capped their achievements with visits to Peking and Moscow.

Threats from these two Communist adversaries were, for most participants and observers, the overriding problem of postwar American foreign policy. Vietnam dominated the sixties. To have negotiated withdrawal from the war and built new relationships with Russia and China is no small set of achievements, even if changing domestic and world political conditions greatly facilitated them all. Moreover, these specific attainments appear to be linked to a broader conceptual approach, an effort to build a "structure of peace" around astute management of relationships among the major world power centers. A five-power world is emerging, Mr. Nixon has suggested. And implicit in this administration's approach is the conviction that the world needs to be managed, and can be managed—much as the post-Napoleonic world had ideally been—by careful dealings among strong leaders of these power centers, leaders politically and institutionally free to bargain internationally, to offer inducements and respond to threats in a flexible (and frequently secret) manner.

An extended analysis of the relevance of this approach to today's world would be beyond the scope of this article. But neither can the issue be ignored. For the real Nixon-Kissinger case for the effectiveness of a closed, "two-man" system for conducting our foreign policy has come to rest not on the once-emphasized distinction between "policy" and "operations." Rather, it depends on the assumption that U.S. relations with a small number of counterpart power centers are what count, that the principal foreign policy issues of concern to the U.S. can be dealt with effectively through negotiating relationships with these power centers, and that top officials in these centers (*and in the United States*) will have enough political weight at home to be able to deliver on the deals they make by getting the requisite actions out of their domestic political systems. To the extent these assumptions are valid, then maybe two men *can* handle this task (with appropriate analytic and operational staff support), and perhaps they can handle it with greater coherence and purpose than a larger number. And maybe most of the day-to-day activities of the foreign affairs bureaucracy can be ignored — as unnecessary for the major enterprises of Nixon-Kissinger diplomacy, and as unimportant enough not to undercut these enterprises. Thus the Nixon-Kissinger system might work even if the "operational" decisions are what policy usually consists of. For the two-man system could dominate the operational decisions that count.

On the other hand, to the extent that power over the issues to be negotiated is widely dispersed, the two-man system will not do. If power is dispersed overseas, then the United States needs many more credible negotiators, able to speak authoritatively for the president and the United States to several levels of many governments. If power is dispersed at home, then the Nixon-Kissinger approach is inadequate also. For the secrecy and masked maneuvers of the closed system tend to conflict with the building of the broader understanding and alliances required for securing sufficient domestic support to sustain the policy.

Obviously, some issues and some relationships will meet these criteria better than others. What is necessary, then, is to distinguish between those situations where a closed, Nixon-Kissinger type approach is likely to be effective, and those where it is not. Logic and experience suggest that the system works well when three conditions are met. It is effective (1) with countries which have strong counterpart leaders with whom to cut deals, (2) in bilateral relationships which are limited in depth and breadth, and (3) on issues where U.S. leaders can personally control the policy outcomes about which they need to deal. Each of these intertwined limits deserves spelling out.

(1) *The need for strong foreign counterparts.* The apparent Nixon-Kissinger preference for dealing with adversary nations has often been noted. And to anticipate a later point, the Nixon-Kissinger difficulties with international alliance relationships are paralleled by their aversion to building and working with strong allies domestically, whether in the bureaucracy, or the Congress, or the broader community of Americans concerned with foreign policy. But the taste for adversary dealings has structural as well as personal roots. For Nixon-Kissinger "diplomacy at the top" requires counterpart leaders in the other major power centers with political weight and flexibility comparable to their own, foreign leaders able to make large commitments and then deliver on these commitments. Without such counterparts, negotiating at the top brings meager results. And if many other foreign officials then need to be dealt with, the system doesn't work. Nixon and Kissinger cannot do all this themselves, and lesser officials have neither the delegated authority nor the understanding of top-level aims that is required.

In the Nixon-Kissinger period it has been the adversary, totalitarian nations where such strong counterparts have been found. They cannot always be found even there—neither Leonid Brezhnev nor Chou En-lai, for example, had a domestic political base in the mid-sixties comparable to what each had developed by 1971. But strong central leadership is far less likely to arise in the advanced industrial, democratic societies of Europe and Japan. In Europe there is no one leader, but a "community" of semi-sovereign states struggling to construct a larger economic and political order. Japan does have a chief of government, of course, and Nixon and Kissinger have sought to use periodic summit conferences to strike binding political bargains with Tokyo. But the Japanese prime minister is hemmed in by a collegial cabinet system, a strong bureaucracy, and a political tradition stressing broad concensus. He is unable to "deal" as Nixon and Kissinger would like, and the result of pressing him to do so has been frustration on both sides.

(2) *The need for relatively unencumbered bilateral relationships.* Another way the Nixon-Kissinger system is better adapted to adversary dealings is its need for relatively simple, unencumbered relationships. China is the ideal example. Since few Americans had any serious ongoing dealings with Chinese counterparts in 1971, there was no network of official relationships and unofficial ties through which signals might be communicated or aims might be pursued which were inconsistent with the clandestine efforts of those at the top. There were not the sort of vested interests in a many-faceted existing relationship which might inhibit, suffer from, or resist major policy changes when the leaders sought to spring them on their astonished publics. But if such an unencumbered "clean slate" minimized the costs of this approach to U.S.–Chinese relations, the "Nixon shock" effects on Japan were multiplied because of many levels and forms of Japanese-American interdependence which the sudden U.S. move toward China seemed to threaten.

And it is the U.S.–Japanese case that seems more characteristic of the modern international system, above all in the relations among advanced industrial societies. Officials deal with one another across a wide range of specialized but intertwined policy issues. Their effective management requires not bilateral summit dealings but complex, many-level, many-issue multilateral negotiations on troop levels, trade barriers, and exchange rates—negotiations that usually need to proceed on regularized, separate, but somehow related tracks.

(3) *The need for issues that the U.S. president can dominate.* Finally, the Nixon-Kissinger system of closed policy making is limited

by the limits of presidential power at home. Spurning broader bureaucratic or domestic alliance building, it tends to work only on those issues
where the president can personally assure the official or unofficial U.S.
action which is at issue. Usually this reinforces the Nixon-Kissinger
bias toward political-military issues and instruments. It is easier to
deliver a B-52 bomb load on Hanoi than to win congressional approval of
a piece of trade legislation.

Again—this time ironically—China is the clearest positive example. The president had the personal power to dispatch his emissary and
arrange the contacts required, and the Taiwan lobby proved to be a
"paper tiger." With Russia, many of the new forms of bilateral cooperation are relatively non-controversial and subject to presidential will.
The SALT agreements, which did need congressional approval, encountered limited difficulty because they were generally consistent with
congressional predispositions. But the promise of most-favored-nation
treatment for Russia on trade lacked effective congressional support,
and seems likely to founder because of American Jewish opposition to
Soviet emigration policies. And there is strong congressional opposition to the large defense budgets that Nixon and Kissinger see as essential to their negotiating strategy.

The most dramatic case of the domestic political limits of the Nixon
approach, however, has been the issue on which he has staked the most
personally—his cherished, oversold Indochina accord. Presidential
rhetoric about "peace with honor" and "peace that will last" was widely
discounted in January. But Nixon apparently meant it, and staked his
hopes for a lasting settlement on the expectation of continued leverage
with Hanoi. In part this was to be exercised through the new relationships with Moscow and Peking. But of critical importance was direct
leverage through the "carrot" of promised large-scale reconstruction
assistance, and the "stick" of further use of the B-52s. Indeed, the
December 1972 carpet-bombing looks, in retrospect, not so much as an
effort to win major changes in the terms of the agreement, as a demonstration to Hanoi that the president was both able and willing to inflict
such punishment, and thus might do it again if the agreement were not
observed.

But as of this writing, domestic politics has taken both options out
of Nixon's hands. The president has been forced by Congress to accept
an August fifteenth bombing cut-off not just for Cambodia, but all of
Indochina. And the only thing with less congressional support than
the bombing is the aid program for North Vietnam.

Thus, these three limitations combine to reduce the range of effectiveness of the Nixon-Kissinger approach to a very limited range of issues. And at least equally disturbing has been the way Nixon and Kissinger have tended to respond to difficulties engendered by these limitations.

One tendency has been to continue to concentrate on those issues and relationships to which the approach is congenial, despite public statements that the priorities are changing. Thus, in the first eight months of their declared "Year of Europe," Nixon and Kissinger still appeared to be giving their prime attention to those adversary relations stressed in 1972. They did not seem to be focusing seriously on those economic questions which are central to any major Atlantic enterprise, partly because they lack substantive interest in these issues, partly because there are no authoritative counterparts with whom to deal on these issues. James Reston has drawn a parallel between Kissinger's "Year of Europe" speech on April 23, 1973 and George Marshall's historic Harvard Commencement Address of 1947. But it is hard to take this seriously, except perhaps as a reflection of the former's rhetorical aspirations.

A second tendency has been to lecture and sometimes punish those foreign governments which do not perform as the Nixon-Kissinger system needs them to. Thus when a Japanese prime minister is squeezed into promising a textile export restraint agreement and proves unable (for predictable reasons) to deliver on his promise, the fault is seen to lie not in unwise U.S. tactics or unrealistic U.S. expectations but in Japanese failure to measure up to the role of de Gaulle-type world statesmen. They are lectured in State of the World messages about the "obligation to keep the specific commitments made to one another." Shock tactics are employed to get the Japanese to stand up and join the five-power world. Thus the needs of the Nixon-Kissinger internal policy-making system and their particular approach to international diplomacy are elevated to the level of moral truths.

It would be remarkable indeed if U.S. pressure could somehow so alter the internal politics of Europe and Japan as to give rise to the sort of powerful leaders with whom our leaders like to play international poker. But while this is unlikely, the opposite is very possible. To the degree that Nixon-Kissinger diplomacy with Russia and China is successful, one major (and apparently intended) result will be to transform the rather simple adversary relationships of the past into multi-issue, multi-level interdependencies much less manipulable through negotiations at the top, and much more affected by broader U.S. domestic politics.

Most disturbing of all the reactions to limits of the system, however, has been the president's typical response when domestic politics keeps him from doing what he wants to do on the world scene. Rather than seeking to broaden his base by mollifying some of his critics, he attacks those whose support he needs as violators of some imagined presidential prerogative of unhampered executive action in foreign affairs, or as advocates of "neo-isolationism" and a total retreat from America's world role. Thus he exacerbates those substantive policy differences (and bad personal relations) which led to his setback in the first place. Appeals over the heads of the "elitists" to the "silent majority" can be tactically effective on occasion. But if unaccompanied by serious efforts at dialogue and consensus building with those congressional leaders and other foreign policy–concerned Americans who would be likely to respond positively to such efforts, such an approach is a prescription for continuing crises, for recurrent threats to that ability to act which the president so prizes, for the nurturing of a strong policy opposition ever-ready to reverse or check him when it has the opportunity to do so. And this opposition's opportunities to prevail have increased because the president, like his predecessor, has squandered a major asset for securing support for controversial actions—his personal credibility.

In sum, the Nixon-Kissinger closed policy-making approach seems effective only in a very limited range of foreign policy situations. And this range is narrowing as our relationships with Russia and China are transformed, as problems of the advanced, capitalist societies come to the fore, and as Americans' tolerance for discretionary presidential foreign policy action diminishes. All of these limitations underscore the need for presidentially linked foreign policy institutions with broader substantive reach and better capacity to coordinate multi-subject and multi-level U.S. negotiating initiatives. All suggest that the Nixon-Kissinger foreign policy-making approach would be looking less and less impressive even had "Watergate" never entered the American political vocabulary. But it has, leaving no U.S. foreign policy institution or issue unaffected. Watergate has weakened the ability of President Nixon to carry out any sort of strong foreign policy, however much he may be trying. And for some, it has also cast further doubt on the desirability of strengthening the presidency for any purpose.

•   •   •   •   •   •   •   •   •   •   •   •   •   •   •   •   •   •

Questions

1. Why did President Kennedy want to eliminate the distinction between "planning" and "operation" in the work of the NSC staff?

2. How successful was President Kennedy in making the secretary of state the agent of coordination for all of American foreign policy?
3. In what ways was the operation of the NSC and the NSC staff changed by President Johnson?
4. Compare and contrast the role of the NSC and the NSC staff in the Kennedy, Johnson, and Nixon administrations.
5. Why does the author believe the Nixon-Kissinger approach to the conduct of foreign policy to be of limited effectiveness?

Presidential Wars: The Convenience of "Precedent"*

Francis D. Wormuth

Francis D. Wormuth is professor of political science at the University of Utah, and is author of *Origins of Modern Constitutionalism* (New York: Harper & Brothers, 1949), and *The Vietnam War: The President vs. the Constitution* (Center for the Study of Democratic Institutions).

The presidential wars in Indochina have been the least publicized events in American history. The war, or rather the unopposed career of carnage, in Laos has never been acknowledged; there has been negligible official, and scanty unofficial, reporting of the military adventures in Vietnam and Cambodia. So obscure has been the history of our involvement that Robert McNamara, then secretary of defense, commissioned a study to discover what had happened. To maintain public ignorance, the Nixon administration unsuccessfully sought to enjoin publication of the study.

There has been even greater official reticence on the constitutional questions involved. In 1966, a year after President Johnson's massive escalation of the war in Vietnam, the State Department supplied the Senate Committee on Foreign Relations with a memorandum, so slight as to be frivolous, in justification of executive war making. The [Nixon] administration has been even less communicative. In various forums, Secretary of State Rogers, Solicitor General Griswold, and former

---

*Reprinted by permission from *The Nation*, October 9, 1972, pp. 301–304, and Francis D. Wormuth.

Assistant Attorney General Rehnquist have defended Mr. Nixon's prosecution of the war; these brief statements exhaust the administration's apologies for its conduct. They do not say much, but they say more than can be defended.

The framers of the Constitution attempted to put the question beyond doubt. At the Constitutional Convention, the committee of detail reported a proposal that the legislature be given the power "to make war." The Convention changed the word "make" to "declare," so that the executive might be free "to repel sudden attacks." This meant that war could be initiated in two ways: by joint resolution of Congress, and by the attack of an enemy. On issues arising from the war with France, 1798–1801, the Supreme Court held that it was for Congress to initiate all hostilities, whether general war or limited war, and that it was illegal for the president to exceed the authorization of Congress. In 1863, in the Prize Cases, the Court held that the president's power to resist sudden attack included response to insurrection; but it said that he had no power to initiate war.

According to Secretary Rogers, it follows from the power to repel attack that "in emergency situations, the president has the power and responsibility to use the armed forces to protect the nation's security." The emergency in Vietnam which purportedly called for independent executive action has never been identified; in any case the Constitution authorizes Congress, and not the president, to determine when the nation's security is imperiled and when it is appropriate to use the armed forces to protect it.

But the Nixon administration places its chief reliance on the commander-in-chief clause. This title was introduced in English military usage in 1639 and is still used by the British to describe the highest ranking officer in a military or naval hierarchy; this officer has always been subject to political superiors. When the Continental Congress made George Washington commander in chief in 1776, it instructed him "punctually to observe and follow such orders and directions, from time to time, as you shall receive from this, or a future Congress of these United Colonies, or committee of Congress." The Constitutional Convention adopted the term in the light of this usage. In 1850 the Supreme Court said of the position of the president, *after* Congress had declared war: "His duty and power are purely military. As commander-in-chief, he is authorized to direct the movements of the naval and military forces placed by law at his command, and to employ them in the manner he may deem most effectual to harass and conquer the enemy."

The commander-in-chief clause does not supplant the war clause, which gives the power to initiate war to Congress. And it must be read together with the clauses of the Constitution which authorize Congress to raise and support armies, to provide and maintain a navy, and to make rules for the government and regulation of the land and naval forces. The Supreme Court has held that only Congress may raise armies, that the president may not require an officer to perform any duty not imposed on him by statute, that he may not alter a salary fixed by statute, that he may not discharge an officer contrary to statute, that court-martial jurisdiction over soldiers is limited to that authorized by Congress, that a soldier when drafted may be assigned duties only in the capacity which subjected him to the draft. Congress has obliged the president to assign command of troops to the highest-ranking officer in the force; it has authorized the use of troops for some purposes and forbidden it for others; on several occasions it has forbidden that troops be sent to specified areas; when Theodore Roosevelt took the marines off naval vessels, Congress obliged him to restore them. As David Dudley Field put it: "To command an army is to give it its orders. . . . To do what? That, and that only, which the laws allow; and the laws are made, not by him but by Congress. His function is executive."

No judicial precedents support the claim that the commander-in-chief clause authorizes the president to undertake acts of war. But the apologists for the war in Vietnam rely on purported executive precedents. This argument developed in a curious way. In 1912 the solicitor of the state department, J. Reuben Clark, published a list of forty-one armed actions or displays of force abroad which had not been individually authorized by Congress. Two were illegal, but the other thirty-nine were naval actions to protect citizens. After "cursory consideration" Clark offered a legal theory to justify these actions, but he warned that "a more detailed and careful study" might not support it. This theory was the proposition that citizens were entitled to protection at international law, that international law was incorporated in the law of the United States, and that in protecting citizens the president was merely executing the laws of the United States. In 1934 the State Department republished Clark's study, updating the list of foreign interventions.

In 1941 there occurred a revolution in legal theory. Defending President Roosevelt's action in sending troops to Iceland, Senator Connally argued that the president as commander in chief might send troops wherever he wished, and cited the eighty-five cases from the 1934 revision of Clark's list as evidence. The commander-in-chief clause thus replaced the president's executive power; the limitation to the protection of citizens disappeared, and with it Clark's misgivings about even this narrowly defined action. In 1950 the State Department used Connally's list of eighty-five cases as precedents for President Truman's unauthorized entry into the Korean War. In 1966 the State Department asserted that there were 125 precedents for President Johnson's unauthorized entry into the war in Vietnam. In 1967 the State Department offered a list of 137 "armed actions taken by the United States without a declaration of war." In 1971 Solicitor General Griswold said that the United States had formally declared war six times and had engaged in hostilities on 155 other occasions as well. On December 18, 1971, Senator Goldwater asserted that he had compiled a list of "192 military actions undertaken without a declaration of war, eighty-one of which involved actual combat or ultimatums tantamount to the use of force."

It is time to set the record straight. Congress has passed not six but thirteen formal declarations of general war against a named adversary. On eight occasions Congress has authorized hostilities short of general war against a named adversary. On thirteen occasions Congress has rejected or ignored presidential requests for authority to engage in limited hostilities. On at least seven occasions the executive has refused to undertake hostile action on the ground that Congress had not authorized it.

In all the lists of purported executive precedents, about half the cases have been brief naval landings to protect citizens or their property in a foreign country in a time of riot or insurrection. All the lists are in error: there have in fact been 116 such landings, thirteen before 1865 and 103 thereafter. The thirteen were legally unauthorized, but in 1862 Congress empowered the secretary of the navy to make rules for the government of the navy, and the rules issued in 1865 contained carefully limited instructions to protect citizens in foreign ports in case of need. The 103 landings after 1865 did not rest on the president's executive power or the commander-in-chief clause. They rested on congressional authorization.

Only fifty-six of these 103 landings appear in the 1967 State Department list. Nine of the other cases listed also had statutory authorization. Of the seventy-two remaining cases, most were trivial. Some were merely minatory demonstrations at sea; some involved merely technical trespass. An unknown number were undertaken by army or navy officers without authorization from their superiors; if they prove anything about the war power, they prove that it belongs to every commissioned

officer. On the other hand, some cases have been presidential usurpa-
tions of great magnitude: six protracted occupations of Caribbean
states, the Korean War, the Vietnamese War. These can be said to
establish that the president possesses the war power only if the mere
repetition of a crime legalizes a sequence of crimes.

However, the Nixon apologists do not rest solely on the commander-
in-chief clause; they also argue that the president's "executive power"
authorizes him to engage in war. Justice Holmes said: "The duty of the
president to see that the laws be executed is a duty that does not go
beyond the laws or require him to achieve more than Congress sees fit
to leave within his power." In the 1952 Steel Seizure Case, three Justices, led by Harry Truman's crony, Chief Justice Vinson, argued that
the president's executive power authorized him to seize the steel mills
in order to maintain military production; but six Justices denied that he
could act without a statute. In 1971 the president sought to enjoin the
publication of the Pentagon Papers, but six Justices held that he could
not do so without statutory authorization. The other three Justices
took no position; they thought it premature to resolve the issues.

Apologists for executive war making invariably refer to what Secretary Rogers has called "the president's constitutional authority to conduct the foreign relations of the United States." Of course, no such
grant is to be found in the Constitution. The president shares the treaty-
making power and the power to appoint ambassadors with the Senate.
He shares the power over foreign commerce and all the war powers with
the full Congress. Only two powers in foreign relations are assigned to
him alone. He is commander in chief; but he acts in this capacity by and
under the authority of Congress. And he has the power to receive foreign ambassadors. Alexander Hamilton said that this function was
purely ceremonial; but it has come to entail recognition, which has legal
consequences. But the power of recognition does not entail the war
power. Presidents Madison, Monroe, Jackson, Grant, Cleveland and
McKinley refused to recognize revolutionary governments in colonial
countries because this might be regarded as an act of war by the mother
country, and only Congress could authorize acts of war.

The 1966 State Department apology asserted that the SEATO
treaty authorized, indeed obliged, the president to go to war in Vietnam. No one had noticed this feature of the treaty for twelve years after
its negotiation in 1954. No treaty made by the president and the Senate
can authorize war. In the Constitutional Convention, Charles Pinckney
proposed that the war power be given to the Senate, but he found no

second; it was given to the full Congress. Nor, if the Senate had the war power, could it delegate it in futuro to the president. Finally, no word of the SEATO treaty requires or permits the president to do anything whatever except to consult with the other signatories. In time of common danger, each signatory is to act "in accordance with its constitutional processes." Today no reliance is placed on the SEATO treaty. As far as this writer has been able to discover, only Presidential Assistant Harry Dent has offered the SEATO treaty as justification for President Nixon's prosecution of the war.

Obviously it is impossible to overcome the constitutional assignment of the war power to Congress. So the argument shifts. During the Johnson administration and the first two years of the Nixon administration reliance was placed on the Tonkin Gulf Resolution of 1964, in which Congress said that the president might do whatever he liked, "including the use of armed force," to assist Cambodia, Laos, "the free territory of Vietnam," Australia, New Zealand, Pakistan, the Philippines, Thailand, Great Britain and France in the maintenance of their freedom. Under Secretary of State Katzenbach called this resolution a "functional equivalent of a declaration of war." But a declaration of war always names an adversary; it makes hostilities mandatory; it specifies whether the war is general or limited. Tonkin Gulf attempted to delegate the war power wholesale to the president, at least as far as Southeast Asia was concerned.

Early in our history Chief Justice Marshall laid down the law of congressional delegation. Certain functions are "strictly and exclusively legislative," and "these important subjects must be entirely regulated by the legislature itself." But Congress may authorize judicial or executive rule making on matters "of lesser interest, in which a general provision may be made, and power given to those who are to act under such provisions to fill up the details."

Clearly the initiation of war is legislative. In 1835 the Senate unanimously adopted a resolution drafted by Henry Clay which rejected a request of President Jackson for contingent authority to make reprisals on French shipping because the war power could not be delegated. Congress rejected for the same reason eight requests of President Buchanan for contingent authority to intervene militarily in Central America and Mexico.

Suppose, however, we agree with the spokesmen for the Johnson and Nixon administrations that choosing an antagonist and launching a war is one of those topics of "lesser interest" on which Congress may delegate the power of decision to the executive. As Chief Justice Hughes said in *Schechter Poultry Corp.* v. *United States*, in making such a delegation Congress must "perform its function in laying down policies and establishing standards, while leaving to selected instrumentalities the making of subordinate rules within prescribed limits and the determination of facts to which the policy as declared by the legislature is to apply." In the Tonkin Gulf Resolution Congress laid down no policy and established no standard; the resolution was, as Senator Fulbright, who sponsored it in the Senate, said at a later date, "a blank check."

But in a strange opinion of 1936 by Justice Sutherland in *United States* v. *Curtiss-Wright Export Corp.* the Court had said that the limitations of the Constitution did not apply in foreign affairs, and that Congress might delegate to the president the power to make rules over foreign commerce without "laying down policies and establishing standards." Both the Johnson and Nixon administrations have argued that the Tonkin Gulf Resolution was a valid delegation of the war power because in foreign affairs the rule against delegation does not apply.

Sutherland's statement was not law but dictum, and has been rejected in every subsequent decision. In *Reid* v. *Covert* in 1956 the proposition that the Constitution does not apply in foreign affairs was expressly repudiated. In two cases involving foreign commerce (the issue in *Curtiss-Wright*) and five cases involving matters "of lesser interest" under the war power (a curfew, price controls, rent controls and contract renegotiation) all decided since *Curtiss-Wright*, the Court has announced and applied the orthodox tests of the validity of delegation: Congress must lay down policy and establish standards. In *Zemel* v. *Rusk* (1965), Chief Justice Warren said that the *Curtiss-Wright* case "does not mean that simply because a statute deals with foreign relations, it can grant the executive totally unrestricted freedom of choice." The dictum in *Curtiss-Wright* has neither paternity nor progeny.

In any case the Tonkin Gulf Resolution was repealed on January 12, 1971. Solicitor General Griswold, deprived of this purported statutory authorization, has argued that congressional appropriations for the support of troops in Vietnam have amounted to an implied ratification of the war. If these acts are ratifications, they too are uncontrolled delegatons. But the argument ignores the law of ratification by appropriation laid down by Justice Douglas for the Court in *Ex Parte Endo:* "the ratification must plainly show a purpose to bestow the precise authority which is claimed." And it ignores the doctrine of the equity of the statute. This doctrine, which goes back at least to the fifteenth century, is the proposition that the policy of a statute must be given effect beyond its literal terms. As Justice Holmes said: "The Legislature has the power to decide what the policy of the law shall be, and if it has intimated its will, however indirectly, that will should be recognized and obeyed." A repealer statute repeals all statutes, though not named, which share the policy of the statute repealed. If earlier appropriation acts carried any implied endorsement of the war, the repeal of the Tonkin Gulf Resolution, to which the appropriation acts were tributary, revoked that endorsement.

Nor has Congress left this in doubt. In the National Procurement Authorization Act of November 17, 1971, Congress declared it the policy of the United States "to terminate at the earliest practicable date all military operations of the United States in Indochina, and to provide for the prompt and orderly withdrawal of all United States military forces at a date certain, subject to the release of all American prisoners of war. . . ." President Nixon in signing the bill announced his intention of defying it. Since then he has repeatedly said that he will end military operations in Vietnam only after an agreement to political terms stipulated by him. The war is being continued, not without Congress but in defiance of Congress. None of the policy arguments for executive usurpation—"emergency" or "national security"—applies to this war. No constitutional provision and no executive precedent justifies the president in continuing a war against the expressed will of Congress. The case is unprecedented.

Since there is no legal case for the Nixon administration, its spokesmen have taken final refuge, not in the law but in the assertion that they are not accountable to law. The courts will not undertake to decide "political questions." Secretary Rogers has said that "There are relatively few judicial decisions concerning the relationship between the Congress and the president in the exercise of their respective war powers under the Constitution. The courts have usually regarded the subject as a political question and refused jurisdiction." Mr. Rogers must know that there are literally dozens of cases in which the courts have decided "concerning the relationship between the Congress and the president in the exercise of their respective war powers under the Constitution." It was never suggested until the Vietnamese War that the war power raised political questions. Rogers himself names only three cases, all concerned with this war. The Court of Appeals for the District of Columbia wrote a brief, confused opinion in *Luftig* v.

McNamara in which it said, among other things, that the legality of the Vietnamese War was a political question which it might not decide. In *Mora* v. *McNamara* the same court followed this earlier decision without opinion. Rogers' third case is *Massachusetts* v. *Laird*, in which the Supreme Court refused to permit Massachusetts to file a bill of complaint to challenge the war. It wrote no opinion and we are left to guess what motive or motives may have prompted the majority. Justices Douglas, Harlan and Stewart dissented.

The first and central test of a political question which the courts may not adjudicate is, to use the language of Justice Brennan in *Baker* v. *Carr*, the existence of a "textually demonstrable constitutional commitment of the issue to a coordinate political department." The Constitution nowhere commits the decision of the constitutional issue of the power of the president to initiate war, or for that matter of the power of Congress to delegate its war power, to the president or to Congress. These are justiciable matters for the courts, which have repeatedly asserted that the president may not initiate war, and that Congress may not delegate legislative power to the president.

But there is a political question of another order, one which demands judicial solution: it is nothing less than the continuance of our Republican form of government. As Justice Davis said, in holding Lincoln's declaration of martial law unconstitutional, "wicked men, ambitious of power, with hatred of liberty and contempt of law, may fill the place once occupied by Washington and Lincoln." Chief Justice Marshall in deciding, in *Cohens* v. *Virginia*, a question more dangerous politically to the Court than the war in Vietnam is to the present Court, said: "We have no more right to decline the exercise of jurisdiction which is given, than to usurp that which is not given. The one or the other would be treason to the Constitution." But our present Supreme Court continues to evade, by denial of certiorari, the most important constitutional question of the twentieth century.

Questions

1. On what basis does the author reach the conclusion that the president's role as commander in chief does not include the right to send troops to Vietnam without congressional approval?
2. How does the author deal with the argument that there are sufficient historical precedents for the presidential right to fight an undeclared war in Vietnam?

3. What does the author mean when he writes: "The dictum in *Curtiss-Wright* has neither paternity nor progeny"?
4. In the author's judgment, can Congress indirectly delegate its power to declare war?

Chapter Three

Congress and Foreign Policy

Over the past twenty-five years a consensus has developed among scholars as well as among many congressmen that Congress ought to confine its participation in foreign policy to establishing the broad outlines of national policy. It is generally argued that Congress does not have the staff capability to maintain a close supervision of foreign policy, but more importantly that such supervision is not a proper legislative function. But the restrictions on the ability of Congress to deal with the details of foreign policy do not apply when Congress turns its attention to the broad outlines of policy. Robert Dahl has suggested why this is so:

> . . . The more closely debate moves toward broad and basic policy, the more competent is the legislative decision likely to be, and correspondingly less competent is the expert. This is not merely because basic policy involved "value" questions which ought to be outside the political authority of the expert in a democracy. It is also because the judgments of "fact" must include more and more complex variables on which the expert, in the present state of social sciences, is probably professionally less competent than the intelligent politician. When questions of military strategy broaden into problems of international politics, as they inevitably will at some point, the competence of the general ought to give way to that of the politician. . . .

Doubt has been cast upon this interpretation of Congress's role by the events of the Vietnam War, which have shown that unfettered executive discretion in the conduct of foreign policy is tantamount to exclusive executive responsibility for foreign policy. If the executive branch is free without legislative supervision to order the armed forces of the United

States into combat, or to conduct the bombing of a neutral country, albeit with that country's permission, without reference to congressional approval, then there seems to be little point in Congress having the power to set general policy guidelines unless it also has the power to ensure that those guidelines will be followed.

Congress is therefore thrust upon the horns of an almost impossible dilemma. If it wishes to exercise close supervision over policy, it has to set itself to achieve a goal that is very poorly structured and ultimately may be beyond its competence. If, on the other hand, it elects to limit its role to the fixing of policy guidelines within which the president is expected to conduct foreign policy, it has little machinery to ensure that those guidelines are not overstepped. There is always the fiscal power that resides in the hands of Congress, but this is a blunt weapon and its use is rarely completely relevant to the problem at hand. This is particularly true when the president commands the support of more than one-third of Congress and can therefore make effective use of his veto. In such cases, it is impossible for Congress to make use of its fiscal powers unless it is willing to bring the life of the nation to a standstill. It would have been possible, for example, for Congress to withhold funds for the prosecution of the Vietnam War. A presidential veto of an appropriation bill with that clause would have meant no funds for national defense. Congress would have been faced with the unenviable choice of either striking the offending clause or cutting off all funds for the armed forces. Faced with these kinds of choices, Congress has been unwilling to use its fiscal power to force foreign policy decisions.

Even if Congress could agree on the concepts that would guide its supervision of foreign policy, there is a major structural problem that Congress must overcome before it can make its voice fully effective in the foreign policy process. This structural problem arises because a division of labor is necessary if Congress is to deal effectively with the broad range of problems on which it must pass judgment. Such a division of labor is, of course, necessary not only for Congress but for all large organizations. It forces Congress to divide its work among various committees whose members with the aid of committee staffs provide the expertise that Congress must bring to the various aspects of the legislative process. However, the recommendations from the various committees must be coordinated if congressional policy is to have an overall coherence and clarity.

We have seen how the executive branch has sought to organize itself using the National Security Council and the NSC staff as a means for integrating the inputs of various executive agencies into a coherent foreign policy. It is precisely this type of mechanism that Congress lacks. The result of this failure is the multiplication of the number of voices within Congress that assert the right to speak for Congress on foreign policy issues, but no congressman can persuade his own colleagues of this right, let alone his own constituents or the executive. This multitude of congressional voices cannot hope to compete with the executive branch, which, although not perfectly unified, presents a relatively solid front to Congress and the nation. The divisions within Congress give the executive ample opportunity to rely on the tried-and-true rule: divide and conquer.

These tensions between Congress and the executive over the control of foreign policy are complicated by the struggle between the major political parties for domination of foreign policy. For twenty years following World War II, the inner party conflict dominated most discussions of congressional-executive relations in the making of foreign policy. Concern for the impact of partisan politics on foreign policy led to the praise of bipartisan foreign policy. Bipartisan, when used in this sense, has stood for the proposition that in the conduct of foreign policy the president would not propose policies that would not be supported by a consensus among leaders of both parties, and that if the president recognized those consensual leaders' limits the opposition leaders would not use foreign policy as a political weapon. Bipartisan foreign policy, however, generally has been interpreted much differently in practice. The party in power has tended to treat it as a carte blanche to follow its party preferences, whereas members of the minority party have asserted that it gave them a veto over policy decisions. Furthermore, the critics of the bipartisan approach allege that it has been one of the major influences that led to the general acceptance of executive dictatorship over foreign policy. What it has done, these critics allege, is to "declare open confrontation off limits. This contributed to the direct delegation of power to the lower-level agencies and nonpolitical bureaucracies without adding power or legitimacy to either the president or the Congress." These critics believe that an independent Congress that can boldly exercise its war and peace powers would be far more dependable and effective than the party system in governing America's international conduct. The dominant relationship between Congress and the president, according to these critics, should be one of confrontation, not cooperation. This would assure that those who oppose policies within the executive branch could gain a meaningful hearing from Congress and that congressional efforts to control and monitor executive foreign policy would be more meaningful.

The first selection in this chapter, "Congressional Resurgence," by Stan A. Taylor, assesses the balance between the executive and legislative branches as they seek to fulfill their constitutional mandate to formulate and carry out foreign policy. Professor Taylor traces the swing of the pendulum of power over foreign policy as it vacillates between Congress and the executive, but accurately notes that the tendency has been for that pendulum to swing further and further into the executive. The second selection is an article by Holbert Carroll on the politics of committees. This article clearly notes that the real work of Congress is done in the committees; therefore, the key to the understanding of Congress and foreign policy is to analyze the way the committees operate and their relationship to the Senate and to the House as a whole. In the final selection, Walt W. Rostow presents the case for executive control of foreign policy, which is answered by Representative Gunn McKay as he presents the case for a much more substantial role for Congress in foreign policy.

Congressional Resurgence*

Stan A. Taylor

Stan A. Taylor, associate professor of political science at Brigham Young University, received his B.S. in political science from Brigham Young University, and his Ph.D. from Fletcher School of Law and Diplomacy. He served as an Administrative assistant to Representative Gunn McKay in 1971–72, and is currently coordinator of the International Relations Program at Brigham Young University.

Much of the literature on the role of Congress in foreign affairs, according to Carl Marcy, chief of staff of the Senate Committee on Foreign Relations, "concludes that what the executive proposes is profound, basically sound, and questioned only by dopes who must be re-elected every two or six years." Moreover, it is widely assumed that Congress will never be able to deal effectively in foreign affairs as long as it has to compete from a position of weakness with an executive branch which by law and tradition is endowed with all of the advan-

---

*Reprinted by permission of the author.

tages. In fact, Congress has usually been considered to be a "crippled eagle" in the field of foreign affairs.

At times that "fact" has been celebrated, but more recently there has been some lamenting. Unfortunately many such discussions, whether celebrations or lamentations, fail to make clear certain assumptions, the blurring of which tend to lead the reader to one, and only one, point of view. Two brief examples may demonstrate this point. Much of the "strengthen the executive in foreign affairs" literature tends to assume that promptness of decision and efficiency of action are very basic values to be achieved in foreign affairs. That assumption ignores the question of ends and focuses rather on means. That is, it is assumed that there is an advantage in quickness and efficiency regardless of the value or wisdom of the policy being executed. On the other hand, the "strengthen Congress in foreign affairs" literature tends to assume that, whether one likes a particular foreign policy or not, the representative nature of Congress results, almost ipso facto, in a more democratic, and hence "better" foreign policy. Yet, many congressional decisions, particularly in the area of defense and trade policies, are singularly undemocratic and unrepresentative and are more in the nature of compromise and favors granted to assist a congressman in his constituent relations.

Perhaps a better approach to the dispute might be to note that throughout American history, the balance between Congress and the executive has swung in a pendulum-like fashion from periods of executive dominance to periods of congressional dominance with the pendulum never quite returning fully to the congressional side. Thus, while congressional-executive dominance has alternated over the years, the axis of the pendulum has drifted toward the executive. The interesting question then becomes, what conditions and developments explain this shift? Why, in fact, has it been difficult for Congress to exert a sustained and powerful influence in foreign affairs? To answer this question, one must consider, among other things, the legal framework, the changing historical setting, the personalities of the primary agents of each branch, and congressional structure. Each of these will be discussed briefly from the perspective of the role of Congress in foreign policy.

The Legal Framework

The constitutional division of responsibilities between Congress and the executive is usually described as "an invitation to struggle."

The framers attempted to avoid the excessive decentralization of authority with which they were familiar under the Articles of Confederation and the extreme centralization they had known in Great Britain. Of course, it is very misleading to assume, as is often done, that this "invitation to struggle" is unique to the field of foreign affairs. The desire to avoid the Scylla of executive dominance and the Charybdis of congressional dominance is present in virtually every substantive allocation of authority in the Constitution.

My own view, somewhat contrary to prevailing wisdom, is that Congress is more favored by the Constitution than is the executive. Consider the distribution: Congress is empowered ". . . to provide for the common defence . . . ; To define and punish Piracies and Felonies committed on the high seas, and Offences against the law of Nations; To declare War, grant Letters of Marque and Reprisal, and to make Rules concerning Captures on Land and Water; To raise and support Armies . . . ; To provide and maintain a Navy . . . ; To provide for calling forth the Militia to . . . repel invasions; To make all Laws which shall be necessary and proper for carrying into execution the foregoing Powers"; and to give "advice and consent" in the making of treaties! The president's responsibilities, on the other hand, are much more administrative in nature. He is empowered to be the commander in chief of the military; however, as Hamilton explained in the 69th *Federalist*, that power was still substantially inferior to that enjoyed by the King of England and was meant to bestow upon the president supreme authority over the armed forces in the field, not to grant him the power to create armed forces where none existed or to unilaterally determine their use in the pursuit of foreign policy. The president may also receive ambassadors, but it is doubtful that that was originally meant to vest sole powers of recognition in the executive branch. The president's remaining powers were to be shared with the Senate—namely, the power to enter into treaty obligations and to nominate ambassadors.

One should not confuse this legal framework with the actual developing practice of conducting foreign relations. As suggested above, even though the pendulum has swung back and forth between the executive and Congress, the axis of the swing has moved consistently and perceptibly toward the executive. Nevertheless, the intent of the framers is probably best expressed by juxtaposing two, sort of summary, constitutional statements. The Constitution gives the legislature the power to "make all laws which shall be necessary and proper for carrying into execution the foregoing powers vested by this constitution in the Government of the United States or in any department or officer thereof," and the executive imperium is that he "faithfully execute" the laws of the land.

Any debate, however, over the intent of the framers is somewhat moot, given the early development of executive power and the continuation of executive prerogative in spite of occasional periods of congressional dominance. In a general sense, the administrations of Washington, Adams, Jefferson, Madison, and Monroe were clearly periods of executive dominance. However, as domestic issues of westward expansion and slavery drew some attention away from foreign affairs, Congress became more important. The power of the executive in foreign affairs then lay in relative abeyance (with some notable exceptions) from Monroe, through Jackson, who had perhaps as much respect for congressional authority as any president, down to Polk, whose unilateral war making with Mexico drew a now-famous attack on presidential war making from Representative Abraham Lincoln. "Allow the president to invade neighboring nations whenever he shall deem it necessary to repel an invasion," said Lincoln, "and you allow him to make war at pleasure."

A brief period of congressional dominance existed from Polk to Buchanan and was followed by excessive presidential superiority under Lincoln. As usual, any strong domination by one branch is usually followed by an opposite reaction. Thus, Congress exercised a heavy influence over foreign affairs until the turn of the century, when McKinley set a pattern of presidential power that has been followed, with some exceptions, down to the administration of Richard Nixon. Roosevelt, Wilson, Truman, Johnson, and Nixon, each in his own way, added arrows to the quiver of presidential power over foreign affairs.

Historical Setting

The foreign affairs power of Congress is influenced by changing historical conditions. This principle becomes particularly apparent when one examines the treaty-making function and the power to make war.

The treaty-making function is significant because it may commit the nation to a particular, and perhaps critical, foreign policy for a long period of time. Terms of alliances, conditions of commerce and trade, peace treaties, arms control agreements, and charters of international organizations are all examples of this power, which the Constitution divided between the executive and the Senate. Article II, Section 2,

Clause 2 states that the president "shall have power, by and with the advice and consent of the Senate, to make treaties, provided two-thirds of the Senators present concur. . . ." Unfortunately, the Constitution suggests neither how nor when the Senate should offer its advice, nor does it discuss when consent is required, to what consent is needed, or how treaties, to which consent has been given, can be changed. Each of these have turned out to be serious questions, the answers to which may have made major differences in U.S. foreign policy. It is also unfortunate that while the intent of the Constitution on this point was probably to provide for democratic control over foreign policy, the most democratic division of Congress, the House of Representatives, is quite openly ignored.

Nevertheless, early administrations appeared to make serious efforts toward utilizing both the advice *and* the consent of the Senate. However, as international relations became more and more complicated and as the technology of war placed greater emphasis on the immediacy of decisions, the executive found an increasing number of ways to ignore or circumvent the advice of the Senate. This particular trend reached a climax when Woodrow Wilson developed plans for U.S. participation in the League of Nations and for the Treaty of Versailles with virtually no "advice" from the Senate, which, so snubbed, refused to offer its "consent," thus greatly lessening the likelihood of a successful postwar organization.

In spite of a brief period of congressional resurgence, the executive, responding to what it has perceived as Senate obstructionism, has resorted to informal agreements, executive agreements, and other types of foreign policy commitments that apparently have not required Senate action. The reputation of the Senate as the graveyard of treaties, though widely held, is probably not true. Since 1789, only eleven treaties have been rejected by a failure to obtain the necessary two-thirds majority. This, of course, omits those not submitted to the Senate because of an anticipated negative reaction. These attempts to circumvent the Senate have continued and sparked a major controversy over executive prerogatives during the Eisenhower administration in the debate over the Bricker Amendment, the purpose of which was to outlaw executive agreements and, in effect, to reaffirm the role of the Senate in treaty making. Although this amendment and subsequent versions died, the long and bitter debate did send a message to the executive office which has, at times, resulted in more courteous relations.

Another interesting effect of the changing historical setting and the foreign affairs powers of Congress is seen in the changing role of the

House in treaty making. While deprived by the Constitution of any treaty responsibilities, the House through its singular power of the purse has played an increasingly important role, not only in the making of treaties, but in the making and supervising of foreign policy. Even from the earliest days of the Republic this possibility was recognized. President George Washington found himself with a treaty to which the Senate had agreed but which required $40,000 to ransom some American captives in Algiers. Much to the objection of the Senate, which was reluctant to share its unique power, the House appropriated the necessary amount and the treaty was consummated.

But it has been only in the post–World War II period that, by and large, the normal conduct of American foreign policy has required large sums of money. This need for money has resulted in a dual shift in the power over foreign affairs. As foreign aid, payments to multilateral agencies, weapons systems developments, the space race, and the financing of undeclared wars became more and more important in American foreign policy, the power of Congress vis-à-vis the executive increased, and because legislation appropriating this money must originate in the House of Representatives, the power of that body vis-à-vis the Senate also increased.

The power to make war, once clearly the prerogative of Congress, has tended to become more and more a presidential prerogative. This, of course, also relates to the changing historical setting. General periods of international crisis favor the executive over Congress. However, periods of crisis-induced presidential predominance have been followed invariably by a reaction of congressional reassertment. Thus, the Spanish-American War, World Wars I and II, the Korean War, and the war in Vietnam all were followed by more or less successful periods of congressional resurgence. Such reassertment, however, normally lasts only until the next crisis.

Of nine fairly significant wars before 1945, Congress "declared" war in five—World Wars I and II, the Spanish-American War, the Mexican War, and the War of 1812. Four were fought without such a declaration—the Mexican-American clashes of 1914–17, the First and Second Barbary Wars (1801 and 1815), and the naval war with France (1798–1800). Since 1945 no declarations of war have been issued, although some major "wars" (Korea and Vietnam) have been fought and a number of foreign commitments have occurred (Lebanon, the Bay of Pigs, the Dominican Republic occupation, and forays into Laos and Cambodia). Some of these, as well as other, commitments have had the "blessing" of a congressional resolution (the Tonkin Gulf, Berlin,

Cuban, Middle East, and Formosa Straits Resolutions); others have not.

In an attempt to reverse this trend, Congress adopted in 1974 a War Powers Bill, the effects of which are as yet unknown but the intent of which is quite clear. The bill (HJ Res 542), one of only five bills passed over President Nixon's veto, established a sixty-day limit on any presidential commitment of U.S. troops abroad without specific congressional approval. It was opposed by some conservatives who felt it tied the hands of the president too much and by some liberals who felt it gave the president something neither the Constitution nor reason gives him—the right to commit troops *unilaterally* for at least sixty days.

The bill also established certain reporting procedures governing the commitment of troops and allowed for a thirty-day extension of the commitment if such were necessary for the safe withdrawal of the troops. Even the sixty-day deadline, however, could be terminated at any time through congressional approval of a resolution to that effect by both the House and the Senate.

The most surprising aspect of the passage of the War Powers Bill over the president's veto was its relatively easy passage in the House. It was a foregone conclusion that the effort would be successful in the Senate, but the House had sustained the president's veto five times earlier in 1973, and neither side was confident of the outcome in the House.

Two events, however, impinged on the House deliberations. First, the ongoing Watergate investigation had created a more favorable climate for limiting presidential power. Specifically, a few days prior to the House debate, the president had fired Special Prosecutor Archibald Cox and had reported the absence of two tapes requested by U.S. District Judge John Sirica. Second, the results of November elections in New Jersey as well as in several cities began to reveal a "Watergate effect" that House members read as a sign of growing dissatisfaction with the president. That perception was translated into a vote to override the president's veto on the War Powers Bill.

In sum, it may be accurate to note that while the changing historical setting has increased the role of Congress, particularly the House, in treaty making, this has been more than offset by growing executive power in other aspects of foreign affairs. Some suggest that even though the relative power of Congress in foreign policy has diminished vis-à-vis that of the executive, the scope of its activities has increased, because foreign policy is now so broadly defined and the number and kinds of foreign concerns have increased. This, of course, may be but a charitable way of saying that Congress is now doing less and less about more and more things. Periods of international tension, incipient conflict, and war normally favor the executive, while periods of relative international stability, postwar periods, and the ascendancy of domestic issues (but *not* domestic crises) and isolationism tend to favor Congress. However tentative that conclusion may be, it is virtually certain that neither the executive nor Congress can claim any primacy of virtue, wisdom, luck, or success in using the war-making power.

Power and Personality

The peculiar intermixing of personalities and personal style also helps explain the changing relationships between Congress and the executive. Of particular importance, of course, are the personalities and styles of the president and his chief foreign policy adviser, whether it be the secretary of state or the chairman of the National Security Council, and of the leadership of Congress, particularly of the relevant committees. It is tautological, but worth noting, that periods of a strong president and weak congressional leadership result in further drift toward executive predominance. It is possible, conversely, to find periods of strong congressional leadership and weak presidential personality, during which the normal drift has been arrested. The absence of a single spokesman for Congress (as well as other factors to be discussed later) is one of the limitations Congress faces in competing with the executive in the foreign policy process. In the period just prior to World War I, when the Speaker of the House "Uncle Joe" Cannon in fact "spoke" for the House, its relative power was enhanced. Following the revolt against such strong centralized leadership, it has been more difficult for the House to field a strong leader.

Similarly, one aspect of the political process in the Senate has inhibited the development of strong assertive leadership in that body. This has been particularly true during the long recent period of Democratic control in the Senate when leadership positions have gone to somewhat undistinguished Western Senators as a result of a compromise between the conservative Southern Democrats and the more liberal Northern Democrats. Thus, in both Houses, any strong leadership that has developed has resulted from the hazards of the seniority process.

The relative ability of the Senate to avoid complete extinction in the field of foreign affairs in recent years is partially the result of the strong leadership of Senator Fulbright. Even there, however, power has resulted not so much from legal and institutional prerogatives as from Fulbright's use of the media as a means of focusing public opinion on several aspects of foreign policy. Hearings before the Senate Foreign Relations Committee have become a sort of nationwide community college course in American and world affairs presided over by Professor Fulbright with a stable of impressive guest lecturers.

The absence of the House Foreign Affairs Committee from the roll-call of power has been noticeable for years. This has been caused, in some part, by the failure of any strong congressman to survive the seniority contest long enough to rise to the chairmanship. On the other hand, the role of the House Appropriations Committee in foreign affairs has increased as foreign policy has required more fiscal appropriations for its success, but not necessarily because of the personality and style of its chairman. Similarly, the role of the House Armed Services Committee has increased, but in this case primarily because of the style of its chairman.

The effect of the personality and style of Wilbur Mills as chairman of the House Ways and Means Committee is a further demonstration of this point. That committee has not had a long history of significant foreign policy input. However, when Mr. Mills became chairman and began to expand its power, Ways and Means became one of the most critical Capitol Hill influences on foreign policy. Mr. Mills became personally responsible for much of American trade policies, even to the point of performing the role of diplomat-negotiator, sometimes with and at other times without White House approval. The precise role of Mr. Mills in 1971 and 1972 in establishing trade and tariff policies with Japan in the critical areas of textiles and steel is still not fully known, yet his impact cannot be denied.

Personality and style can be so important in Congress that the anticipation of certain developments may become cause for action or inaction. Early in the 92nd Congress an attempt was made by a coalition of liberal congressmen to lessen the effects of the seniority system, particularly as it applied to committee and subcommittee chairmanships. Prior to this effort a congressman could lead one full committee plus as many subcommittees as he wanted. The thrust of the liberal attack was to require that a congressman could chair no more than one full committee *or* subcommittee. This reform would have opened approximately thirty-five subcommittee chairmanships. The conservative and moderate congressmen wanted to modify the proposal so that a congressman could chair a full committee *and* one subcommittee, which would have opened up only fifteen subcommittee chairmanships. As the Democratic caucus was preparing to meet and vote on these proposals, word began to float around that if the complete liberal reform was accepted, it would result in the removal of a moderate congressman from a significant defense-related subcommittee and allow the ranking majority member, who was a militant cold warrior, to assume leadership. Moreover, it was rumored, were he allowed to assume that leadership, he would have the United States "at the gates of the Kremlin" in six months. This specter was enough to frighten the liberals into retreating to the moderate proposal so that committee chairmen could retain both a full committee and one subcommittee chairmanship.

Congressional Structure

The institutional structure and processes of Congress also have played a significant role in the degree of influence Congress has been able to utilize. While it is obvious that the Senate Foreign Relations Committee and the House Foreign Affairs Committee were meant to be the congressional committees most influential in foreign policy, this actually has been the case only in the Senate, where the Foreign Relations Committee has been one of the most prestigious committees on Capitol Hill. Primarily because of its jurisdiction over treaties, the committee has been the most sought-after committee assignment in the Senate and, until recently, one of its major centers of power. Nevertheless, there are at least twelve of the Senate's seventeen standing committees that have some jurisdiction over legislation impinging more or less directly on foreign affairs.

In the House, the Foreign Affairs Committee has never held the stature of its counterpart in the Senate. Lack of jurisdiction over treaties and the absence of strong leadership have relegated the Foreign Affairs Committee to lesser importance. The House also suffers from a proliferation of committees dealing with foreign policy. Of the twenty standing committees of the House, thirteen have some jurisdiction. Of particular importance in the House has been the Appropriations Committee with its control over all expenditures, the Ways and Means Committee with its jurisdiction over trade legislation, and the Government Operations Committee through its Subcommittee on Foreign Operations. This proliferation of congressional committees, each with some jurisdiction in the foreign affairs field and each very jealous of that responsibility, has resulted, particularly in the House but also in the Senate, in a chorus without a conductor and has greatly lessened congressional impact in foreign affairs.

In recent years there has been a great deal of talk about creating a "supercommittee" to allow for greater coordination in the foreign policy field. This has already been done in the economic field with the creation of the Joint Economic Committee, consisting of ten congressmen and ten senators. This committee has been moderately successful in its efforts, largely as the result of the vigorous leadership of the senior senator on the committee. Other such efforts, in the areas of atomic energy, congressional operations, defense productions, budget control, federal expenditures, and taxation, have been less successful. There is normally considerable opposition to the creation of joint committees unless their powers are severely limited by statute. Even the Joint Economic Committee has no legislative jurisdiction and relies, often in vain, on other committees for appropriate legislation. There is little likelihood at the present time for a Joint Foreign Affairs Committee, given the relative decline in foreign policy interest in the post-Vietnam period.

There is, however, greater likelihood that the House will adopt a major reorganization plan being debated in 1974. If so, it will be the first major reorganization of committee jurisdictions and structure since 1946. A bipartisan select committee headed by Representative Richard Bolling of Missouri was created to accomplish this, and its recommendations, if adopted, would make far-reaching changes in virtually every area. In the foreign affairs area it would give trade, international finance, and other new responsibilities to the Foreign Affairs Committee. This would have the effect of centralizing responsibility by ending some of the proliferation that now exists as well as by strengthening the Foreign Affairs Committee.

Unfortunately, the proliferation of jurisdictions is not the only structural problem Congress faces. The inability of Congress to deal strongly in foreign affairs is also the result of staff limitations and of traditional intercommittee jealousies. It is difficult for Congress to discharge its overseer responsibilities with any great care and precision when the foreign policy agencies, operations, and processes over which it has responsibility themselves are so large and dispersed. The Senate Foreign Relations Committee has a total staff of 33 and the House Foreign Affairs Committee one of 35, yet they are expected to produce appropriate legislation, conduct hearings and briefings, and carry out overseer responsibilities in areas for which the executive branch has the National Security Council, the State Department, the entire intelligence community, and some parts of Labor, Commerce, and other assorted executive agencies. The House Appropriations Committee, for example, which has the responsibility of overseeing all federal expenditures, has a professional staff of 42 whereas its counterpart in the executive branch, the Office of Management and Budget, has a professional staff of 660.

Moreover, there is a debilitating lack of cooperation within Congress itself. It is often difficult for a congressman to obtain foreign policy information he may need from a committee of which he is not a member. Even interstaff cooperation is limited, and that which does exist is a result of personal friendships and ties with no legal or continuing base. Much of this problem is created by the way staff personnel are hired. Because virtually every staff person holds his position because of an appointment by a congressman or senator and with his continuing approval, staff loyalties are very strong and are directed first to his patron, second to the subcommittee, then to the full committee, and then to other members and other committees and staffs.

Moreover, given the almost inherent advantage of the executive branch because of its single leadership, Congress faces a difficult task in trying to reverse the somewhat inexorable drift of the axis of the pendulum toward the executive. Even the post-Watergate period, when there appears to be widespread acceptance of the need to limit the powers of the president, has produced only one such reform—the War Powers Bill. As mentioned above, the success of that effort remains to be seen. The most significant area of congressional reform will probably be in the budget area with the creation of a more coordinated budget process between both Houses. As Lloyd George once remarked about the division of powers in British government, "Parliament has really no control over the executive; it is a pure fiction."

Nevertheless, some congressional reorganization would alleviate, at least partially, some of the conditions that restrain congressional effectiveness in foreign affairs. It is enlightening, if not also discouraging, to observe the radical changes that have occurred in the structures and processes by which the executive branch conducts foreign policy and national security policy over the last thirty years and to observe the glaring absence of any concomitant congressional changes.

Conclusion

The constitutional basis of the division of powers and responsibilities in foreign affairs favored Congress much more than have subsequent developments. With the exception of the post–World War II development, of foreign policy requiring large sums of congressionally appropriated money, nearly every other factor discussed above has resulted in a lessening of congressional influence. Of course, it is not difficult to celebrate this development and to point out numerous instances of destructive intervention by Congress into foreign affairs. But it is equally easy to cite instances of constructive congressional activity. The wisdom of the Founding Fathers was great, and their creation of a separation of foreign policy powers was neither accidental nor incidental. In the American nonparliamentary system, Congress is in some ways given the role of a "loyal opposition." Recent insight into the nature of complex decision-making systems suggests there may be considerable wisdom in multiple advocacy, which itself requires strong and informed, yet competing, centers of power.

While nothing will ever replace the value of wisdom, one can hope that the right coincidence of personalities, reorganization, and international events may encourage a reassertment of congressional authority in foreign affairs—not, of course, at the expense of a strong executive. To return to a metaphor used earlier, American foreign policy requires, among other things, strong healthy wings on both sides of the eagle for successful flight.

Questions

1. What effect do you feel the war in Vietnam had on the traditional argument that the slowness of congressional action renders Congress less suited for participation in foreign affairs? Why?
2. How do you evaluate Taylor's argument that the Constitution favors Congress more than the executive in foreign affairs?
3. As more and more foreign policy decisions become subject to cost-effectiveness analysis and as America becomes more cost-conscious, do you think the role of the House will change? Why? What may be the effect of worsening domestic conditions?
4. What do you feel would be the most effective way for Congress to become more efficient and play a beneficial role in foreign affairs?
5. Do you anticipate that any of the so-called abuses of executive power that contributed to the resignation of President Nixon may alter future foreign policy decision making? Why?
6. Does the rather sustained popularity of Secretary of State Kissinger support or detract from Taylor's argument concerning the role of personalities in foreign affairs?

The Politics of the Committees*

Holbert N. Carroll

Holbert Nicholson Carroll was educated at the University of Pittsburgh and at Harvard. He was a consultant to the Brookings Institution, Washington, D. C., and is presently chairman of the Department of Political Science at the University of Pittsburgh.

The House sits, not for serious discussion, but to sanction the conclusions of its Committees as rapidly as possible. It legislates in its committee-rooms; not by the determination of majorities, but by the resolutions of specially-commissioned minorities; so that it is not far from the truth to say that Congress in session is Congress on public exhibition, whilst Congress in its committee-rooms is Congress at work.

Woodrow Wilson[1]

In that happy age of innocence before World War II, the myth persisted that a high wall separated domestic from foreign policy. Participation in a major European war and involvement in scores of minor skirmishes had not yet taught the American people that they had never been as isolated as they supposed. Only one house committee regularly dealt with "foreign affairs." Even this group, so its historian has recorded, was not busy.[2]

The Committee on Foreign Affairs now competes with eighteen other standing committees and miscellaneous select and special units for all the foreign policy business of the House of Representatives. All of these committees are at least indirectly concerned with foreign affairs. More than half of them regularly consider important foreign policy matters, usually in jealous isolation from one another.

Indeed, it is not uncommon for several committees to dabble with one problem. An alert refugee abroad interested in settling somewhere

---

*Reprinted from *House of Representatives and Foreign Affairs* by Holbert N. Carroll, by permission of the University of Pittsburgh Press. © 1958 by the University of Pittsburgh Press.

1. *Congressional Government* (New York: Meridian Books, 1956), p. 69. This book was first published in 1885.

2. Albert C. F. Westphal, *The House Committee on Foreign Affairs* (New York: Columbia University, 1942).

or just in getting fed, for example, should at a minimum keep an eye on the activities of the Committees on Judiciary, Foreign Affairs, and Agriculture as well as several subcommittees of the Committee on Appropriations. It would also pay him to examine stray clauses in bills sponsored by two or three other committees such as Armed Services. Few, if any, representatives could give a coherent picture of what Congress has provided for assorted refugees, displaced persons, migrants, expellees, and orphans about the globe.

Woodrow Wilson's observations of 1885 are still sound. The House continues to devolve immense powers upon its committees and to serve mainly as a ratifying agency for their decisions. But in 1885, tiny tricklets of legislation flowed from many standing committees to form a small stream of business for the lower chamber. Today, the standing committees and numerous less regular streams pour out an ocean of legislation. The relationship among hundreds of bills is more intimate now than then. Domestic and foreign policy merge into one policy. Military and budgetary considerations impinge upon all areas of policy. Yet the processes of the House for coordinating its control over this vast ocean of business are not much more efficient than in 1885.

To be sure, Congress has periodically reorganized itself. In the reorganization of 1946, strengthened staff services were provided for Congress as a whole, and the committees were encouraged to employ professional staff assistance.[3] The number of standing committees was sharply reduced, and the members of the House, with minor exceptions, were assigned to only one of the new combinations. Committee jurisdictions were broadened and somewhat rationalized in the process.

This modest reorganization helped to improve the quality of legislative control of foreign affairs. Serious deficiencies in the organization and procedures of the House and its committees were not touched, however, and some of the opportunities provided by the act have been but half-heartedly exploited. Only about half of the committees, for example, are well-staffed with competent professional assistance. More important, this reorganization failed to correct the situation . . . of divergent and sometimes contradictory committee behavior in foreign affairs. Uncoordinated control of foreign affairs characterizes the behavior of the House of Representatives. Before plunging into this problem of coordination, it is necessary to probe into the anatomy of a congressional committee.

---

3. P. L. 601, 79th Cong.

The Anatomy of a Committee

Formal and Efficient Parts

Writers of books on American government generally appreciate the role of committees in the legislative process. The half dozen or so committee decisions required, the resulting decentralization and, in many instances, disintegration of leadership and power, the curious but often tragic consequences of the seniority system, the powerful influence of the committee chairmen, government by a multitude of little governments as Wilson so interestingly described it in 1885—all of these features have been properly stressed.

The tendency in following this textbook analysis, however, is to look upon committees primarily as institutions, as monolithic bodies of thirty or so men, bodies roughly equal in power and respect in the eyes of the House and men equally attentive to their duties. A committee, to use a distinction made famous by Bagehot in another situation, has its dignified, ornamental, or formal parts and its efficient parts.[4] An appreciation of this distinction, as well as certain other features of congressional committees, is essential for an understanding of the role of these little legislatures in foreign affairs.

The formal part of a committee consists of the chairman and the party majority, a part of the committee which usually sticks together on procedural matters. In short, the formal part of a committee consists of those who in theory supply the initiative and leadership. They may formally approve legislation in the committee and support it with their votes on the floor, but they do little of the real work. On occasion, though, the formal part of a committee may be the efficient part.

The efficient part of a committee consists of a core of members, usually only a handful of men representing both political parties. These men actively participate in the hearings, propose the amendments that are accepted, and shape the legislation. They write parts of the committee's report, or at least take the time to slant it to their satisfaction. The efficient element then takes the bill to the floor and fights for it. Their knowledge of the subjects within the committee's jurisdiction may be more specialized than that of the witnesses from the executive branch who appear before them. Department and agency heads and

---

4. Walter Bagehot discussed the dignified and efficient parts of English government in *The English Constitution* (World's Classics ed., London: Oxford, 1928).

their top assistants are viewed as mere transitory figures by representatives whose service extends over more than one administration. More than one witness has been confounded by questions and observations drawn from the vast reservoir of knowledge gained by individual congressmen over decades.

The efficient element of a committee is rarely composed of a majority of the members even though it must carry a majority with it. Probably less than ten members of the thirty-two man Committee on Foreign Affairs, for example, persistently and actively participate in the deliberations of the group. Indeed, in some instances the efficient element may be just one man. This monologic situation is not unknown in subcommittees of the Appropriations Committee, where occasionally just one member has been present to take important testimony to overwhelm his less attentive colleagues.

The efficient part of a committee, moreover, may change from one piece of legislation to another as the interests of the members wax and wane. Each piece of legislation is in a class by itself. The efficient part of a committee, in sum, is the part which wields influence and power. The fruit of its efforts is embodied in statutes and not merely in bills. The men who compose it are the leaders who determine whether the House will play a responsible role in foreign affairs in its committee rooms, on the floor, and in conference committees.

Selection of Members

Chance, modified occasionally by purposeful intrusions by the formal party leaders of the House, determines the quality of a committee's efficient element. Vacancies on committees are formally slated for the Democratic party by the Democrats serving on the Committee on Ways and Means. The Committee on Committees, composed to give representation to the geographical distribution of the party, performs this function for the Republicans. Geography, seniority in the House, the wishes of an applicant, and the desires of the ranking members of the committee with an opening are the major factors weighed when these party agencies slate members for a vacancy.

All of these factors were weighed, for example, when a Democrat from the South serving on the Foreign Affairs Committee was defeated in a primary in 1954. Representatives from the region of the defeated committee member approached Democrats on the Ways and Means Committee to suggest the name of a replacement. The candidate's seniority in the House was adequate for assignment to an important committee. The ranking Democrat on the Foreign Affairs Committee was consulted, and the candidate was informally cleared as satisfactory to the formal party leaders. His foreign policy voting record was checked by some of the more careful Democrats on the Ways and Means Committee. Surviving these tests, the candidate was slated and elected to membership in 1955.[5]

·   ·   ·   ·   ·   ·   ·   ·   ·   ·   ·   ·   ·   ·   ·   ·   ·   ·   ·

Those who slate members for Republican vacancies weigh the same factors as the Democrats, but the Republicans are faced with a greater diversity of foreign policy viewpoints that demand representation. Thus, senior Republicans in the House as a whole, and the party leaders in particular, tend to be more active in slating for vacancies on the foreign policy committee. In 1953, following Eisenhower's election, the two top Republicans of the Foreign Affairs Committee were virtually ignored in the process of filling vacancies on their committee. The Republican leaders of the House made certain that the isolationist element of the party composed about one-fourth of the Republican membership of the committee.

Unfortunately, the foreign policy views of a representative, although not always ignored, are not an important factor weighed in the process of filling vacancies on committees other than the foreign policy committee, despite the fact that they handle a large volume of foreign business. Powerful domestic factors enter the picture. Representation on the Agriculture Committee, for example, is not only carefully balanced by regions of the country but also to some extent by crops. The Merchant Marine and Fisheries Committee is liberally packed with representatives from the major inland and ocean ports of the country. Whether a responsible foreign policy element sits on committees of this sort is thus a matter of chance.

The Environment

From another angle the committees emerge as something more than the bloodless bodies they appear to be in the highly compressed language of the textbooks or even in the hearings and reports. The polished hearings are often artificial and always edited. The real work of a committee is accomplished in executive sessions away from the glare of

---

5. This process was described to the writer by a Democrat serving on the Ways and Means Committee.

publicity. The member's public and printed behavior is often different from his private behavior and influence in the very human yet political environment behind locked doors.

Within a committee human beings work together, the majority of them from small-town law offices. They frequently do not adequately appreciate the needs and problems of a large bureaucracy. All of them come from single-member districts. They come to the House as individuals, not as players on a team. They often lack the national viewpoint so essential for the responsible consideration of foreign policy matters.

Committees also function in a political atmosphere as do all committee organizations to some degree. Less than one-tenth of the bills debated in Congress arouse intense party controversies, but politics, including the politics of the nation, the states, the local communities, and between the committees, colors all committee action. Grievances and power are much more likely to be vented and exploited at the committee level than at the more disciplined and rule-ridden floor level of the House. Since the decisions of committees normally become the decisions of the House, pressure groups work most avidly at the committee level.

To assure proper perspective, it should be mentioned, in addition, that the influence of the committees on the floor of the House varies sharply. Except in times of crisis or when tremendous sums of money are involved, foreign affairs matters bore the members of the House. They sometimes respond with resentment because of the time consumed by such matters. The prestige and influence of the Committee on Foreign Affairs still ranks fairly low in the House. In contrast, some committees, like the Committees on Agriculture and Merchant Marine and Fisheries, have a powerful domestic clientele which they serve with extraordinary bipartisanship. On the floor, they wield tremendous power, sometimes to the detriment of American foreign policy.

Staff

Finally, the staff of a committee must be kept in mind in probing its anatomy. Staff politics is as complex as committee politics. Able professionals, clerks of widely varying competence, some of whom have themselves become institutions, political henchmen of members—all these are scattered among the staffs of the committees of the House of Representatives. Some of these staff people exert extraordinary influence on policy, and it is not unknown for a zealous staff to capture a committee until the committee amounts to little more than its voice. . . .

Party Leadership at the Committee Level

An important factor in discussing the politics of the committees in foreign affairs is the role of party leadership. Leadership in the House of Representatives is dispersed. The machinery through which the party leaders work to coordinate party attitudes constitutes only one part, but a significant part, of the leadership picture in the House. The role of the parties and their leadership at the committee level reflects the well-known looseness of the American party system.

The speaker, the majority floor leader and the chief whip, a few loyal chairmen, and the majority on the Committee on Rules compose the key elements in the party picture for the majority. The minority floor leader and his assistant are the key figures for the minority party. On some matters, certain other party agencies play a part: a steering committee on occasion; the caucus or conference rarely; and on committee assignments, the Republican Committee on Committees and the Democrats serving on the Ways and Means Committee. The Democratic leaders rarely utilize any steering or party policy committee, but the Republican leaders regularly consult with a policy committee composed of the formal party leaders, the Republicans serving on the Rules Committee, and ten other Republicans selected on a geographical basis.

The president keeps in touch through his regular and informal chats with key representatives and occasionally, as will be noted later, through persuasion directed at various groups in stages of the legislative process. Congressional party machinery, however, is almost totally divorced from the national party machinery. In Congress, moreover, there is a meager liaison between the party leadership of the House and of the Senate.

Although important at other levels of action in the House, the role of the party leadership is weakest and least significant at the committee level. The scene might open with the majority floor leader, whether a Republican or a Democrat, emerging innocently from his office in the Capitol into the middle of a group of eager reporters. They want his opinion as a party leader on the action of the Foreign Affairs Committee, let us say, in revising the foreign aid legislation. The leader will usually hesitate until the newspapermen indicate by their questioning what the committee has done. He may then offer a vague comment. This scene is likely to be repeated in other parts of the building with different actors, the Speaker and the minority floor leader for instance. Over at a White House press conference, the president may be feeling his way through the same fog.

The party leaders are not surprised or even much bothered by these little scenes. They are not unusual. The substance of even critical legislation before the committees is strictly committee business, so the tradition runs. Occasionally, a party leader may have advance information as to what a committee intends to do or has done. Otherwise, the leaders, like the public, must depend on the newspapers for their information or perhaps pick up something from people working with the committee on the matter in question. No party leader makes any systematic effort to keep track of committee business and the status of legislation. They have no staffs for these purposes. Their work is almost wholly ex post facto. They come into the picture when bills are ready for the floor.

Occasionally, the party leaders may referee disputes between chairmen, conciliate in some other fashion, attempt to blast a bill from committee, and dabble in the selection of committee members. In 1954, for instance, some Republicans from the Foreign Affairs Committee visited the majority floor leader to complain about what they regarded as an intrusion into their jurisdiction by the Agriculture Committee. The farm committee was considering a bill for the disposal of surpluses abroad that was similar to provisions incorporated in bills reported in previous years by the Foreign Affairs Committee. The floor leader was unwilling to do anything to unravel this jurisdictional dispute, and shortly the more powerful Agriculture Committee had its way.

Normally, the party leaders prefer to stay clear of involvement in committee business. Representatives emphasize with pride that the party leaders, the caucus, and the steering committee do not "interfere" with the committees. The theory is that each committee is in charge of a party leader who supposedly looks out for the interest of the party, as worked out with other party leaders and with the responsible executive branch officials, and coordinates his committee's activities with those interests. The ranking minority committee member, in theory performs a similar role for his party.

Committee chairmen wield tremendous power, even if lacking talent and ability. The chairman usually determines what the committee will consider and when; he may control the membership of subcommittees; he is the formal spokesman for the committee to the press and to the executive branch; he is the formal leader on the floor and controls the time and lists of speakers for the majority party in debate; and sometimes he is the man who supplies the appropriate cues to those who desire to know what the executive branch wants. The chairman's role is a dual one. In theory, if not always in fact, he is a party leader, and thus a leader for the administration if his party is in power. On the other hand, he is the committee chief, and his committee's views may or may not coincide with those of the administration. A chairman's influence depends a great deal upon his ability to reconcile this dual role.

Is the chairman a party leader? Is he influential? A leader at all? Does he have followers? That depends on the accidents of seniority. His job is the result of his talent in keeping alive and his ability in getting the support of a plurality of less than one-four-hundredth of the nation's voters. No tests of party regularity or of talent are prerequisites for the job.

The seniority system elevates some very capable and influential men to the chairmanships, men who have a sense of party, or at least program, responsibility. Not infrequently, the committee leader may be weak, lacking influence, and unsympathetic with policies supported even by majorities of both parties. Or he may be a strong and influential man with immense retaliatory powers. The Republican victory of 1952, for instance, elevated Representative Daniel A. Reed (R., N.Y.) to the chairmanship of the Ways and Means Committee, a powerful figure generally out of harmony with the foreign trade policy views of the president. And to the chairmanship of the Committee on Foreign Affairs it brought Congressman Robert B. Chiperfield (R., Ill.), a man with an isolationist voting record almost in total opposition to the foreign policy views expressed by the president and other Republican party leaders. Fortunately, Chairman Chiperfield shed his isolationism to support the president in foreign affairs.

Both political parties, in short, like the followers of Adam Smith in economics, operate on the assumption of the natural identity of interests among those who wear the party label. The free enterprise system functions at the committee level. A few of the entrepreneurs, by conviction or otherwise, work with the party leaders.

In committees led by weak chairmen, an "efficient" element frequently takes over and attempts to work out policy with some attention to party responsibility.

Summary

Ordinarily, a committee is regarded as an institution, as a corporate body with a unitary voice or at most, majority and minority voices. A committee is in a sense an institution. The continuity provided by senior members who pass the biennial political tests, staff people who survive

periodic turnovers of personnel, committee tradition, history, and prerogative—all these serve to bind human beings into a collective body.
But beneath the surface, a committee is but a few men who make decisions, men who are blessed with no unique capacities beyond those
given to other mortals, who deliberate in a very human but intensely
political environment, and who, like other men, are sometimes lazy and
indifferent, overwhelmed with other business, or devoted to duty.

These committees work in jealous isolation from one another and
compete for the foreign policy business of the House. Commonly, the
scheme of the separation of powers maintained by checks and balances
is discussed in terms of the judiciary, the president, and the Senate and
the House. But the House of Representatives is afraid of its own power.
A scheme of checks and balances has evolved throughout the House,
and especially at the committee level. This scheme is not embodied in a
clear theory but is nevertheless part of the fabric of the lower chamber.
It aims at preventing the massive accumulation of power and decision
anywhere in the House. Facets of the scheme include the weak position
of party leaders in dealing with committees, the allotment of business
among several committees, many of which work simultaneously and at
cross-purposes in the same general area of foreign affairs, and the inher-
itance of committee leadership according to seniority.

Many other facets mark the scene. Its ramifications penetrate to the
executive branch. It is not uncommon for a congressional committee to
develop intimate relations with leading pressure groups and with the
agencies of the executive branch in which it has a special interest. The
attachment may be sufficiently powerful to defy the best efforts of the
president to coordinate and control the executive branch. The Committee on Foreign Affairs, for instance, enjoys a clientele relationship with
the Department of State, but the foreign policy viewpoint,they support
may vary quite sharply from that emerging from another committee in
deliberations with its clientele. The combination in foreign affairs may
be quite weak in bucking the combination of the Department of Agriculture, farm groups, and the Committee on Agriculture or the combination of the shipping interests, the Maritime Administration, and the
Committee on Merchant Marine and Fisheries.

These features of the politics of the committees of the House of Representatives and the effects of these complex relationships in foreign
affairs can best be appreciated in the context of specific examples
involving major foreign policy areas. . . .

Questions

1. In general, how are members of committees selected? Is it a process you would institute if you were to set up legislative rules of procedure?
2. Does the House Committee on Foreign Affairs enjoy less prestige than its equivalent in the Senate? Why is this so?
3. What is the role of party leadership in the House with respect to foreign policy?
4. The seniority system has been called "the measurement of a man's ability by the length of his beard." Discuss this in terms of the foreign policy process.

A Debate:
Congress and Foreign Policy*

Walt W. Rostow

Walt W. Rostow is professor of economics and history at the University of Texas at Austin. He served as presidential assistant for national security affairs under Lyndon Johnson and as head of the Policy Planning Council in the Department of State during the Kennedy administration. He is the author of the *United States in the World Arena* (New York: Harper, 1960), and *The Stages of Economic Growth* (Cambridge: Cambridge University Press: 1960).

Who should make foreign policy in this delicate period when, to use President Johnson's language of January, 1967: "We are in the midst of a great transition: from narrow nationalism to international partnership; from the harsh spirit of the cold war to the hopeful spirit of common humanity on a troubled and threatened planet"?

Foreign policy is, of course, now made by the president, in a relationship to the Congress more complex, perhaps, than the Founding Fathers envisaged. The austere "concurrence of Senate" in Section 2 of

---

*Reprinted by permission of the author from *The Washington Star,* February 20, 1972.

Article II of the Constitution has ramified out into a maze of briefings and consultations, formal and informal.

The "congressional leadership"—the leaders in both houses of both parties—has assumed an almost constitutional role in this consultative process on key issues. In addition, foreign and military policy have become extremely expensive; and congressional control over the purse strings has become a major factor shaping foreign policy.

The armed services committees play a large role in military policy and the Joint Atomic Energy Committee on issues that, in the past, have set important limits on both military and foreign policy.

In the wake of the war in Vietnam, these relationships are all under examination; and there are evidently those who would dilute the president's powers in various ways and seek a new balance between the president and the Congress in these matters.

I am against such dilution on the basis of both past experience and future prospects.

The Founding Fathers gave much attention to this matter, as we all know. The incapacity of the nation to conduct foreign affairs effectively through congressional committees in the 1780s was, of course, a major reason for the formulation of the Constitution.

I believe the issue of foreign affairs was decisive to the reluctant acceptance of the Constitution by the individual states. The deep and understandable suspicion of excessive executive authority nevertheless left in the Constitution very great powers in the hands of Congress in foreign affairs.

I would certainly suggest no change to diminish congressional authority in foreign affairs; but we should all face the fact that this authority has not always been used with wisdom.

In this century, for example, congressional opposition to two presidents helped cause the second World War. First, there was the rejection of the League of Nations, in which the Senate played a crucial role; and then, in the 1930s, resistance through rigid neutrality acts to President Roosevelt's efforts to deter the Axis by throwing American weight into the balance.

Congressional pressure to pull our forces out of Europe and unilaterally demobilize our military strength helped encourage Stalin, in 1945–47, making the cold war inevitable.

The conduct of the Korean War was gravely complicated at a critical stage in 1951 by extraconstitutional communications between a general and a senior member of the Congress.

The shifting position of the Congress on Southeast Asia, despite the SEATO Treaty and the Southeast Asia Resolution of 1964, will, I believe, be judged in history as one major factor in prolonging the war in Vietnam.

Why, for almost two centuries, has the collective behavior of the Congress in foreign affairs been quite often less than satisfactory? The answer is, I believe, two-fold.

First, the president and the members of Congress have different constituencies. The latter are elected from states and districts which have strong local interests that demand representation in Washington. They may also have narrow particular foreign policy interest. But no member of Congress is elected with a primary duty to weigh the nation's interest as a whole.

Second, the people do not look to the Congress to make foreign policy and do not hold its members responsible. They look to the president, knowing that his constituency is national and that he is amply checked by the treaty-making powers of the Senate, the congressional control over the purse strings, and other restraints on willfulness or bad judgment.

Every four years the people can and do make their own assessment of the president's performance in foreign as in domestic affairs. And if the president does not run, they make the best assessment they can of the policies, character, experience, and judgment of the candidates, knowing one of them will have to act for all of us in a complex and dangerous world.

If a president passively bowed to the will of the Congress on a major issue of foreign policy and things went badly, the American people would not exonerate the president and vote out the offending members of Congress: they would get themselves a new president.

I understand with sympathy the argument of some that further restraints on the executive might encourage a responsible partnership between the president and the Congress in foreign affairs. Occasionally that kind of partnership has happened; for example, as between Senator Arthur Vandenberg and Presidents Roosevelt and Truman; Senator Lyndon B. Johnson and President Eisenhower; Senator Everett M. Dirksen and Presidents Kennedy and Johnson. But that kind of relationship cannot be legislated.

In the period 1961–69 I had the privilege of observing the process of congressional consultation with the president on many occasions, formal and informal, in large groups and small. I emerged with great respect for members of the Congress and have heard them make wise and helpful observations, both critical of the president's course and supportive.

They often left the room, after such sessions, with authentic expressions of sympathy for the burdens the president carried, one of the most notable such expressions being: "Mr. President, you have more trouble than a dog has fleas."

And, in the end, they are the president's fleas; for when views had been candidly exchanged, the members of Congress walked away from the White House relatively free of responsibility. The president was left essentially alone, with the burden of decision. That is the way the Constitution is written; that is the way the people expect it to be; and that, in my view, is the way it should remain.

In carrying his inescapable responsibilities, the president needs and deserves the limited protection his constitutional prerogatives, as now interpreted, afford. Proposals now being considered would diminish the president's authority without in any way diminishing his responsibilities.

As for the use of armed forces, the record will show, I believe, that on such contentious issues as the Korean War, the Dominican Republic, and Vietnam the president's initial commitments were made after congressional consultation and overwhelmingly supported by congressional opinion and public sentiment. The problems—notably with respect to Korea and Vietnam—came later, as the pain of using limited force for limited purposes over a protracted period weighed down the spirit of a nation whose style lends itself more easily to an all out, uninhibited application of its powers.

I will not argue here whether or not the policies of Presidents Truman and Johnson were wise, once the basic commitments were made. But surely, wars cannot be conducted by recourse to monthly opinion polls or the changing moods of the Congress, which will have their effect in our system as elections come around.

Further, I do not believe that an increased congressional role in determining the use of our armed forces would, as many believe, lead to a more temperate and reserved application of our military power. The congressional advice President Kennedy received on the eve of his missiles-in-Cuba speech of October 22, 1962, was for example, to go immediately beyond his limited and selective quarantine. That has been and, I suspect, will be the tendency of congressional feeling in crises sufficiently serious to induce a president—always contrary to his basic political interests as well as his human feelings—to engage Americans in armed conflict.

If it is military restraint we're looking for, we're more likely to get it from the president than from the Congress.

Looking ahead to the complex transitional problems of moving towards stable peace in a world of diffusing power—where cold war impulses are waning but not yet tamed, where raw and violent nationalist feelings have not yet been disciplined by the habits of stable regional partnerships—I believe we shall have to rely on the responsibility and judgment of our presidents at least as much as in the past.

* * * * * * * * * * * * * * * * * * * *

A Reply to W. W. Rostow*

Representative Gunn McKay

Representative Gunn McKay is a native of Huntsville, Utah. He attended Weber State College and Utah State University where he received his B.A. He served in the Utah Legislature from 1962 to 1966, and from 1967 to 1970 he was administrative assistant to the Governor of Utah. He was elected to the 92nd Congress in 1970, and re-elected in 1972.

W. W. Rostow's article, "In Defense of the President's Foreign Policy Powers," which appeared in these pages on February 20, begins with an acknowledgment of the "complex" executive-congressional relationship in the field of foreign affairs and follows that acknowledgment with one of the most simplistic and misleading analyses yet published on that subject.

After reaffirming the constitutional superiority of the executive over the congressional branch, and after condescendingly suggesting no diminution of congressional powers, Mr. Rostow proceeds to blame the defeat of the League of Nations, World War II, the cold war, the Korean War and the prolongation of the Vietnam conflict on Congress!

Anyone familiar with U.S. diplomatic history will immediately recognize not only serious oversimplification but perhaps even intentional distortion. Each of Mr. Rostow's charges against Congress warrants further exploration.

---

*Reprinted from *The Washington Star*, March 12, 1972, by permission of the author.

Failure to Consult

While the Senate did play a role in the defeat of the League of Nations at the conclusion of World War I, it is wrong to fault the Senate solely; there were a number of other contributory factors.

First, President Wilson's blatant failure to consult the Senate *in any way* during the drafting of the terms of both the Covenant and Peace Treaty was a monumental failure in human judgment.

How Wilson, and for that matter most of his sucessors in the Oval Office, can expect to have bipartisan support of foreign policies when Congress not only is denied information but is actually misled about foreign policy is a question which perhaps can be answered only by persons more familiar with psychoanalysis than I.

Mr. Kissinger's recently revealed desire to find some way of getting aid to a foreign country without letting Congress know about it is only the most recent manifestation of this attitude.

Franklin Roosevelt's success in securing virtually unanimous agreement on the U.N. reveals not so much an improvement in the U.N. over the League as it does his skill in involving Congress in the initial planning for the U.N. Wilson's stubbornness prompted him to ignore some early compromises which may have saved the League in America, to ignore Congress in every aspect of U.S. planning for the League, and to refuse to take a single Republican with him to Paris.

Each of these mistakes was serious. Together they virtually guaranteed Senate defeat of the League.

Secondly, the Senate vote on Wilson's League was a reflection of an overwhelming isolationist attitude which captured the mind of America and only awaited another election to be reflected in presidential as well as congressional thinking. To blame the Senate for being responsive to the mood of the country is to confuse symptoms with causes.

This mood was inflamed to astronomical proportions under the rhetoric of the Republican party in 1920. While presidential candidate Harding waffled beautifully on both sides of the League issue, Hughes, Root, Taft and Simpson advocated joining a gutted League while Senator Borah said the Republican party would not join a league of any kind.

Immediately following his election, Harding announced that his victory was a mandate against American participation in the League of Nations in this country. I find it difficult to agree with Rostow that Congress, in this case the Senate, scuttled the League.

Isolationism

Rostow also charges that Congress was responsible for the isolationism of the 1930s. This allegation is even further from the truth than is the first.

Whatever moods seized the Senate in the 1930s were, to a considerable degree, merely a reaping of the harvest of thirteen years of intense isolationism nurtured by a succession of Republican administrations aided and abetted by a Republican majority in both the Senate and the House.

Secretary of State Charles Evans Hughes, under President Harding, immediately reversed most of Wilson's foreign policies. Hughes' actions included a complete renunciation of the League and all of its activities.

A cropping out of the perennial executive syndrome in this period was the Harding administration's secret preparations for the Washington Naval Disarmament Conference begun in late 1921. Hughes kept all planning for the conference not only a secret from Congress, but also a secret from our major ally in the conference, Great Britain.

And for economic nationalism during the interwar period, we again must point more towards the executive than Congress. While Wilson had believed that sound economic recovery and expansion of Europe was wholly interwoven with the requirements for global stability, the Harding, Coolidge, and Hoover administrations steadily increased tariffs and pursued policies of economic nationalism at home which were, in turn, used by Germany to justify her failure to pay reparations.

Even the Reciprocal Tariff Act of 1934, which attempted to reverse the trend of economic warfare, was passed by Congress only under pressure from Roosevelt and Hull.

The specific neutrality legislation to which Mr. Rostow refers was begun by Congress in 1935 and reached its apex (or better put, nadir) in 1937. After a decade of encouragement by the executive, it was difficult for Congress to change direction quickly.

It is important to understand that these laws were enacted with bipartisan support in Congress and with the encouragement of a majority of the American people. This kind of widespread support was not the result of a congressional misuse of power so much as it was a natural consequence of a decade of isolationism preached by the executive branch and the Republican party and readily received by a majority of the American people.

The most serious congressional failure during this period was not giving Roosevelt the amendments to the Neutrality Acts of 1936 and 1937 which he wanted.

Even here, however, primary blame must be laid at the feet of Roosevelt and Hull, who failed to provide strong leadership in behalf of the attempt.

If Rostow is blaming World War II on Congress because it failed to lift the arms embargo in 1939, then he has forgotten that the pending war was virtually inevitable at that point. After all, Japan had gone to war in Asia in 1931, Italy attacked Ethiopia in 1934, and Hitler had reoccupied the Rhineland in 1936 and seized Austria and the Sudetenland in 1938.

Cold War

Mr. Rostow's charge that "congressional pressure to pull our forces out of Europe and unilaterally demobilize our military strength helped encourage Stalin, in 1945–47, to make the cold war inevitable," is even more incredible than his previous charges.

It ignores two basic facts. In the first place, whatever degree of inevitability there was about the cold war was a consequence of Stalin's desire to seize Eastern European countries in order to provide security for the Soviet Union. It did not exist because of a misuse of congressional power! In fact, whatever happened to U.S. foreign policy from 1945 up through 1947 happened, by and large, because of executive-congressional cooperation and a bipartisan approach. Few periods of American diplomatic history have been marked by such a high degree of both inter-branch and inter-party cooperation.

Mr. Rostow's two final accusations can only be called absurd. He blames a congressional misuse of power for "gravely" complicating the conduct of the Korean War.

He admits that this misuse of power amounted to "extra-constitutional communications between a general and a senior member of the Congress," but nevertheless he deduces from the activities of one "senior member of the Congress" that Congress cannot be trusted in the field of foreign affairs.

It is absolutely mind-boggling to read Mr. Rostow as he concludes by attributing the prolongation of the war in Vietnam to the "shifting positions of Congress!"

Rarely in the history of our foreign relations has Congress been found less at fault. While no one has clean hands over Vietnam, Congress has at least had serious second thoughts about its earlier Pavlo-vian responses to executive bell-ringing. The errors of Congress in regard to Vietnam are not due to a misuse of its power but to its unwill-ingness and inability to assert its proper role.

When America finds itself fighting for nearly ten years at an enor-mous human, moral and economic expense without a congressional dec-laration of war, Congress cannot be blamed for a misuse of power! If any single branch of government has misused its foreign policy powers in America's recent history it is the executive branch.

No one should deny that Congress is cumbersome, somewhat erratic, petulant, and deliberate; it sometimes moves too fast and some-times too slowly; it remembers some things too long and forgets other things too fast; it can be frugal when it should be lavish and lavish when it should be frugal.

But for all its faults, Congress as a collective unit is the most repre-sentative element in our governmental system. It is closer to the people than any other branch of the federal system. Only when our presi-dents learn that both houses of Congress should be consulted and kept informed about the development of our foreign policies will the confi-dence and credibility which the executive so needs in foreign affairs be restored.

No, Mr. Rostow, Congress is less guilty of either arrogance or ignorance than is the executive. This is the fact we should all face.

Questions

1. On the basis of your understanding of the Constitution, whose argu-ment—Rostow's or McKay's—makes more sense from the viewpoint of the framers?
2. Does one argument or the other seem more logical when you consider the changing international system?
3. Rostow suggests that the unwise use of foreign affairs powers by Con-gress supports his executive supremacy argument. Is that a two-edged sword? Why? On a "national scoreboard" that measured the wisdom of each, Congress and the executive, in the use of power in foreign affairs, which would come out ahead?
4. How would you evaluate Rostow's argument that we are more likely to get restraint of the military from the president than from Congress? Can you think of any recent incidents that either support or detract from that argument?
5. Does the McKay argument possibly reflect the bitterness that might be

expected from a member of the "slighted branch" of government? Does this detract from its intrinsic worth?

6. Rostow argues that only the president is elected nationally, and thus he is better qualified to decide foreign policy matters, whereas McKay argues that Congress, because its two-year terms and large numbers make it closer to the people, is better qualified. With which do you agree? Why?

Chapter Four

Diplomacy, Diplomats, and Secrecy

We have already traced some of the problems created by the constitutional division of powers over foreign affairs between the president and the Congress. A fragmentation of function also characterizes the foreign policy process within the executive branch. The cause of this intrabranch fragmentation is in part the influence of the constitutional system, but fundamentally it stems from the complex nature of foreign policy problems. This complexity determines the nature of the policy-making process, as well as the structure and relationships of the governmental institutions responsible for foreign policy.

Until World War II, the foreign policy process in the United States was almost exclusively the concern of the president and the Department of State. Every effort of other government agencies, including the military, to win recognition of their right to be consulted about foreign policy was rebuffed. Traditionally, foreign policy had not required large sums of money, nor had it needed substantial military forces to make it effective. In those simpler times, war was war and peace was peace; American business had not yet developed large overseas markets; Near Eastern and South American oil was not yet a prize to be protected; and international affairs centered in London, Paris, Vienna, Moscow, and Berlin, not in Washington. Slowly at first, then rapidly during World War II, all of this changed. Once, it was possible to draw sharp lines between peace and war, between domestic and foreign affairs, and between public and private policy; now, these lines are blurred beyond recognition.

As foreign policy problems began to cut across geographical and functional lines, the traditional division of organizational responsibility was called into question, since a single department no longer could assert an exclusive right to make policy. As a consequence, the policy process became one of shared responsibility and overlapping authority.

In the reexamination of the State Department, three questions emerged: (1) should the Department of State be expanded to include all nonmilitary, foreign policy–related issues and hence to bring them under one organizational roof; (2) should the emerging aspects of foreign policy be assigned to newly created organizations; or (3) should existing governmental agencies and departments be permitted to expand their functions to include foreign policy–related issues. The organizational problems generated by these questions can clearly be seen in the emergence of information and propaganda as a major foreign policy instrument. The first impulse was to house these activities in the Department of State, but for a variety of reasons this decision was later reversed, and a new agency— the United States Information Agency—was created. This same decision had to be made about foreign aid, intelligence activities, and much of our financial and economic involvement abroad. The general pattern has been, not to expand the Department of State but to solve the organizational problem by adopting one of the other alternatives. Thus the department has lost considerable operational control over foreign policy making, and thus it belies its public image as the sole originator of foreign policy. At best it has a preferred, not an exclusive, position in the ranks of presidential advisers on foreign policy.

It is in the context of this reduced operational authority that the discussion of the effectiveness of the Department of State must begin. It is, of course, popular to criticize the department for being tradition-bound, rigid, excessively slow in reaching decisions, and hostile to new ideas. Criticisms of the department fall into two general classes. First, there is that which finds fault with the kind of people employed by the department and the Foreign Service. These arguments range from sophisticated analyses of the organizational style of department officials to the more familiar and popular criticisms of them as self-perpetuating, cookie-pushing snobs. Politically, the criticisms extend from the rantings of the radical right about the legacy of Alger Hiss and the secret influence of Communists in the department to the charges of neo-fascism from the new left. In each case, the cure is to alter the behavior of the people employed by the department.

A second group of arguments lays the blame for the inefficiency of the Department of State on the nature of bureaucracy and on the complexity of foreign policy issues. These critics stress the fact that the problems faced by the department cut across geographical boundaries and functional divisions. Hence, decisions necessarily involve two or more geographical offices as well as two or more functional offices. Decisions in this environment can be reached only after following a complicated clearance process, to assure that all relevant questions have been raised and all material interests consulted. Secretary of State Dean Rusk has spoken eloquently about the problem of "layering," by which he means the number of offices that must be consulted as a decision moves from the bottom of the bureaucracy to the secretary's desk. The faults of the department, these critics allege, are those of any large bureaucracy. The able people who serve in the department and the Foreign Service are victims of the system.

Seen against the complexities of the foreign service policy issues, the Department of State's normal, day-by-day operations do not appear to be less effective than those of other large bureaucracies. If the problems of foreign policy were so simple that they could be handled solely within one geographical or functional office, most of the organizational problems of the State Department would be greatly simplified. Given, however, the nature of the foreign policy process, many criticisms of the State Department reveal less about its ineffectiveness than about the naive assumptions of the critics. Most criticisms do not mention the department's own awareness that its normal decision-making procedures are not effective in crises. In serious, but not acute, crises, the department has hit upon the "task force" as a solution to more rapid decision making. The task force is a group of officers relieved of their daily duties and assigned to the problem that has created the crisis. This task force then assumes full responsibility within the department for the solution of the problem. When the crisis subsides, the task force is disbanded, and the problem again becomes the concern of the geographical and functional offices.

The acute crisis calls for a still further modification of the organization. In some cases the secretary of state assumes direct operational control of the crisis and, in effect, represents, along with a small group of advisers, the entire Department of State. During the Suez crisis of 1956, Secretary of State Dulles bypassed the upper levels of the bureaucracy to deal directly with the crisis at the desk level. Situations such as the Cuban missile crisis are so dangerous that policy making is confined to the presidential level and the department as an organization does not play an important role in making the decisions, although individual members of the department may serve as presidential advisers.

How to coordinate military strategy and foreign policy with intelligence (knowledge about other nations, their capabilities and intentions) has also been a central issue posed by the transformation of the foreign policy process. One of the traumatic experiences of World War II was the realization that the United States intelligence services had been totally inadequate. The task of rectifying this inadequacy became a major order of business after the war. Because control of the intelligence function was a potential source of influence over policy, there was no lack of claimants for the task of organizing and directing its revitalization. But the very existence of these conflicting claims meant that none of them could be successful. A new organization, the Central Intelligence Agency (CIA), was created to undertake the task.

The role of the new agency was to be passive; it was to provide information upon which policy might be based, but it was to eschew any policy-making role. The National Defense Act of 1947 that created the CIA also etablished the Department of Defense, the National Security Council, and the Joint Chiefs of Staff. The Act assumed that the various strands of foreign policy—military, diplomatic, and intelligence—would be strengthened by these organizational changes and would be woven into the finished fabric through the National Security Council. It was intended that the military and diplomatic would be the active agents; intelligence would be the passive member. This model has not been realized in practice because the expectation that intelligence experts would refrain from entering the policy arena was unrealistic.

From the beginning CIA has had a dual role: (1) providing the intelligence data required by the decision makers and (2) conducting "cloak-and-dagger" activities that have clearly had profound policy implications. The full extent of the policy orientation of this part of CIA functions was revealed by the investigations following the failure in 1963 of a CIA-sponsored and -planned invasion of Cuba by a group of refugees. These investigations showed that the CIA officials not only planned the invasion but originated it and served as its advocate in the policy councils of the government. This fusing of the intelligence and policy functions is not necessarily the result of a "plot" by CIA officials to extend their influence but stems primarily from the basic truth in the old saw, "Knowledge is power." There is an almost irresistible tendency on the part of those who know to intrude into the policy process, despite resistance from policy makers. This tendency reflects the fact that the policy-making and the intelligence functions are not separate operations. They are parts of a dynamic process and are locked in an inseparable interaction. The expectation that they can be assigned a sphere of action and that sharp demarcation lines can be drawn between them is fully unrealistic. However these functions may be assigned, one must take into consideration the reality that they cannot be isolated from each other.

The history of the past twenty-five years shows how difficult it is to provide an organizational structure that will give full expression to the complexity of the policy process. Neither the Department of Defense nor the CIA has been able to refrain from usurping, to some extent, the primary foreign policy role of the Department of State. This blurring of roles and functions has resulted, as we have seen, primarily from the nature of the problem, but it has also been influenced by the people who have articulated the roles. During the tenure of Allen Dulles, CIA could operate relatively unfettered, not only because it was effective but also because Mr. Dulles' brother was the secretary of state, and both had great influence with President Eisenhower. The Department of Defense has played a significant role in shaping Vietnam policy, not only because that policy requires the use of military force but also because McNamara was a forceful secretary of defense upon whom President Johnson relied. The Department of State necessarily has had to share its influence over foreign policy with the Department of Defense because foreign policy has become only one component of national security policy, and also because Secretary Rusk was not John Foster Dulles.

The first two articles in this chapter reflect the two explanations of the ineffectiveness of the Department of State. Professor Scott argues that the cause is the life-style of a dominant elite—the Foreign Service—and Mr. Campbell that it is the size of the bureaucracy as well as its structure. The third article, by Professor Hickman, reviews the link between diplomacy and negotiation and suggests how diplomacy differs from other forms of negotiation. The last article, by Professor Ransom, is concerned not only with the problems of creating an effective intelligence system but also with the more fundamental question of the role of that system in a free society.

The Problem of the State Department*

Andrew M. Scott

Andrew Scott is professor of political science at the University of North Carolina. He is the co-editor of *Readings in the Making of American Foreign Policy* (New York: Macmillan, 1965).

*"The Department of State: Formal Organization and Informal Culture," by Andrew M. Scott, is reprinted from *International Studies Quarterly*, Vol. 13, No. 1 (March 1969), pp. 1–18, by permission of the Publisher, Sage Publications, Inc., Andrew M. Scott, and *Foreign Service Journal*.

Every organization exists in an environment and interacts with it to some extent. When the environment changes in a significant way the organization usually goes through a process of adaptation which, allowing for time lag, corresponds in some way to the environmental change. If sufficient adaptation does not take place, strains will develop and the organization will begin to move toward irrelevance, extinction, or some form of abrupt, forced, change. Some organizations adapt to change more readily than others. This article deals with an organization—the Department of State—which has found adaptation extremely difficult.

To note that the department has been insufficiently adaptive is not to suggest that it has been changeless. The Foreign Service Act of 1946 and the integration of State Department officers into the Foreign Service in 1953, for example, represented efforts to make the department and the Foreign Service more effective instruments of American foreign policy. Such changes have usually resulted from external pressures rather than internal.

Interestingly enough, during the period since World War II in which the adaptation of the Department of State was altogether inadequate, the foreign affairs system as a whole showed an impressive capacity for adaptation. Foreign aid began in the post–World War II period with the modest goals of relief and rehabilitation. Governmental agencies were formed to administer aid programs, and the concept of what might be done with economic aid gradually expanded to encompass the economic rebirth of one continent and the economic development of others.

The concept of technical assistance emerged as a response to needs and when it was funded and supported, a new instrument of statecraft was born. The United States government wanted to carry its story to other nations during the cold war and so yet another instrument of statecraft, the United States Information Agency, came into being.

Various forms of military aid were developed—the use of military advisers, the training of foreign officers in the United States, the development of civic action programs, and so on. Just as new weapons altered the nature of war and the way that men thought about it, they also altered the way that men thought about peace: the Arms Control and Disarmament Agency was created, and the White House was organized to play a more important role in the foreign affairs process. But in the midst of all these developments, the Department of State showed only minimal adaptation.

The starting point for understanding the department lies in an appreciation of the nature and dominance of the Foreign Service corps.

Only 15 percent of those employed by the Department of State are Foreign Service officers but they set the tone for the whole. The Foreign Service has the characteristics of a typical career service including entry at the bottom, resistance to lateral entry, career tenure and regular advancement through grades if qualified, competition with others for advancement, esprit de corps, and a tendency toward corps self-government.

The Foreign Service has developed an internal culture of its own consisting of an interrelated set of ideas, behavioral norms, and operating practices, including several of those enumerated above. The norms and ideology associated with this culture permeate the department and govern departmental responses in a variety of important areas.

This subculture contains elements which satisfy short-term needs of the career service and individuals in it but which do not necessarily satisfy the long-term needs of the Department of State nor the requirements of American foreign policy. These elements include hostile or condescending attitudes toward research, planning, management, and "outsiders." Their dysfunctionality often takes the form of promoting attitudes and behavior that tend to insulate the organization from full and free contact with its environment, which reduces pressure to adapt to it. The short-term functionality of these elements is usually to be found in the way in which they soothe and reassure members of the subculture, protect them from critics and criticism, help smooth interpersonal relations within the service, and promote discipline and order.

One aspect of the Foreign Service subculture is the extent to which it encourages officers to become inward looking and absorbed in the affairs of the service. Perhaps all career services tend to do this, but the Foreign Services carries it to an extreme. When an individual finds himself in an environment that places great emphasis upon rank and status, he usually learns to concern himself with matters of assignment, promotion, the impression he makes on fellow officers, the position he takes on shifting alignments in the service, and the like. Learning to adapt one's behavior and reactions to expectations of the organization is an important part of being molded into it. The fully adapted individual has learned the organization's norms and expected behavior patterns so well that he conforms to them without thought. If this pattern were universal, the internal affairs of the service would move smoothly and without a hitch, but it would be detrimental to American foreign policy.

Given the importance to the individual of the internal workings of the service it is understandable that he may become as concerned with these workings, and their relation to his career, as with the organization's success in dealing with the external world. If an officer fails to do well in internal competition he will be directly penalized, but if the organization fails to cope effectively with its environment he may not suffer personally at all because the responsibility for the failure will be diffused throughout the entire organization. It is not surprising, therefore, that an individual may become more concerned with office holding than with organizational accomplishment, more concerned with trying to *be* something rather than with trying to *do* something. There is no invisible hand that makes it inevitable that the internal processes of an organization must necessarily produce results that are in harmony with the formal objectives of the organization. The two may easily drift into conflict and when this happens it is as likely that the formal goals of the organization will suffer as that organizational imperatives will be disregarded. The very absorption with service matters that molding encourages, and almost requires, can be counterproductive from the point of view of the conduct of foreign policy.

If an organization is dealing with a relatively stable and unchanging environment, an insulated mode of operation may work fairly well, but if the environment is highly dynamic, as in the international environment, insulation is likely to entail high costs. For one thing, it hinders the development in the organization of a determination to do what it can to shape events. Attitudes toward planning provide a case in point. The ideology teaches that planning is usually futile because each situation is unique and cannot be anticipated. That being the case, the best that one can do is to play things by ear and improvise creatively when events require it. Ideology, therefore, is one reason the department is often incapable of a serious planning effort.

A nation with widespread interests should be constantly planning for the future. Those responsible for policy must ask what actions should be taken today and tomorrow and next month in order to bring about a desired result some time in the more distant future. If the Department of State is not prepared to undertake this activity some other organization is likely to try to fill the vacuum. During the Robert S. McNamara era it was the Department of Defense, to a degree. The changing role of the president's staff has been more important. The White House is not insulated from its environment but is, on the contrary, a focal point for a great many pressures. The members of the White House staff do not belong to the State Department subculture, do not share its attitudes toward planning, and hence are free to plan. Furthermore, they are at the president's elbow and a president is likely to feel the need for effective policy planning.

The White House staff has been important in the foreign affairs field from the time that John F. Kennedy assumed office. The explanation for this is, in part, that the presidents of the 1960s have been strong or interested in foreign affairs. At the outset President Kennedy expected to operate through the State Department and established the McGeorge Bundy operation only when that expectation was disappointed. Lyndon Johnson had great confidence in Secretary Rusk but that did not prevent W. W. Rostow from becoming a powerful figure in foreign affairs. Henry Kissinger, foreign affairs adviser to President Nixon, is shaping American policy more visibly than the Department of State and has made a point of drawing certain planning functions to himself and his staff.

Foreign affairs staff members in the White House have become important because the times have demanded action and the Department of State has not been able to gear itself for action. There is significance in President Kennedy's happy daydream of "establishing a secret office of thirty people or so to run foreign policy while maintaining the State Department as a facade in which people might contentedly carry papers from bureau to bureau."

It may seem strange to speak of the department as insulated from its environment when its officers all over the world file millions of words annually, but the term is nevertheless appropriate. If a scale could be developed showing the extent to which public organizations interact with their environments the department would be found toward the lower end of that scale. It is insulated in that the Foreign Service is:

- A career service with little lateral entry.
- Its members have a high level of interaction with one another and a relatively low level with significant figures in the outside environment—congressmen, individuals in other departments and agencies, young people, corporate executives, academicians, and certain categories of foreigners.
- It is unresponsive to changing circumstances and to the emergence of new skills, new information, new ideas, and new problems.
- It defines what is relevant to its mission in a parochial way.
- It has developed ways of explaining away outside criticism and has learned to ignore or sidetrack most demands for change.

It is easy to understand why individuals in an organization may try to shield the organization from its environment. When the organization is insulated, the need for disruptive adjustments to the environment is reduced and uncertainty and felt pressure are minimized. Isolation makes life easier. Men can do things the way they are accustomed to, and they can think accustomed thoughts.

The drive toward isolation can be seen in many organizations but has been particularly apparent in the Department of State. Since changes in the international environment in which it operates are many, complex, and follow one another in rapid succession, the attractiveness of holding that environment at arm's length is particularly great. Since the Washington environment is also complex and changing and, in addition, is somewhat threatening and critical, it is not surprising that the department should have developed fairly elaborate defense mechanisms.

Structural characteristics of the career system also impede easy adapation. When entry into the services is primarily at the bottom, the carriers of new ideas are apt to be young and to be low in rank, status, and influence. Power in the organization will rest in the hands of older men who are likely to be imbued with traditional ideas. During a workshop in 1966, junior Foreign Service officers identified a number of departmental problems, including the following:

- Assignment to jobs is based more on seniority than on competence;
- The service is not making use of modern organizational training and assignment practices;
- Older officers prevent progressive, adaptive action by younger officers;
- The service reserves decisions to the highest levels and suppresses ideas from lower levels;
- Fear of criticism and retaliation inhibit dissent and the expression of non-conformist ideas.

Each of these "problems" represents a feature of the Foreign Service system that is functional from the point of view of a senior officer's conception of the smooth operation of the service, i.e., a seniority system, personalized management, caution and conservatism on the part of senior officers, deference on the part of junior officers, the absence of vigorous debate that might mar interpersonal relations. Yet each of these features is also counterproductive from the point of view of the service's long-term future and its formal purposes. Order and discipline within the service are purchased at the cost of imagination, flexibility and organizational drive.

The argument set forth here is that departmental officers have crip-

pled the Department of State by promoting insulation and by furthering a variety of counterproductive doctrines. If this line of analysis is
correct, it means that the subculture these people represent will have
to be substantially modified before the department can play its proper
role in foreign affairs. The historical record of the department discour-
ages optimism. Examples of bureaucratic self-renewal are few and far
between and certainly the Department of State does not have a history
of success.

Nevertheless, in recent years there have been stirrings that may
prove to be important. In 1967 a group of Young Turks in the Foreign
Service gained control of the American Foreign Service Association to
use it as an instrument for service reform. Some of the reforms that the
association's leadership is concerned with—improved training, more
effective use of research, rapid promotion of able younger officers,
altered assignment practices—would have the effect of weakening the
hold of a number of the doctrines that now tie up the department.

The leaders of the association have also indicated that they intend to
open the Foreign Service to its environment. One of the ways they propose to do this is by giving Foreign Service officers experience in the
nongovernmental sectors of the foreign affairs community.

Many individuals work professionally in foreign affairs outside the
government. Together with those in the government, they make up a
"foreign affairs community." Members of this community not in the
government represent a resource that governmental agencies could
utilize more fully. Conversely, members of the community in the government represent a resource from the point of view of overseas busi-
nesses, foundations concerned with international affairs, banks, nongovernmental organizations with international interests, and academic
institutions.

A larger degree of lateral movement of personnel among the various
sectors of the community could be a net gain for all concerned. The
attractiveness of the Foreign Service would certainly be increased and
its competitive position would be improved if movement in and out of it
were made much easier. At present, a young man considering the Foreign Service is asked to choose a way of life once and for all because the
decision to go into the service usually forecloses other options. An able
young man would be more likely to opt for the service if he knew that
he could move out of it for a few years with comparative ease and then
back in if he chose.

Perhaps, in time, young men may be able to plan for a career in foreign affairs that will involve relatively easy movement among the various sectors of the foreign affairs community. An individual's career would not have to be tied to a particular organization, such as the Foreign Service, but could be planned with an eye to the broad arena of foreign affairs. Perhaps also, in time, the Foreign Service and the other governmental services will be merged into a single foreign affairs service. This would do a good deal to overcome any tendency toward parochialism and would certainly open up the Foreign Service.

The leaders of the Foreign Service Association are interested in opening up the service by making greater use of lateral entry. This would have a number of advantages, particularly if it could be coupled with short terms of service. At present the Foreign Service does not have enough technical specialists. Given the service's predisposition toward the "generalist," such specialists are not likely to be developed within the Foreign Service and must therefore be recruited from outside. Many of the specialist candidates for appointment might not be interested in giving up their professional careers in order to spend a large part of their lives abroad but might be interested in entering the service for four or five years. The adoption of a different philosophy with regard to lateral entry would make it easier for the service to draw on the vast reservoir of trained men in the middle years of their lives. More important, these men might be a valuable leaven in the Foreign Service since they would be likely to have perspectives varying from those normally found in the Service.

Some Foreign Service officers have misgivings about the extension of lateral entry on the ground that it will tend to undermine the concept of a career service. Their instincts are probably right. The guild-like characteristics of the service would be strained by extensive use of lateral entry. If a choice must be made between a closed service, on the one hand, and an open, adaptable service on the other, however, there can be no doubt where the long-term interests of the nation and of the Department of State lie.

One of the features of the Young Turk rebellion that makes it encouraging is that it has received the backing of the secretary of state and of Under Secretary Elliot Richardson. The under secretary has endorsed a number of ideas of the American Foreign Service Association, has instituted some changes and is considering others. If a working alliance can be achieved between top appointive officials in the department and the dissident elements in the Foreign Service, the entire situation in the department could become malleable. Together they might be able to do that which neither could do alone.

The external environment in which the Department of State must operate is going to become more rather than less demanding with the passage of time. The department is charged with conducting the foreign policy of one of the world's most powerful nations and the insulation and lack of effectiveness that were irritating but tolerable in the era before World War II are too costly and dangerous to be tolerated any longer. The costs associated with nonadaptation, errors made, imagination not exercised, problems not understood, and opportunities overlooked are not borne by the department alone but by many people, in the United States and elsewhere, whose destinies will be shaped to some extent by the successes and failures of the department.

Questions

1. What is an informal organization and how would it differ from that of the Department of State?
2. Why does the author believe that reorganization of the Department of State will not lead to basic changes in its effectiveness?
3. What are the principal reasons the author advances to explain why the Department of State shows little interest in basic foreign policy research?
4. Assess the author's judgment that the goals and objectives of the "subculture" within the department often conflict with those of the department.
5. What are the consequences, in the author's opinion, of the view he ascribes to many State Department officers, that there is "no 'theory,' only practice"?

The Disorganization of State*

John Franklin Campbell

John Franklin Campbell served as a Foreign Service officer in the Department of State. He resigned to become the editor of the journal, *Foreign Policy*. He died at the age of 31 in 1971.

---

*Chapter 5, from *The Foreign Affairs Fudge Factory*, by John Franklin Campbell, © 1971 by Basic Books, Inc., Publishers, New York. Footnotes have been omitted.

Secretary of State William Rogers, several months into his new job in 1969, confessed to newsmen: "I don't feel I have an action group at my command as they do in other departments. Sometimes I have a feeling things aren't going to get done." His complaint was hardly new. What is remarkable is that recent secretaries of state have not realized that the size of their staffs, the confusing structure of their department, and inattention on their own part are the heart of the difficulty.

Perhaps this charge is less than fair to the present secretary, for he is presiding over a reform program of sorts. On July 21, 1970, the *New York Times* reported that officials of State, "concerned by what they consider to be its declining role in foreign affairs," had made "468 recommendations to strengthen the department." Five months later, on December 8, 1970, the list had grown to 508 and was published in a compendious 600-page document entitled *Diplomacy for the '70s*. This document was drawn up by thirteen task forces employing 250 personnel, who had been ordered to study flaws in the system. One of the task forces devoted itself to "openness in the foreign affairs community," another to "the role and function of diplomatic missions," and yet another to "stimulation of creativity." . . .

Task Force Reform Proposals

The motive behind this latest reform wave is decent enough. It all started with a Young Turk movement of Foreign Service officers, which was formed in 1967 to agitate within the system. The dissidents were bureaucrats in their thirties and forties, later joined by men in their fifties (which shows how "youth" is defined in the State Department lexicon). The Turks, young and old, won control of their company union, the American Foreign Service Association, in the fading days of the Johnson administration. They published articles and manifestoes suggesting that General Maxwell Taylor's Senior Interdepartmental Group be strengthened, that a career man be appointed to the new permanent position of "Executive Under Secretary of State," and that younger men be given more interesting and responsible jobs. But the timing, even for such small changes, was premature.

· · · · · · · · · · · · · · · · · ·

Shorn of trivia, the 600 pages of *Diplomacy for the '70s* consist of a series of hortatory appeals for "a new spirit" in American diplomacy. It is time, the authors say, "to shake off old habits, old ways of doing things, old ways of dealing with each other. What we are proposing is a change of outlook and method." This is all very elevating, and no doubt even useful; the trouble is, the new outlook and method are described in only the vaguest way. What do recommendations for "a more dynamic and aggressive style" and for "increasingly close and effective coordination" really mean? One is not sure that the would-be reformers have any idea.

. . . .

The prose gets muddier and muddier as one reads along. What the reformers clearly want to stress is change and novelty, a new style for themselves and a new effectiveness for their organization. How to change the system they are unhappy with, however, escapes them. All they can come up with are high-sounding, but mostly meaningless or self-contradictory slogans, a rhetorical rehash of the Kennedy and Johnson reform programs.

They do not get to the bottom of the problem, or even close to it, because they do not touch structure and size. They fail to redefine State's relationship to the White House, the Pentagon, and the CIA. They speak broadly of "management," without ever defining the word, but not at all of diplomacy. Ten years too late they praise counterinsurgency and program budgeting.

The reformers might have done a better job if they had paid more attention to a speech given in the State Department by John Kenneth Galbraith on October 24, 1969. Galbraith urged that reform begin with an awareness of changes in foreign policy. Few Americans, he noted, still retain the "illusion" that their country has "a massive capacity to affect the destinies of other countries and a desperately urgent need to do so. . . ."

Surely by now, Galbraith continued, we have "discovered that the need to influence these countries is far less than we imagined." We now know that the economic development of the poor countries will be "very slow," that most of the CIA's "detection and prevention of communism, in countries where we can do nothing about it—and where it wouldn't greatly matter if we could—may well be the greatest make-work activity since WPA." We must bring our foreign operations "back into accord with the modern reality," lest much of our diplomatic establishment become "a bloated, unnecessary, and redundant bureaucracy," which "employs itself only in the wrong things."

Like so many intelligent critics before him, Galbraith was arguing for changes in structure and cutbacks in size and function for the whole machine, with particular attention to military and intelligence operations. The trouble with most of the critics, and with State's own reformers-from-within, is that they have not bothered to look closely at the institutions they would change, to learn where and why the cuts must come. Above all, they have not paid attention to the history of the problem, to the twenty-year story of how the bureaucracies have strayed from their original purposes.

Postwar Decline of the State Department

Three men have contributed heavily to the postwar decline of the State Department: Franklin Roosevelt, Senator Joseph McCarthy, and Henry Wriston. FDR, like many politicians and much of the American public, regarded the diplomatic service as a playground for dilettantes and socialites. He distrusted Foreign Service officers, referring to them sarcastically as the profession of perfection. In a memorandum to Cordell Hull he remarked of career men, "You can get to be a Minister if (a) you are loyal to the service, (b) you do nothing to offend people, (c) if you are not intoxicated at public functions." During World War II Roosevelt turned almost entirely to his military commanders and a few close political advisers for diplomatic advice, virtually ignoring the State Department. Foreign Service officers (FSOs) were drafted into the armed services, and there was no new recruitment of diplomats in the years 1940–1945.

Still, the career service had a brief flowering during the Truman years of 1947–1950. Men who had entered the new profession in the 1920s, many of them Russian specialists such as George Kennan and Charles Bohlen, were used by two strong secretaries of state, George Marshall and Dean Acheson. They shaped and carried out the 1947 revolution in foreign policy, when America broke with 150 years of isolation to rebuild a shattered Europe and to check expanding Russian power. Other members of the Rogers' Act generation of the 1920s—Llewellyn Thompson, Robert Murphy, Foy Kohler—served alongside Bohlen and Kennan as skillful negotiators and advisers to every postwar president well into the 1960s. Diplomats do not make good culture heroes, and none of the five names mentioned above are exactly household words. But each of them has made a contribution to the solution of tough international problems and to a wiser understanding by our presidents of the nature of power and the imperatives of peace. Except for Murphy, who nearly resigned at the time of the Berlin Blockade of 1948 because he favored sending a tank column up the *Autobahn* rather than the less risky airlift, most of these men have usually been a restraining influence on their bosses. That, after all, is the diplomatic tradition.

. . . .

The McCarthy Era

Attacked in 1953 by Senator Joseph McCarthy, Bohlen survived a close Senate confirmation vote and stayed in the Foreign Service when a number of his colleagues under greater pressure, including Bohlen's brother-in-law, Charles Thayer, were resigning. Kennan, who had incurred the displeasure of John Foster Dulles, was "retired" from the service in the same year at the height of his career at age forty-eight. Although McCarthy could not substantiate his public charges, made first in 1950, that the State Department was "thoroughly infested with Communists," he succeeded in ruining professional careers, destroying public confidence in State, and killing Foreign Service morale. He offered a simple theory to explain the "loss" of China and the frustrations of the Korean War, and millions believed him. As late as January 1954, the Gallup Poll reported a 50 percent "favorable" response to McCarthy, while 21 percent had "no opinion."

The Truman administration, McCarthy said, was guilty of "stupidity at the top—treason just below." The State Department was full of "the bright young men who are born with silver spoons in their mouths" who were trying to "diminish the United States in world affairs, to weaken us militarily, to confuse our spirit with talk of surrender in the Far East and to impair our will to resist evil." Former Secretary of State George Marshall, McCarthy alleged, was "A man steeped in falsehood . . . always and invariably serving the world policy of the Kremlin." Democratic presidential candidate Adlai Stevenson was "an out-and-out pro-Communist." During the 1952 campaign McCarthy promised, "If you will get me a slippery elm club and put me aboard Adlai Stevenson's campaign train, I will use it on some of his advisers, and perhaps I can make a good American of him." The domestic hysteria was spread in the columns of major newspapers as well. The *Chicago Tribune* called Secretary of State Acheson "another striped-pants snob" who "ignores the people of Asia and betrays true Americanism to serve as a lackey of Wall Street bankers, British lords, and Communistic radicals from New York." Senator Butler of Nebraska declaimed against Acheson, "I look at that fellow, I watch his smart-aleck manner and his British clothes and that New Dealism . . . and I want to shout, Get out, Get out. You stand for everything that has been wrong with the United States for years." After the Republicans came to power in 1953, Vice-President Richard Nixon announced, "We're kicking the Communists and fellow travelers and security risks out of the government . . . by the thousands." The new security chief of the State Department, Scott McLeod, cautioned, "Not *all* New Dealers are necessarily security risks." Richard Rovere has reported that "when it came to appointing ambassadors and hiring and firing department officers," Secretary Dulles first "cleared everything with McLeod, who cleared everything with McCarthy."

John Paton Davies, Jr., one of the Foreign Service's foremost Asian experts who was fired after being attacked by McCarthy, wrote of the effects ten years later, "The violence and subtlety of the purge and intimidation left the Foreign Service demoralized and intellectually cowed. With some doughty exceptions, it became a body of conformists. . . . and many cautious mediocrities rose to the top of the service." The China specialists were particularly hard hit, with the result that by 1961, when Vietnam came to a boil, the State Department lacked a cadre of senior men having East Asian experience. The few left behind had no desire to share the fate of their discredited brethren: McCarthyism had made honesty and brilliance akin to bureaucratic recklessness. A White House staffer of the 1960s has written that "the American government was sorely *lacking in real Vietnam or Indochina expertise*" in the Kennedy years, and that "career officers in the department, and especially those in the field, had not forgotten the fate of their World War II colleagues who wrote in frankness from China and were later pilloried by Senate committees for critical comments on the Chinese Nationalists. Candid reporting on the strengths of the Viet Cong and the weaknesses of the Diem government was inhibited by the memory."

The McCarthy purge cut down some of the ablest men of the Rogers Act generation, America's first generation of career Foreign Service officers. It occurred at a time when newer Washington agencies in the foreign affairs field, including the integrated Defense Department and CIA, unscathed by McCarthy, were just three to five years old and beginning to flex their independent muscles. Just as damaging as the dismissals and resignations of experienced officers, the purge spread fear throughout the bureaucracy. Recruitment into the Foreign Service stopped from 1951 to 1954, and special "security teams" were sent from

Washington to overseas diplomatic posts to review the records of all personnel. A bad word from a neighbor or colleague, a record of political activism in college, a former teacher, friend, or acquaintance of "left-wing" views, even a well-stocked library of political philosophy were enough to make a man a potential "security risk." FSOs waited in Washington for months, sometimes for more than a year, to learn the outcome of their security clearance investigations before they were permitted to tavel to assignments abroad. A new generation of diplomats was taught the virtue of caution and conformity.

The Wriston Committee

On the heels of the McCarthy purge came the Wriston flood. Henry Wriston, the president of Brown University, headed a reform panel in 1954 to recommend ways to reorganize State and restore its flagging morale. Without mentioning McCarthy by name, the Wriston report noted wryly, "For a variety of reasons, which need no elaboration, public confidence in the State Department was shaken in recent years." Given just two months to propose sweeping changes, the Wriston Committee took a meat-axe to the personnel system of the Foreign Service. Its intentions were benign, but its effects unsettling. To "democratize" the service and end rank distinctions between Washington civil servants and overseas employees, the Wriston Committee believed that a "direct infusion of needed talents from outside, especially in the middle and upper officer grades," was required, and that the two distinct groups should be integrated into a single, larger Foreign Service. The "single service" had been proposed five years before by the Hoover Commission, but had not yet been acted upon. Now action occurred with a vengeance, with new employees from the State Department's civil service and other government agencies brought into the Foreign Service at middle grades without competitive examination at the bottom. By 1957, when the program ended, the service had tripled in size.

Like FDR before him, Wriston believed that the Foreign Service needed to be "Americanized" lest it become an out-of-touch expatriate elite. The committee thought it "unfortunate" that "the Foreign Service is in effect in a condition of exile abroad," and concluded, "it has been a serious mistake to keep so much of the Foreign Service orbiting overseas so long." There were also complaints about an overly narrow geographic spread among FSO candidates. In the 1920s about half of all new recruits to the service came from Ivy League colleges, in the forties and fifties the figure was closer to one third, and since Wriston's reforms it has fallen to below one quarter.* Measured by place of birth and education, the Foreign Service continues to be heavily overrepresented by East and West coasters, who in 1964 made up 75 percent of the FSO corps, and to be underrepresented by Midwesterners and Southerners.

Broadening the base of national recruitment was a reasonable reform, but the Wriston influx of 2,500 outside bureaucrats at middle ranks over a two-year period, coming shortly after the havoc of McCarthyism, spread chaos and uncertainty. It also destroyed one of State's most useful assets—a permanent, Washington-based staff of civil servants. Civil service employees were importuned to "integrate" and take foreign posts lest they lose the better salaries, ranks, and pension rights that could be obtained only in the Foreign Service. It is not hard to see why Dean Acheson, a man who doesn't mince words, thought the Wriston reforms "contemptible."

In addition to favoring much greater "lateral entry" into the Foreign Service by men and women from other government agencies and occupations, the Wriston Committee recommended the annual recruitment of 500 new officers at the bottom. The former policy was pursued in the late 1950s and the early 1960s, but the latter was not. Today only 100 to 150 new men and women come in annually at the bottom, and the highest annual intake—in 1965—was only about 250. Over Wriston's strenuous personal objection, State Department administrators further lowered entrance standards in 1956 by dropping the requirement that all new recruits have a speaking knowledge of at least one foreign language before being hired.

The long-term effects of "Wristonization" have created a curious generation gap in our professional diplomacy. In 1954, only about 400 officers out of a total Foreign Service of 1,200 had entered the profession prior to 1945. In the Wriston service of 3,600 officers, the few prewar first-generation American diplomats were thoroughly swamped by newcomers. Since most recruitment in the 1950s was via lateral entry of middle-aged men, and since promotions were many and retirements few in the 1960s, today's Foreign Service is seriously "overage." There are

---

*Prior to 1925, 64 percent of all American diplomats had attended Harvard, Yale, or Princeton. By 1936–39, these three schools were providing 26 percent of new recruits into the Foreign Service, a figure which fell to 15 percent for the years 1957–62 and 9 percent in 1969–70. Of the 103 new Foreign Service officers in 1969–70, 24 of them attended Ivy League schools as undergraduates.

many more men over forty-five than under thirty-five in the service today, and two times *more* officers in the top four than in the bottom four ranks, rather like an army with more colonels than captains.

Responding to the inverted pyramid, most State Department and embassy jobs have had to be reclassified an average of two grades upward over the past fifteen years, creating more positions for chiefs but fewer and fewer responsible posts for Indians. (In late 1966, when I called this anomaly to the attention of Under Secretary Katzenbach, he raised the matter with Secretary Rusk. Rusk rationalized the accidental imbalance as follows: "We're a policy business. We *need* more chiefs than Indians.") Another incalculable result of the Wriston "direct infusion" of 2,500 new officers was a lowering of training standards and a loss in the continuity of professional traditions, for relatively few senior men were left who had served in the prewar era and could educate young men coming in at the bottom. Although some of the Wriston lateral entrants brought useful "new blood" to diplomacy, the majority of them had a lower level of competence than the entrance standards of the career service would normally allow. By 1962, the Herter Report noted: ". . . present leadership in the State Department, both at home and overseas, includes only a minority of officers who entered and progressed in the Foreign Service by the orthodox examination route. . . . in Washington, fewer than one-fifth of the executive positions . . . are held by officers who entered laterally and the remainder are filled by Reserve Officers, civil servants and political appointees. In 1962, lateral-entry officers held about one-third of all U.S. ambassadorships and two-thirds of the number two "deputy chief of mission" posts in embassies. By 1970, even fewer men who came in at the bottom by competitive examination were reaching the top: 67 percent of all FSO-1s and 65 percent of all FSO-2s today are men who have entered the service laterally.

However one judges the Wriston program of 1954–1957, it profoundly changed the character of the Foreign Service and of State Department officialdom. The 1924 Rogers Act had enforced by statute a fixed balance between the upper and lower ranks of the service, assuring that there would always be many more men on the bottom than on the top rungs of the ladder. The Wriston program, and subsequent personnel policy in State, totally reversed that balance, creating an inverse pyramid and overcrowding at the top. The combined shocks of McCarthy and Wriston seemed designed to produce a surplus of cautious organization men and a shortage of trained diplomats. Today, nearly two decades later, most senior Foreign Service officers are either the survivors or the beneficiaries of McCarthyism and Wristonization.

Organization of the State Department

Structural flaws in the system encourage the tendency to duck responsibility. At the top of the State Department there are five principal officers: the secretary of state, the under secretary, the under secretary for political affairs, the deputy under secretary for economic affairs, and the deputy under secretary for administration. The four top men and their staffs and the officers attached to them, who all reside on the seventh floor of the State Department Building, had a total population in late 1969 of 342 persons. These included the office of the secretary of state and attached staffs (89 personnel), the executive secretariat (120), the policy and coordination staff (32), the office of the under secretary (33), the under secretary for political affairs (17), the deputy under secretary for economic affairs (11), and the inspector-general for foreign assistance (40).

Next in the chain of command (leaving aside the administrative area, which amounts to half of the department's personnel) are fifteen geographic and functional bureaus, all headed by assistant secretaries (each of whom has between three and seven deputy assistant secretaries as well as a personal office staff of ten to twenty people and, typically, technical advisers on public affairs, labor, and other specialized subjects). In the five geographic bureaus, fifty "country directors" form the next level, each responsible, on the average, for a staff of ten (five officers and five clerical workers). Presently the bureaus headed by assistant secretaries or their equivalents are double the number that existed at the end of World War II.

Within these policy bureaus of State there is a "buried administrative factor," since between 20 and 25 percent of the personnel of each bureau are, in effect, liaison officers from the administrative half of the department. Another 10 to 15 percent of the bureau staffs comprise the deputies and office help and special and technical staffs of the assistant secretaries. In all, administrative and staff overhead of each of the policy bureaus thus accounts for about 30 to 40 percent of total bureau personnel. This figure is doubly high when one considers that nearly half of the department (2,580 personnel) is already compartmentalized into administration, and that on State's seventh floor there is an Executive Secretariat of 120 persons that exists, along with the other top-level staffs, to coordinate the work of the various bureaus as a channel between them and the four highest officers of the department. Below the assistant secretaries is the "working level." This consists, in the geographic bureaus, of country directors and, in the functional bureaus, of office directors who are generally FSO-2 Foreign Service officers (or the equivalent of GS-15 civil servants). An example in the African Bureau would be the country director for Algeria, Libya, Morocco, Spanish Sahara, and Tunisia, who is State's responsible officer for those countries and has four or five lower-ranking FSOs working for him.

The normal flow of work and chain of responsibility would seem to go from the top level (the secretary or under secretary) to an intermediate level (15 assistant secretaries) to a working level (about 150 country or office directors) to an expert level (roughly 500 "desk officers" for specific countries and functions) as well as back and forth between all levels and ambassadors in the field. In fact it is not that simple.

At every level staffs get in the way, and at every level a custom has evolved of "coordinating" or "clearing" horizontally with other bureaus and offices before going *up* the chain of command. To send a cable to our embassy at Lisbon concerning the U.S. naval bases in the Azores, the country director for Spain and Portugal must first "clear" his draft message with several other offices—perhaps with the African and International Organization Bureaus because of colonial and UN ramifications, perhaps with the NATO office of the European Bureau since Portugal is a NATO member, perhaps with the Bureau of Politico-Military Affairs (and through it with the Defense Department) since this is a military matter. After these "lateral clearances" are obtained, the story is not over. The drafter may then try to consult his assistant secretary (going through one of several deputy assistant secretaries and a bureau staff). If the matter is of sufficient importance, the assistant secretary may pass the draft up through the Executive Secretariat to the under secretaries or the secretary of state on the seventh floor, who may want the opinion of other assistant secretaries. The White House and other agencies such as the CIA and the Treasury may be consulted. A time-consuming process such as this requires telephone calls, committee and staff meetings, and continual rewriting or amendment of the original draft message by however many colleagues are consulted about its contents. The horizontal clearance system is a most cautious way of doing business. It reflects an institutionalized desire to diffuse responsibility among many different offices and colleagues rather than to accept responsibility oneself. . . .

In the African Bureau, 44 of its 166 personnel, or 27 percent, were administrative staff dealing with such matters as budget, personnel assignments, selection of supplies for our African posts, processing of official travel between Washington and Africa, and the like. But separate and much larger department-wide administrative offices already existed for all of these functions under the deputy under secretary for administration. Thus, much of the work was duplicated and "coordinated" between two distinct offices, adding an extra layer. Another 22 positions, or 14 percent of this bureau's personnel, accounted for the 3 deputies of the assistant secretary for Africa, their office staffs, assistants, and liaison officers from other bureaus as well as specialists in labor and cultural affairs.

This pattern existed and exists in every policy bureau of State. Its practical effects should be obvious. It contributes to slowing down work, to requiring extensive and elaborate "permanent staff meetings" to keep everyone informed of what his neighbor is doing, to introducing extra buffers between different bureaus that may have a common interest in a single problem, and to delaying the process of up-and-down communication and work flow between the seventh floor, the assistant secretary, and his country directors. It results, too, in wasteful and frustrating attempts to "coordinate" and compromise disputed questions of policy at the lowest possible level, rather than transmitting a clear-cut choice of alternatives to a higher level, reflecting honest disagreement among different lower-level officers or bureaus. It contributes to excessive preoccupation with daily operational detail that leaves expert- and working-level officers no time for reflection on the wider implications of a policy.

This says nothing of the difficulties and misunderstandings caused by the distance and number of layers through which information must travel. From the secretary of state to his country directors and desk officers is a long way. The route from the bottom to one of the top policy makers may include the alternate or "deputy" county director, the country director, a deputy assistant secretary, an assistant secretary (via his staff), the Executive Secretariat (and possibly the policy and coordination staff), and finally one or all of four top officials (through their personal staffs). *And*, on the way up, any policy recommendation must normally receive clearance from all concerned horizontal layers.

Stalemate is a clear and present danger in this kind of system, as is an easy acceptance of the status quo as the best of all possible worlds. Altogether, a more cautious way of doing business could not have been invented. And it is important to recall that this one is no man's invention; it has just "happened" in a way that no president or secretary of state consciously intended during the fast-paced postwar years.

Proposals to create more coordinating committees and superstaffs to assist harried policy makers are temporary palliatives that ignore the larger structural problem or assume it to be insoluble; yet substantial reductions could plausibly be made in the size of the entire foreign affairs machine. Rather than resulting in any loss of effectiveness, a reduction should result in improved performance. Until size and structure are recognized as *problems*, the central issue will continue to be evaded and more trouble, or at least more foul-ups, are built for the future. Above all, the system weds itself to policy assumptions of the past, with little scope or time for questioning the rightness or necessity for continuing policies in the 1970s first devised during the "national emergency" atmosphere of the 1940s and 1950s.

In pure structural terms, as one student of government has stated, the present framework "violates all the basic rules of bureaucratic organization: duties are not clearly assigned, the diffusion of authority slackens responsibility, the same job is done by different people, the proportion of staff services to the rest of personnel is unsound . . . top officials have too many subordinates reporting to them, and comparable activities are dispersed among various agencies."

•   •   •   •   •   •   •   •   •   •   •   •   •   •   •   •

Administration of the State Department

Traditionally, "administration" as defined in State and the Foreign Service has had a very limited and special meaning. It concerns itself narrowly with "housekeeping" and physical support of the efforts of diplomats and officials to form and carry out foreign policy. Unlike any other cabinet department, State's main budget outlay is simply for the salaries of its employees and not for physical plant or programs. Administration hence has a rather lowly place in the State hierarchy, for it exists only to support the intangible, intellectual effort of diplomats and policy makers to ply their craft of political communication. The demands on the time of the secretary of state, other senior State officials, and ambassadors have been such that administrative tasks have been delegated to a specialized class of "administrators" remote from the policy process. The secretary of state probably pays less attention and has less of a personal role in formulating his own department's annual budget than does any other cabinet officer. He devotes his time to "policy" and leaves the "administrative details" to distant underlings. His budget, compared with that of the secretary of defense, or of health, education, and welfare, varies little from year to year and is not a crucial consideration. It is also one of Washington's smallest budgets.

Before World War II, however, it was much smaller, only 3 or 4 percent of today's total, and its administration was much more informal. But the vast expansion of the foreign affairs bureaucracy in the postwar years posed new administrative requirements. A new machinery evolved to meet the need.

It is headed in Washington today by a deputy under secretary for administration, currently the number-five man in State's hierarchy, and run in the field by counselors of embassy for administration, who are generally the fourth- or fifth-ranking men in our embassies. Within the Foreign Service, administrative specialists are generally expected to remain in their narrow field and are considered out of the running for more prestigious "policy" jobs. Administration has become a compartmentalized and esoteric skill.

The tasks of administration are varied but they include some of the following: preparation of the annual budget, assuring organizational efficiency, paying 25,000 U.S. and foreign employees, determining all foreign and domestic assignments and promotions of personnel, arranging for shipment of supplies and of the personal effects of employees between Washington and foreign posts, providing housing and medical services, and in some cases running schools and food and clothing stores abroad for employees and their dependents, providing secure cryptographic telegram facilities connecting Washington with our foreign missions and a secure courier system for transmitting mail, running and staffing a training institute in Washington to teach languages and other job skills to Foreign Service personnel, protecting the security of embasssy buildings overseas, arranging evacuation of U.S. officials and families from foreign trouble-spots in times of crisis, building embassies and leasing foreign properties for official use abroad, and keeping U.S. missions supplied with all of their needs from paper clips to motor vehicles to electricity and typewriters. In Germany during the mid-1960s, one administrative officer and his staff of local helpers were responsible, among other things, for stocking, storing, and shipping a regular supply of American toilet paper to our missions in Eastern Europe.

These are complicated jobs, partly because of their nature and partly because of the extremely large number of U.S. officials (especially of Defense and AID) stationed abroad, for State's administrators in the field provide services not only for State personnel but also on a "shared-cost" basis to representatives of many other government agencies. Nonetheless, State's elaborate administrative practices are in many cases indirectly harmful to the *policies* State attempts to carry out abroad. By segregating administration from policy, the department has failed to filter out those aspects of administration that require attention at high policy levels from those other aspects that require only low-level "housekeeping."

To reduce the State Department's present high overhead and inefficient administration would reverse trends that were initially set in motion by the expansion of our foreign affairs agencies after World War II. It also means beginning to pay some attention to the ways other countries organize their diplomacy. None of the European foreign services provide the kind of massive, prepackaged services to their embassy staffs that American administrators offer. They find it necessary to assign specialized "administrative officers" only to their very largest overseas missions. In an American embassy, on the other hand, the administrative section is typically larger than the diplomatic and consular sections combined. Most field administrative work done at German, French, and British embassies is handled by low-level clerical personnel, under the supervision of the number-two or -three diplomatic officer of the mission.

To adopt this course in U.S. embassies of necessity would require other major changes. It would presuppose major cuts in the total staff, particularly the personnel of agencies other than the State Department. It would mean putting an end to what has been called "the PX Culture." Instead of having U.S. supermarkets, schools, and housing compounds supervised by administrative officers, we should have to cut back these direct services and compensate our diplomats, the same as every other major nation does, with allowances to cover their expenses. A small clerical staff would still be needed to handle routine "housekeeping" functions, but U.S. diplomats would have to become more self-reliant in housing and feeding their families.

The idea of large military post exchanges and food commissaries and housing projects for Americans abroad originated with the U.S. armed forces in Europe and Japan after World War II. When Germany was occupied in 1945, the economics of scarcity and of conquest made it necessary to import U.S. products and construct American housing colonies for our military families and civil administrators. A shattered local economy was hardly able to support the local population, let alone handle the needs of a vast influx of foreigners with a much higher standard of living.

That era is long since past in Europe and Japan, yet the PX Culture remains. It has been extended throughout the world, not only to U.S. military bases but also wherever a sizeable American diplomatic mission exists. It effects are pernicious both to American officials and their families and to their foreign hosts, for the system encourages isolated ghetto living that deepens American provincialism based on what foreigners see as "special privilege." In parliamentary debates in Rome, Italian legislators have pointed with mock disbelief to wives of U.S. officials in their country who may purchase American-made spaghetti in American military supermarkets. When the staff lives together in a housing compound, U.S. officials inevitably find themselves spending more time entertaining each other than mixing with the people to whom they are accredited. By making the American officials stationed abroad more self-reliant, we could help make them better representatives at the same time. As long as U.S. military personnel outnumber State Department personnel at our overseas missions, however, military administrative requirements will set the pattern of life at a majority of our embassies.

Another difficulty in employing and looking after large official staffs in foreign countries is that the very size of their presence can become provocative, breeding frictions locally that undercut the purposes of our foreign policy. Having much larger diplomatic missions than any other country, the United States strains the reciprocal basis of international law and the credulity and hospitality of other governments and peoples. An immense diplomatic presence implies, often falsely, a high degree of political influence with the host government while willy-nilly generating an impression of American interference in domestic matters that is not always intended. In some cases, of course, American interference *is* intended, but even then an ostentatious staff is rarely the best way to achieve influence. Forbearance would suggest not sending large, unskilled official staffs to areas about which Americans have little knowledge, experience, or political insight, which means most of the less-developed world. It is the limit of American wisdom as well as the limit of our power that should teach us the folly of too large or conspicuous a diplomatic representation.

In Washington the outstanding fact about the administrative structure is that it has become so confusing that few people within State are able to grasp the intricacy of its design. Although there are uniform administrative regulations, they are not uniformly applied. Whim and intrigue replace certainty and responsibility. The "operator" who is able to navigate through a tangled paper underbrush, or slice through it with random personal contacts, is the rare and bureaucratically admired individual.

Instead of routine personnel decisions being made in one place, they are now made in six or seven, for the personnel offices under the deputy under secretary for administration must deal in turn with their liaison staffs under the assistant secretaries for Europe, Africa, the Near East, Latin America, the Far East, and international organizations. This duplication is multiplied many times over when one considers all of the executive and liaison offices scattered around State, each lobbying for funds, "warm bodies" (the bureaucrat's ghoulish slang word for "personnel"), and supplies, each seeking new "clearances" and each enmeshed in its own committee syndrome.

Personnel policy—the method of recruiting new officers, training them, and determining their assignments and promotions—has always received special attention in State. "Let me control personnel," George Kennan has said, "and I will ultimately control policy. For the part of the machine that recruits and hires and fires and promotes people can soon control the entire shape of the institution, and of our foreign policy. That is why it is a curious blindness of secretaries of state . . . when they delegate administrative parts of their responsibility to outside 'specialists.'" What Kennan complains of has long been a fact of life. The daily "nuts and bolts" of personnel policy are attended to with care in the lower reaches of the bureaucracy but there is practically no long-range planning and no attention at the top.

Few organizations devote so much time to their promotion and job assignment systems as does the Foreign Service. Indeed, one has the impression that the next promotion and the next assignment are things constantly on the minds of most FSOs. The five-to-ten page "efficiency report" each officer receives annually from his boss is a document of real and ritual significance. It is a report card on every facet of the man's personality, competence, and "potential for development," and it is also likely to explore such extraneous matters as his wife's ability in the kitchen, his hobbies, and his "attitude toward the Foreign Service." By contrast, French diplomats use a single sheet of paper to rate their subordinates each year, wisely confining themselves to the more demonstrable question of job-performance.

The elaborate mechanics of State personnel administration in the 1950s and 1960s may have contributed to the molding of a conformist career mentality. Constant preoccupation with one's next promotion can easily breed sycophancy toward superiors and a patronizing attitude toward subordinates. In any case these things are a diversion from the main job of getting on with the public business. Short-term pressures toward "getting ahead" gear the system to a one-year rather than a ten- or twenty-year cycle: thus, the unplanned, unwanted bulge of underemployed senior officers today grouped around ranks FSO-1, 2, and 3.

"Selection out"—the process envisioned in the 1946 Foreign Service Act whereby the lowest performers of each rank of Foreign Service officers would be forcibly retired each year—has not been rigidly enforced. The Wriston Report in 1954 noted that selection-out was nearly a joke—only an average of sixteen men had been annually released in the first eight years of the program. Ten years later a larger Foreign Service was just as lenient. It seemed that the concept of selection-out was too ruthless a method to be practically administered by bureaucrats. Personnel boards with the power to use it charitably refrained from doing so. Indeed they did just the opposite, giving gift promotions to men approaching the selection-out line in order to protect their jobs. Thus the selection-out provision of the law has had a perverse rather than a constructive effect. Instead of keeping the service lean and fit, it has strengthened seniority and featherbedding.

It is little wonder that by the late 1960s the Foreign Service began to have trouble maintaining its traditional appeal to able graduates of American universities. In part, this reflected the wider unpopularity of recent foreign policies in the under-thirty age group, and the youth attack on Establishment institutions. Bureaucratization and State's declining reputation, however, may have been just as much of a factor. The heavy preponderance of senior officers in a reverse-pyramid Foreign Service, leaving little room for responsible work by younger men, and the public image of State as a place of excessive paperwork, rigid indoctrination, and stultifying bureaucracy have bred cynicism about diplomacy as a career. Anyone who remembers the American campus scene of 1960 and has troubled to talk with students and professors of 1970 knows that a great change of attitude toward the Foreign Service has taken place over the last ten years. Students are well aware of the limited possibilities for advancement and the many personal constraints in today's professional diplomacy, and they have heard a growing number of teachers and former public officials recommend *against* a Foreign Service career. They point out that the way to be "effective" in foreign policy is to pursue a career in academic life, or the law, or some other agency of government where chances for advancement are greater and the organizational framework is looser and less inhibiting. After rising rapidly in another field, a young man may become qualified for lateral entry into the State Department at a higher and more responsible level more quickly than following the "career route."

In December of 1969, when the Foreign Service exam was given for the first time since 1967, there was a drop of nearly 50 percent in the number of total applications. An average of 7,000 persons applied to take the test annually in 1960-1967, but only 3,875 applicants were heard from in the last year of the decade. More ominously, the "raw scores" of those who pass the test declined notably during the 1960s, indicating progressively lower academic preparation among those who took the test. If the trend is not just temporary or accidental, one might predict a "stupidization" of American public service in the 1970s, a vicious cycle of fewer and fewer people of progressively lower abilities joining the government. A career official who worries about these things said to me, only half in jest, in April 1970, "We're taking the best secondraters we can get."

History as well as common sense suggests that a declining curve of ability in recruitment into the most prestigious sectors of government is something to worry about. The example of Imperial Russia in the late nineteenth century may be an extreme case of this phenomenon, but it is one worth pondering. An unpopular government, trying fitfully to reform itself, lost touch with the ablest of its university students and logical future leaders. Recruitment into the bureaucracy was designed to meet high educational standards, but with each passing year fewer and fewer of the brightest students were motivated to apply. As "stupider" newcomers entered the administration each year, the regime became increasingly less responsive to the needs of the society and ever more heavy-handed. Growing incompetence in government bred growing cynicism and repression and a failure to address the serious problems of the nation, which made more and more of the intellectual elite go underground to fight the system. Revolution replaced reform as the only decent aspiration for the best of the nation's youth.

Questions

1. The author lists three "villains" who have contributed to the disorganization of the Department of State. Compare his criticism of each man. Are there any common elements?
2. Explain why the author believes that the structural flaws in the system encourage people in the Department of State to "duck "responsibility."
3. What has been the meaning of "administration" in the Department of State? How has this traditional meaning affected the conduct and formulation of foreign policy?
4. Describe the "practical effects" that the author believes result from the existing organization of the Department of State.
5. Why does the author stress the importance of personnel policy in the administration of the Department of State?

The American Diplomat: The Search for Identity*

Martin B. Hickman

The publication of the State Department study *Diplomacy for the 70s* raises once again questions about the nature and function of diplomacy. This study is only the latest in a series of studies of the American Foreign Service and diplomacy that have been undertaken since World War II. Each study has struggled with the nature of diplomacy, the relation between the structure of the Foreign Service and the tasks of diplomacy, and finally the problems of recruitment, promotion, and training. Many Foreign Service offices have become cynical about such studies, which seem to them only harrassments that keep them from doing the job they could do superbly well if they were just

---

*Footnote references omitted.

left alone. On the other hand, a growing number of Foreign Service officers have joined the critics of Foreign Service and have taken the lead in demanding a reassessment of the Foreign Service, the Department of State, and other agencies involved in the administration of foreign affairs. The studies of the foreign affairs establishment contained in *Diplomacy for the 70s* reflect the efforts of the department and the Foreign Service to initiate internal reforms before they are forced on them from outside.

The recommendations for change contained in *Diplomacy for the 70s* are far-reaching and foresee some drastic changes in all phases of the department's responsibilities. The purpose of this paper is not to review those recommendations but to look closely at the concept of "diplomacy" to determine what meaning it has in the modern world.

What emerges from the pages of *Diplomacy for the 70s* is an explicit assertion that foreign relations covers the entire range of "interests and activities" within the jurisdiction of the executive branch. This includes "diplomatic problems in the old and narrow sense" but ranges well beyond into the emerging technological and economic questions of vital interest to the United States. This definition of foreign relations, it is alleged, requires new skills that traditional diplomats did not need. In addition to what the studies call the "core skills" of diplomacy—"the ability to negotiate, to observe carefully and report accurately and precisely, to analyze and synthesize"—the administration of foreign relations now calls for mastery of "agriculture, labor, commerce, finance, developmental economics, science, information and the like." Moreover, it is alleged that a crucial skill—identified in the studies as management capability—has been sorely lacking in the Department of State and the Foreign Service. The result has been that the effectiveness of the Department of State as the "director and coordinator" of American overseas activity has been limited. The failure to develop management capability coupled with a stubborn reliance on "generalists" who concentrated on the core skills has "eroded the confidence of their federal agencies in the department's ability to exercise leadership in the conduct of foreign policy."

On first reading, the authors of *Diplomacy for the 70s* seem to be making a sharp distinction between diplomacy and foreign relations. This distinction rests on a specific ordering of the relationship between the two, with diplomacy becoming a subset of a larger set of activities encompassed in foreign relations. This conceptual ordering is confused, however, by the introduction in the same report of the term "the new diplomacy." As this term is used it seems to be synonymous with foreign relations. Therefore, when "diplomats" master all of the skills that the conduct of foreign relations requires they will then be the "new" diplomats ready to practice the "new diplomacy." The "old diplomacy" only required a diplomat to master the core skills; the new diplomacy requires in addition to the core skills a knowledge of all the "new activities . . . which have become a standard part of our diplomatic operations abroad."

This distinction between the "old diplomacy" and the "new diplomacy" is also a distinction between process and content. The core skills relate almost exclusively to the process of international interaction—negotiation, reporting, and analysis. The additional skills required by the new diplomacy are for the most part substantive skills that relate to the content of the process. The explicit assumption on which this distinction rests is that in the past diplomats have needed only to understand the process to be successful; the implicit assumption is that negotiating, reporting, and analyzing did not require mastery of content or that content was immaterial.

It is true that traditional definitions of diplomacy have identified diplomacy with the process of international interaction. Harold Nicolson in his well-known study, *Diplomacy*, adopts the definition of diplomacy given by the *Oxford English Dictionary:* "Diplomacy is the management of international relations by negotiation; the method by which these relations are adjusted and managed by ambassadors and envoys; the business or art of the diplomatist."

The *Oxford* definition of diplomacy differs in detail from definitions used by most writers on international affairs but the essentials are the same. All definitions either explicitly or implicitly contain three elements: (1) The concept of process, which is usually called negotiation. In some definitions skill in negotiation is stressed, as in that of Sir Ernest Satow who says that "Diplomacy is the application of intelligence and tact to the conduct of relations between the governments of independent states. . . ." But in none is the process element absent. (2) The identification of the principals in negotiation as "nations" or "states" or "independent states." (3) The existence of agents—diplomats—who represent the principals in the negotiating process.

In addition to these three elements some definitions of diplomacy also introduce a representation function, an information-gathering function, and an information communication function. Thus it has been said that diplomats have a dual function: "they represent their own nation abroad and they report home conditions prevailing in foreign countries." In the same vein, Georg Schwarzenberger cites a British White Paper that defines diplomacy as "making the policy of His Majesty's Government, whatever it might be, understood and, if possible, accepted by other countries."

Implicit in the identification of diplomacy with the process of international interaction is the assumption that diplomats understand the issues at stake as well as the process itself. The authors of *Diplomacy for the 70s* do not, therefore, place limits on or otherwise specify the content of the process; diplomats, they assume, might negotiate agreements on any possible subject in which their government has an interest. Diplomats have for centuries negotiated agreements that solved problems involving economic, financial, agricultural, technological, and military issues. What was thought to be crucial was mastery of the negotiating process and the politics of the situation, not expertise in the subject matter of the agreement.

The authors of *Diplomacy for the 70s* are somewhat unfair then to imply that mastery of subject matter was irrelevant in the "old diplomacy." It is indeed true that the content of international negotiations may have changed and that some diplomats cannot operate effectively in these negotiations until they become familiar with the subject matter, but the relationship between process and content has not changed and hence the new diplomacy is not all that new.

Still other authors have attempted more sophisticated definitions of diplomacy. In a recent paper a former ambassador, Leon Poullada, has distinguished between the procedural aspects of diplomacy—"such as the refinement of protocol, diplomatic draftery, press relations, yes, and even gastronomy"—and what he terms substantive diplomacy—"conflict management, problem solving, cross-cultural interaction, negotiation and program management." Substantive diplomacy, he argues, is distinguishable from similar behavior in other situations by the cross-cultual environment in which they occur. Indeed the essence of the diplomat's skills is "that they are exercised in trans-national and trans-cultural milieu."

This emphasis on the "trans-" or "cross-" cultural milieu of diplomacy is the theme of an earlier article by Robert Rossow on which Poullada has relied heavily in his own definition of diplomacy. For Rossow the service rendered by the diplomat is the *"minimizing of distortion and friction in cross-cultural communication and operations."* To perform this service the diplomat must acquire a knowledge of other cultures that will permit him to "interpret them accurately and to operate smoothly in their milieus."

The addition of the cross-cultural element in these definitions of diplomacy only makes explicit what is implicit in the more traditional definitions that identify "states" or "nations" as the principals in the diplomatic process. Furthermore, Rossow's and Poullada's treatment of the cross-cultural element in diplomacy is really a discussion of the skills of the diplomat, an important problem but one which should be kept separate from the definition of diplomacy.

Nor does the distinction between substantive and procedural aspects of diplomacy suggested by Poullada clarify the definition of diplomacy. Although the five functional areas he names may be sharply distinguished from what he calls the procedural, they clearly suggest process rather than content. If problem solving is substantive rather than procedural, what name should one give to the disciplines of economics, agriculture, and the others which the authors of *Diplomacy for the 70s* identify as being part of the "new" diplomacy? Furthermore, except for program management, Poullada's substantive diplomacy can be subsumed easily under the core skills identified in *Diplomacy for the 70s*. What is conflict management or problem solving, other than the adjustment of disputes by bargaining and negotiation, or the ability to analyze or synthesize? Poullada himself suggests, and correctly so, that reporting is really problem solving, not simply straightforward intelligence gathering.

It is clear, however, that the use of the term "core skills" in *Diplomacy for the 70s* and the emphasis on process in the older definitions of diplomacy suggests that whatever changes have taken place in the content of diplomacy, there is a set of skills that have remained constant over time and have characterized diplomats. It is the persistence of these skills that has led diplomats and scholars to identify diplomacy as a profession, and to distinguish between amateur and professional diplomats. The best history of the emergence of the American Foreign Service is called *Professional Diplomacy in the United States*, and a recent study of Foreign Service personnel is entitled the *Professional Diplomat*. This coupling of these two concepts—professional and diplomacy—creates a deceptive image. We believe we understand clearly what is meant by each of them. Yet on closer examination, they are both ambiguous concepts that require careful definitions before they can be used with any degree of precision.

We have seen some of the difficulties that the authors of *Diplomacy for the 70s* encountered in defining diplomacy. But this definitional problem has plagued the Department of State and Foreign Service for some time. The question has usually been raised by asking: Is any government employee stationed abroad a diplomat? If not, where does one draw the line? Historically, international law has drawn a distinction between embassies and consulates, and at one time diplomats were those who performed the work of embassies and consular officials worked in consular offices. The distinction between embassies and consular offices remains today, but with the Rogers Act of 1924 the separate personnel systems that the United States had developed around this historical distinction were amalgamated into one personnel system. Each Foreign Service officer now receives two commissions, one as a secretary in the diplomatic corps and one as a consular officer. Which hat he wears is determined by the functional role to which he is assigned.

Implicit in the Rogers Act is the assumption that diplomacy includes all representation of the government abroad and that diplomacy is synonymous with foreign relations. This assumption finds expression also in the Foreign Service Act of 1946. Yet it is abundantly clear that the task of political and economic reporting as well as negotiation of international agreements is substantially different from the work of issuing visas, administering passport regulations, and protecting American citizens abroad. Nevertheless the Foreign Service for the past forty-seven years has been based on the premise that all of these functions are part of diplomacy and that it is possible to rotate officers not only from post to post but from function to function as the needs of the service dictate.

Since the end of World War II the assumption that a diplomat is anyone who represents the government abroad has been increasingly called into question as the United States provided foreign aid to all parts of the world, participated in the complex international agreements on economic and financial issues, and began an active information program. Where do the people who administer these programs fit into the Foreign Service? Are they diplomats, or are they merely civil servants temporarily assigned overseas? The tendency was at first to treat the agencies that administered these programs as temporary and to create temporary personnel systems. As it became clear that they were not temporary, permanent personnel systems separate from the Foreign

Service have been established. The upshot has been the explicit assertion in *Diplomacy for the 70s* that foreign relations is not synonymous with diplomacy and that diplomats are only some of the many who must contribute to successful administration of foreign relations. Yet no sooner was this distinction drawn than it was obscured again by the introduction of the term "new diplomacy," which is but a synonym for foreign relations.

Even if one accepts the more traditional definition of diplomacy, as a process, definitional problems remain. First one might raise the question that if diplomacy is essentially negotiation, and all that term implies in the way of conflict management and problem solving, how does it differ from other forms of negotiation? In these definitions is negotiation intended to be a generic term that covers all situations regardless of the issues and principals involved? If so, can one fairly infer from these definitions that skill in negotiations is transferable from situation to situation so that skilled negotiators can readily operate effectively in any given situation? If this is an unwarranted assumption, what is there about diplomacy that makes it different from other negotiations?

If, in response to the last question, one reaches the answer that it is not possible to distinguish diplomacy from other negotiating situations, is it then the principals in the process that makes the difference? Does the "right" of nation states to resort to force if negotiations do not promise a satisfactory solution to their problems make diplomacy something other than mere "negotiation"? And, if the character of the principals makes diplomatic negotiations more momentous than other negotiations, does it follow that the character of the principals changes the nature of the skills required of a successful negotiator?

What emerges from these questions raised by a careful review of the various definitions of diplomacy is that they imply more than they say. What they say is that diplomacy is the conduct of relations between principals called "nations" or "states" by agents called "diplomats." What they imply is that the conduct of these relations is somehow different than the relations between any other possible principals. The ways in which the conduct is different are left unspecified, as if by giving human behavior a special name it becomes different.

It is undoubtedly true that diplomacy resembles other forms of negotiation so closely that one must concede that negotiation skills learned in other situations are probably transferable to the diplomatic setting. Yet it is going too far to say that diplomacy does not have some unique aspects that justify treating it as a very special kind of negotiation and that requires very specific skills. There are at least five characteristics of diplomacy that set it apart from all other negotiations and that justify special concern for the personnel system that selects and trains diplomats.

1. Diplomatic negotiations are conducted in a system in which there is no central enforcement agency. Unless diplomats clearly understand the constraint that this type of system imposes on the negotiating process they are likely to rely too heavily on legal solutions to complex problems. Moreover, decentralized enforcement means that agreements among or between nations must offer sufficient rewards to each party to ensure enforcement through self-interest. Where a nation's self-interest shifts substantially over time, agreements cannot be enforced except by the unilateral use of force. One has only to examine the post–World War II agreement relating to Berlin to see the ineffectiveness of agreements that became detached from the self-interest of one of the parties.

2. Diplomacy involves negotiation in which the issues are substantially more difficult and complex than in other negotiating situations. These issues cannot be resolved without taking into consideration economic and social as well as political factors. Diplomatic agreements affect the relationship between the parties but also affect the domestic affairs of those nations involved as well as each party's relationship with third states. The complex network of interrelationships that are affected by diplomatic negotiation strains the analytical capabilities of even the most knowledgeable and experienced participants.

3. Closely related to the second distinguishing feature of diplomacy is the importance of the issues involved. Not only are the issues difficult and complex, but they also affect the most important aspects of human existence. Surely no issue in any other situation can match the saliency of the question of peace. True, not all diplomatic negotiations concern the question of war and peace, but all are related to that issue either directly or indirectly. But even where war and peace are not directly involved the issues at stake in diplomacy are vital to the life of a nation. International

economic issues particularly are central to national existence in ways unmatched by any but the most unusual of negotiations on the domestic scene.

4. The number of people affected by diplomatic negotiations also sets those negotiations apart from other negotiations. Labor disputes may have consequences that involve most of the people in a nation, but diplomacy crosses national boundaries to affect the people of many nations, not just one. This widespread impact of diplomacy is as true for the lesser issues with which diplomats must deal as it is for the central issues involved in war and peace. This is not to say that all diplomatic issues are vital to all people; they certainly are not, and they may not even affect most of the people in the nations directly involved. What is true is that as diplomatic issues approach the upper end of the complexity and importance spectrum they affect more and more people in ways that are increasingly central to their very existence.

5. Finally, diplomatic negotiations do involve a cross-cultural element that complicates the communication process. Traditionally diplomacy has sought to overcome the cross-cultural barrier by the development of a common diplomatic language and code of behavior. The assumption was that these diplomatic skills transcend cultural lines and that if a diplomat mastered them he could be effective in a variety of environments. A corollary of that assumption was that all diplomats, whatever their country, shared these skills, and it was the sharing of these skills even more than the skills themselves that facilitated diplomatic negotiations.

The more recent literature on cross-cultural communication suggests that the traditional diplomatic skills are not sufficient to overcome the barriers to such communication. This literature insists that the diplomat must understand the language, the philosophy, and the lifestyle of the people before he can effectively communicate across cultural barriers. Implicit in this insistence on the need for diplomats to have a wide understanding of other cultures is the assumption that diplomatic skills are relevant only when the larger cultural context has been grasped. Hence the problem is not how to choose between the traditional diplomatic skills and cross-cultural understanding but how to relate these two bodies of knowledge to each other. A decision has to be made as to whether diplomatic skills fit in the larger setting of cross-cultural knowledge, or whether the reverse is true.

Whatever the merits of the opposing views on this issue, it is clear that the cross-cultural setting of diplomacy poses negotiating problems for diplomats that other negotiations do not have. Even those who insist that diplomatic skills are primary must take into consideration the environment in which those skills are exercised. Moreover, the importance of cross-cultural factors is becoming more important as the community of nations widens to include nations that do not accept the norms of the diplomatic community that had its origins in Western Europe. Ironically, the rejection of those norms began with the emergence of the United States, and the evolution of alternative diplomatic styles is still under way.

Questions

1. Identify what the author means by "core" diplomatic skills.
2. What elements are shared by many definitions of diplomacy?
3. Make a list of the reasons why you think a skill in "cross-cultural" communications is required for a diplomat to be successful.
4. Compare diplomacy with other kinds of negotiation with which you are familiar, to test the author's arguments that diplomacy has some unique aspects.

CIA: Clandestine Services in an Open Society*

Harry Howe Ransom

Harry Howe Ransom teaches political science at Vanderbilt University. He has also taught at Harvard, Princeton, Vassar, and Michigan State. Educated at Vanderbilt and Princeton, Mr. Ransom was a congressional

*From *Can American Democracy Survive the Cold War?* by Harry Howe Ransom. Copyright © 1963 by Harry Howe Ransom. Reprinted by permission of Doubleday & Company, Inc.

fellow of the American Political Science Association and research associate and senior staff member of the Harvard Defense Studies Program. He is the author of *The Intelligence Establishment* (Harvard University Press, 1970).

One

The Central Intelligence Agency presents a particular paradox among the many stemming from the conflict between security and liberty. At the entrance to the CIA's new headquarters building near Washington is the biblical inscription: "Ye shall know the truth and the truth shall make you free." Were he permitted through the entrance so decorated, a seriously inquiring citizen would, however, soon discover the agency's operating principles:

. . . the Central Intelligence Agency does not confirm or deny published reports, whether good or bad; never alibis; never explains its organization; never identifies its personnel (except for a few in the top echelons); and will not discuss its budget, its methods of operations, or its sources of information.

So the citizen, as far as CIA's managers are concerned, cannot in fact know "the truth" about a very large, expensive, and increasingly important government agency, the directorship of which has been described as "second in importance only to the president."

The existence of a large, secret bureaucracy sometimes pivotally important in making and implementing national policies and strategies raises special problems. At the level of democratic ideals, the problem is the existence of a potential source of invisible government. At the level of representatives of the people—executive and legislative—the problem is primarily how to control a dimly seen instrument, so hot that if not handled with great skill it can burn its user instead of its adversary. The problem for the scholar is access to verifiable information for objective analysis.

The secrecy officially proclaimed by the CIA and affiliated intelligence agencies, and required by the statutes establishing them, quite obviously has not been absolutely maintained. America's open society, particularly the separation of governmental powers, the pluralism of the administrative bureaucracy, and a free press, have made complete secrecy impossible. Journalists and scholars have been able to produce a considerable amount of literature, much of it speculative. The volume has increased as a result of a series of misfortunes or misadventures in recent years, particularly the U-2 incident, the defection to Moscow of two National Security Agency employees, and the abortive attempt to invade Cuba in 1961. These events removed, temporarily at least, the cloak of secrecy to an unprecedented degree. Even with these disclosures, however, our view remains a partial one. One simply cannot apply the usual rigorous standards of data gathering and documentation to this subject. But within limitations, one can analyze some of the dilemmas presented by the existence of a secret intelligence apparatus in a democratic society.

· · · · · · · · · · · · · · · · · · · ·

In gathering information, Intelligence* must have the objectivity and detachment from policy that will assure the most forthright possible reporting on world affairs. But this detachment should not be such that Intelligence either develops its own policy preferences or loses contact with the informational needs of the policy makers. Its duty is to report objective facts without regard to whether they spell good or bad news for existing policy preferences, but with appropriate regard for policy alternatives. In its operational (political warfare or overseas counterintelligence) missions Intelligence must serve always as an instrument of foreign policy and never be allowed to make its own policy.

Knowledge, however, conveys power. Secret knowledge can become secret power. A secret intelligence apparatus, claiming superior knowledge from undisclosed sources, and operating—because of legitimate secrecy claims—outside the normal check-reins of the American governmental system can wield invisible power either in the policy-making process or in clandestine operations in other countries.

· · · · · · · · · · · · · · · · · · · ·

Two

A policy maker must contend with three major considerations in reaching a decision: First, what are the policy objectives or goals being sought and what are the risks or probable costs in seeking them, in terms of alternative values that might have to be sacrificed? In other words, if a certain value is placed on military security as an objective, must

---

*Intelligence with a capital "I" will be used here to denote the system; lower-case "intelligence" will denote the information "product."

other policy objectives, such as self-determination and economic development, be sacrificed in some calculable degree? Second, what are the pressures and forces likely to shape world affairs whatever course of action is adopted? Put another way, what are the calculable facts and the most probable trends in world affairs? Third, how may one assess the potentialities and limitations of the alternative instruments by which the environment may be influenced in the most favored direction? In other words, with national objectives and world trends in mind, how can we best go about attaining our ends?

Traditionally, the intelligence services are concerned only with the second of these and not with national values, ends, or means. Yet all are inextricably entwined. . . . An agency charged with supplying secret information about the state of affairs in the Soviet Union can be a source of great influence in the policy process. To assume that the USSR is "mellowing" in its objectives calls for one American foreign policy; to decide that she intends to conquer the world soon, either by surprise attack or otherwise, for quite another.

There are, to be sure, checks on the growing influence of secret intelligence. In the American governmental system, long-range policies or major shifts in existing policy are determined normally only after an elaborate consensus-building effort. An intelligence estimate, no matter what its assumed degree of accuracy, cannot alone determine major policy outcomes. Yet the rapidly changing, increasingly complex nature of world politics seems to be leading to more and more Intelligence participation in national decisions. The senior intelligence professionals in the interdepartmental policy planning units, though in theory they "advise" and do not "recommend," have already come to have great influence. And since intelligence professionals are usually more permanent members of the advisory and policy planning units than are representatives from the State Department or the armed services, who are constantly "rotated" through such assignments, their prestige increases all the more.

. . . .

The ultimate power and the ultimate restraint of democratic government is an informed electorate. While it would make no sense to publish information about legitimately secret intelligence operations, the principle must be maintained that the citizen, or at least his representatives, be as completely informed as possible. A corollary requirement is that the citizen know something about the source and process by which intelligence is produced. There ought to be public confidence in the professional competence of the intelligence services, but in recent years this has been badly shattered.

Three

The product generated by the vast machinery of the loosely confederated intelligence community is distributed according to a governmental "need to know" concept. With a few exceptions, neither the product nor the system's organization, functions, and costs are matters of authenticated public record. The rationale for secrecy is that intelligence activities are particularly sensitive in three respects: First, sources of certain types of data would immediately "dry up" if disclosed. Second, espionage and other illegal forms of information gathering should not be officially acknowledged as a government function. In the intelligence tradition, governments always strive to be in a position to "plausibly disavow" espionage. Acknowledgment by top United States officials, in May 1960, of U-2 espionage flights over Russia sharply violated this precedent. Third, underground political actions, which since 1947 have been within the jurisdiction of the CIA, must be secret.

Inevitably and perhaps logically, the executive branch monopolizes the control of information on all these activities, and within the executive, the intelligence community has its own inner-circle monoply. This inner circle can dole out intelligence reports or information on clandestine activities to groups or individuals having, in the opinion of the leaders of the intelligence establishment, a need to know. Although intelligence reports and estimates go regularly and routinely to important decision-making units, their flow is tightly controlled. Information on some sources and some activities, it may be assumed, is never communicated beyond a small group. Some very high-ranking government officials, it turns out, did not know of the U-2 flights over Russia.

. . . .

This situation confronts the American system of government with a two-sided problem: How can there be public control over functions that require secrecy; and how can the effective operation of a two-party system of government be assured when control of the executive branch gives the party in power a potentially exclusive access to essential information in the field of foreign military policy?

. . . .

No longer a secret, as a consequence of "accidents," are the facts that: espionage activities and clandestine political action overseas on a large scale and by every possible means have been an expanding American government function since 1947; under the cover of weather research and in the ostensible employment of a large private aircraft corporation, American CIA operatives spied on the Soviet Union with long-range aerial cameras and other devices between 1956 and 1960; and by means of a large and complex organization comparable in estimated size and cost to the CIA, the National Security Agency has for some years been operating or supervising a massive network for electronic eavesdropping on adversaries and allies as well.

·   ·   ·   ·   ·   ·   ·   ·   ·   ·   ·   ·   ·   ·   ·   ·   ·   ·   ·

It is often asserted that the CIA has its own foreign policy. Little direct evidence can be brought forth to prove this. The more likely situation is that the CIA has moved on its own in a policy vacuum. Standard operating procedure is for the ambassadors on the spot to be fully cognizant and in control of clandestine operations. It is hoped that this principle is forcefully applied and will always be. "Civilian control" is as important here as in the use of the military instrument for policy aims.

·   ·   ·   ·   ·   ·   ·   ·   ·   ·   ·   ·   ·   ·   ·   ·   ·   ·   ·

Four

The Central Intelligence Agency's operations, like those of the National Security Agency, are financed by annual congressional appropriations. Until the sensational disclosures of recent years, however, most congressmen knew little about the nature and functions of either agency. They know even less about the amount of money annually expended.

Congress as a whole has voluntarily walled itself off from detailed information by statues requiring secrecy at the discretion of the CIA's director. In establishing the CIA in 1947, Congress prescribed its organization and functions in general terms, giving the broadest possible definition to "intelligence," in current usage a term covering a number of distinctly different functions. Wide discretion was left to the National Security Council, for which the agency was to work, and to the CIA director. Congress made the director responsible for "protecting intelligence sources and methods for unauthorized disclosure."

In the CIA Act of 1949 Congress went even further, exempting the CIA from existing statutes requiring publication or disclosure of "the organization, functions, names, official titles, salaries or numbers of personnel employed by the agency." The director of the budget was proscribed from making the usual reports to Congress. The standard procedures regarding the expenditure of public funds were waived, and the director's personal voucher alone became sufficient for expenditures for purposes of a "confidential, extraordinary or emergency nature."

The Bureau of the Budget has since established special review procedures for the CIA, and most of the CIA's funds are said to be audited in a regular, albeit classified, manner by the General Accounting Office. The unvouchered funds expended at the discretion of the CIA director, running to tens of millions of dollars annually, are said to be audited also, but by an even more secret process. The CIA must also participate in the annual cycles of rigorous budget "justifications" within the executive hierarchy.

. . . .

The discovery that the CIA was sponsoring aerial reconnaissance flights deep within the borders of the Soviet Union in the 1956–60 period was as much a shock to almost all congressmen as it was to the man in the street. But the CIA leaders could cite congressional statutes as authority for withholding such information.

. . . .

This was not, however, a dark secret to every congressman. A few were privy to some details. One such privileged member spoke up on the other side of Capitol Hill the next day. Representative Clarence Cannon, a Democratic congressman since 1923, as chairman of the House Committee on Appropriations told his colleagues that, although members were unaware of it at the time, they had earlier appropriated money for the U-2 program and other unspecified espionage missions. . . .

To justify the fact that some senior appropriations committee members as well as the more junior congressmen had been hoodwinked into approving camouflaged appropriations for secret intelligence operations, Representative Cannon cited "absolute and unavoidable military necessity, fundamental national defense." He explained that the privileged subcommittee that knew of and approved the U-2 flights included for the most part the same legislators who were privy to the secrets of the atom bomb in World War II. The U-2 flights were, he said, the CIA's response to insistent congressional demands that the nation be forewarned of enemy attack. Presumably they were also in response to the Strategic Air Command's demands for better target information to bolster "deterrence." Tight secrecy about such matters was required, Cannon implied, because "some incautious member of a congressional committee or its staff" might disclose highly sensitive information.

Cannon's House appropriations subcommittee is not the only House group concerned with intelligence. A special House armed services subcommittee was activated in 1958 by Chairman Carl Vinson, Democrat, Georgia, amidst Capitol Hill discontent with intelligence performances. This committee is composed of four members of the majority party, three from the minority, and reviews CIA activities, according to its spokesman, "to the fullest extent it deems necessary."

A similar group exists in the Senate. The Senate Armed Services Committee has, since 1955, maintained a formal subcommittee on Central Intelligence composed of five of its highest ranking members of both parties, all of whom are also senior members of the Senate Committee on Appropriations. This subcommittee receives "information on the magnitude of the CIA appropriation and the purposes for which this money is spent." Its chairman, Senator Richard B. Russell, Democrat, Georgia, said in 1960 that the CIA was "very cooperative," and that he "knew in advance of the U-2 aircraft and its capability." The group, like the others concerned with the CIA, holds its meetings in secret; no record of subcommittee actions has ever been released.

. . . .

A Hoover Commission task force headed by General Mark W. Clark made a detailed survey of the central intelligence system in 1955 which resulted in two reports. One, dealing with organizational aspects, was published. The other, dealing with secret operations, was top secret. The Clark Task Force made special note of the CIA's freedom from the public surveillance normal to our governmental system. Believing this potentially dangerous, it recommended the establishment of executive and congressional watchdogs. The executive group would be a presidential board of distinguished private citizens. The congressional group would be a "Joint Congressional Committee on Foreign Intelligence, similar to the Joint Committee on Atomic Energy."

The joint congressional committee idea was not adopted because of presidential opposition and a similar coolness among senior legislators. But the first recommendation led to the creation, in February 1956, of the President's Board of Consultants on Foreign Intelligence Activities. Its specified duties were to "conduct an objective review of the foreign intelligence activities of the government and of the perfor-

mance of the functions of the Central Intelligence Agency . . . and
report its finding to the president semiannually or at more frequent
intervals. . . ." The board's jurisdiction covered not only CIA but all
government intelligence agencies. The director of central intelligence
was required to reveal to board members any information demanded,
and board members were sworn to secrecy.

After the 1961 Cuban fiasco President Kennedy reconstituted this
board, changing its name to the President's Foreign Intelligence Advisory Board. On May 2, 1961, James R. Killian was reappointed chairman, a post he once held under Eisenhower.

Concurrently, President Kennedy summoned former Army Chief
of Staff General Maxwell D. Taylor to make a special study of the Cuban
failure and of America's capabilities for paramilitary operations and
guerrilla warfare. General Taylor was assisted in this study by Attorney General Robert Kennedy, Chief of Naval Operations Admiral
Arleigh Burke, and CIA Director Allen Dulles. The aftermath was a
delayed but major shake-up in the top leadership of the CIA. Within
a year after the Cuban affair, the director and deputy director had
retired and were replaced by John A. McCone, former shipbuilder,
air force official and chairman of the atomic energy commission, and
Major General Marshall S. Carter, a career army officer. Functional
deputy directors for "plans" (secret operations) and "intelligence production" were also replaced within the year. But major organizational
changes, as of this writing, have not been disclosed.

One point to note about surveillance is that the executive has not
usurped monopolistic control of the CIA. Rather, Congress voluntarily, by statute, gave the president and the National Security Council
wide and undefined discretionary authority. Only a few specific statutory restraints were placed on the agency: that it have no policy or
internal security functions; that it not foreclose or usurp the foreign
intelligence work of existing departments and agencies; and that it be
given access to FBI files only upon written request from the CIA
director to the FBI director.

Five

Who determines specific policies and operating programs for the
Central Intelligence Agency? Because the CIA is but a central unit
among various overlapping, duplicating, and inevitably competing
intelligence agencies, who arbitrates the jurisdictional disputes? The
working constitution of the intelligence system is a set of National

Security Council Intelligence Directives, stemming from Congressional statutes of 1947 and 1949. While such directives bear the imprimatur of the NSC, this may be little more than "rubber stamp" approval of working rules and jurisdictional assignments made under the leadership of the director of central intelligence among the various cooperating (or competing) units of the intelligence community. These directives, codified in 1959, set forth the operational and organizational principles of the CIA and assign functions among the various other intelligence units of government. From these basic NSC directives, director of central intelligence directives are formulated to guide the operations of the agency and to coordinate government-wide foreign intelligence activity, in the hope of preventing duplication or gaps in essential information.

The "public interest," then, is represented by the president, advised by the NSC; a handful of senior legislators on Capitol Hill; and the President's Foreign Intelligence Advisory Board. The latter group is not statutory and serves, on a very part-time basis, at presidential discretion. The question remains: Is this system for surveillance adequate, given the scope and importance of the intelligence function and the potentially explosive nature of some types of operations that have come under the rubric of "intelligence"?

· ·

. . . It is my own belief that the system would benefit rather than suffer from additional external surveillance, because of the inherent value within a government bureaucracy of the feeling of external responsibility and the fear of being embarrassed or called to account.

Perhaps 80 to 90 percent of the activities of the intelligence community could be scrutinized by a joint congressional committee to the same degree that existing committees oversee the defense establishment, foreign affairs, and atomic energy policies and programs. These fields too contain highly sensitive elements from a security viewpoint. The record of Congress in keeping secrets given to its various committees in "executive" (secret) session is good. Probably more secrets have deliberately "leaked" from the executive branch than from Congress.

· ·

In her search for democracy America produced a government system that fragments and diffuses power. To recommend giving Congress a more institutionalized role in overseeing central intelligence is not to recommend more diffusion of power but less. A joint congressional committee on central intelligence would be a center of countervailing power, and should help to focus responsibility and authority. There is also the troublesome question of whether meaningful debate can occur, particularly in national elections, when sometimes crucial information is in the control of the party in power. During the 1952 election campaign, President Truman established the precedent that the presidential and vice-presidential nominees of both parties receive foreign intelligence briefings from the Central Intelligence Agency. His purpose was to assure foreign policy continuity, regardless of the candidate elected. Since such information is highly classified, however, it may be used for background purposes only, and this limits debate on decisive issues. Aware of this, General Eisenhower, in accepting Truman's offer, did so with the understanding that, except for security information, it would "in no other way limit my freedom to discuss or analyze foreign programs as my judgment dictates." . . .

Six

The foregoing analysis suggests some guidelines that may be useful in assuring that the intelligence services are as efficient as possible and under the control of responsible authority. Operational intelligence activities must, above all, never be more or less than instruments of national policy, and even as such should not be overrated. Some missions are better left to diplomats. In their informational function, intelligence services must preserve their objectivity. At the same time, Intelligence must serve policy in a staff role rather than attempt to persuade decision makers, openly or subtly, on particular courses of action. And there must be mutual understanding and a close working relationship between the policy makers and the intelligence professionals.

While the control of Intelligence must remain primarily the president's responsibility, Congress must assume a more active and clearly defined role, and the Department of State must participate aggressively in weighing gain from success against cost of failure in every proposed major secret operation. A strengthened Department of State is a prerequisite to putting Intelligence in its proper place.

The CIA is misnamed. More than an intelligence service, it has become a multipurpose organization, engaged in a number of disparate "strategic services." The informational mission of the intelligence system should be organized separately from the clandestine political mission. For when operational planners also supply the ultimate decision maker with the information required to justify a plan's feasibility, great risks abound, with the self-fulfilling prophecy perhaps the most common danger. Planners and operational commanders are notoriously prone to view their proposed plan as an end in itself. As experiences in the Korean War, Laos, and Cuba demonstrate, selecting only those bits of "intelligence" that justify a given plan's practicability courts disaster.

Another problem involves secrecy and the frequent "leaks" that have occurred in this country. Certain strategic services by definition require the utmost secrecy. The United States can impose a higher degree of legitimate secrecy in two ways. First, the leadership of the intelligence community must resist the many temptations to mount the public speech-making rostrum. Wisdom suggests that they cultivate a passion for anonymity. Second, a restoration of confidence in the professional quality of the intelligence system and in the *fact* of its unquestioned subordination to responsible political authority will automatically produce greater self-restraint on the part of Congress and the press.

Perhaps the most fundamental problem, reflected in the apparent bungling in recent times of supposedly secret operations, has been the lack of a clearly defined national purpose and a national consensus on American foreign policy objectives. A clarified national purpose is the most commonly recommended nostrum for the nation's ailments in foreign affairs. Intelligence has borne the brunt of criticism for many policy and operational failures. The blame ought to be shared with the presidency, State Department, and Congress. Many of the problems of the intelligence system would be self-solving, given a positive consensus on foreign policy aims other than the natural concern for self-survival. In this regard the Communists have an advantage in conducting clandestine political action, for a democracy cannot enforce an ideological dogma. However, dogma places totalitarian regimes at a disadvantage—witness Nazi Germany and now Soviet Russia—because intelligence reports processed through an ideological filter are likely to be inaccurate and misleading. Even with vast intelligence services, Stalin refused to believe that Hitler was about to attack Russia in June 1941; Hitler in his later years habitually refused to hear "bad" news from his intelligence services; and more recently Khrushchev has misapprehended the United States. All leadership suffers from this malady; totalitarians perhaps to the greatest degree.

Some Americans argue that we must refrain from clandestine illegal operations overseas, adhering instead to high moral principles of conduct. While diplomacy is preferable, and usually more reliable and effective than subversion, the United States cannot realistically abstain from espionage or follow an absolute principle of non-intervention in the internal affairs of other nations. Cold war is by definition a stage in international politics that is neither war nor peace. In this situation, and short of a reign of international law based upon the consent of the governed, the United States may sometimes have to engage in clandestine activities to protect the national interest. The nation cannot accept the claim, in every situation, that the existing government or regime in every foreign country is the legitimate one. The national interest and the common defense may require intervention, even though this confronts us with legal and moral problems. The United States rarely faces comfortable alternative choices in support of foreign regimes. Often we must accept the lesser evil because circumstances fail to provide an ideal option.

America can neither unilaterally resign from the cold war without unacceptable risk to all nations sharing democratic ideals, nor cynically adopt an "ends justify means" rule for action. Intervention or espionage should occur only when no alternative exists, and should be undertaken with a precision and a purpose, determined always by responsible, identifiable political leaders, that have been lacking in the past.

Questions

1. Critics have argued that the function of the Central Intelligence Agency should be limited to information gathering, that the CIA should not be the advocate of specific policies. Do you agree?
2. What might be the advantages of having a secret intelligence service? What might be the dangers?
3. The CIA budget is hidden in various appropriations for other government agencies. Because Congress has responsibility for the budget, should it have knowledge of the way in which the taxpayer's money is spent? This, of course, would involve disclosure, which Senator Henry M. Jackson has said "may be unwittingly giving aid and comfort to the enemy." What is your view?

Recent Trends in American Foreign Policy: An Epilogue

Martin B. Hickman

Introduction

The melancholy era bracketed between the twin tragedies of the assassination of John F. Kennedy and the resignation of Richard M. Nixon has been one of traumatic change for American foreign policy. Few could have predicted that Richard Nixon, the dedicated cold warrior of the Eisenhower administration, would preside over the liquidation of American involvement in Vietnam on terms less than victory, initiate a rapprochement with the Soviet Union, and journey to Peking at the invitation of Mao Tse-tung. Those changes have not only been dramatic, they have been represented in the mass media as personal victories of President Nixon and his secretary of state, Henry Kissinger. Given the aura of personal diplomacy that surrounds current American foreign policy, it is inevitable that Gerald Ford's ascension to the presidency will raise speculation as to the future of American foreign policy. At best all one can do is speculate, because at this writing President Ford has not had sufficient time to give foreign policy his own stamp. Certainly his decision to retain Henry Kissinger as secretary of state suggests a continuation of past policies. But there are reasons other than the personality of the secretary of state for believing that in the next decade foreign policy will be relatively constant. Those reasons are linked to the reality that revisions of foreign policy are mainly the result of fundamental shifts in the structure of the international system. Thus the sharp changes in the international system that have taken place in the last fifteen years are likely to determine the mood and thrust of American foreign policy for the foreseeable future just as they provided the environment from which the Nixon doctrine emerged. It is important then to understand the nature of those changes, and the way in which President Nixon and Henry Kissinger adjusted American foreign policy to make it relevant in a changing world.

The new departures in American foreign policy initiated by Nixon and Kissinger must be seen against the background of the previous twenty-five years to be fully appreciated and understood. Those years were themselves years of near-revolutionary change. They marked the final end of the "splendid isolation" that had been the cornerstone of American foreign policy. The end of isolationism as a viable foreign policy option meant that the American people were finally psychologically prepared to accept what had been a reality for at least a half century: that the United States was a strong world power. What was not immediately apparent was that there were only two great powers—the United States and the Soviet Union.

The reality of the bipolar world penetrated only gradually the consciousness of the American public and policy makers alike. The conduct of World War II, the planning for the United Nations, and our immediate postwar diplomacy all were based on the assumption that except for Germany and Japan the major European powers, along with China, would resume their prewar roles in the international system. But the classic international system organized around the existence of several major powers was a victim of World War II. What emerged was a bipolar world dominated by the United States and the Soviet Union, whose economic and military resources were so much larger than those of other nations that they soon became recognized as superpowers. This recognition of their unique status was hastened as each of them developed atomic, and then thermonuclear, weapons, along with missile-based delivery systems.

The polarized structure of the post–World War II world made substantial conflict in the international system an ever-present possibility; the resurrection of ideology as an important factor in international affairs made that conflict inevitable. Not since the religious wars of the fifteenth and sixteenth centuries, with the exception of the interlude of the French revolution, had nations divided into ideological camps. But a deep ideological cleavage between the two superpowers was to become a distinguishing feature of the post–World War II world. Thus the conflict that was inherent in the emergence of the two superpowers became explicit and pervasive.

Open conflict between the opposing ideological camps emerged gradually in the period 1945–50. The conventional historical interpretation is that this conflict resulted from the aggressive, expansionistic policies of the Soviet Union that left the United States no choice but confrontation and a policy of containment. That view has been challenged by a school of revisionist historians who find the causes of the conflict in the policy choices of President Truman and his advisers. These historians allege that Truman deliberately abandoned Roosevelt's policy of cooperation with the Soviet Union in favor of a policy of hostility and confrontation. It is not necessary to settle that debate to recognize that by the outbreak of the Korean War in June 1950, the cold war was a harsh reality of international affairs.

Because of the cold war the dominant images of American policy makers were those of a "free world" confronted by a communist monolith bent on world conquest. American foreign policy sought to stem communist expansion, for in the language of the Truman Doctrine, "Totalitarian regimes imposed on free peoples, by direct or indirect aggression, undermine the foundation of international peace and hence the security of the United States."[1]

This belief that opposition to direct or indirect aggression was in the national interest of the United States led to extensive United States assistance in rebuilding Western Europe. The same logic was extended, after the Korean War, to Asia and other parts of the world. American economic and military aid was given to virtually any nation that appealed for protection from communist subversion or domination.

This cold war image based on a policy of containment was reinforced in 1957 by the successful Soviet launching of an earth satellite called Sputnik. The military implications of this scientific achievement were immediately apparent. The Soviet Union might well develop an arsenal of intercontinental ballistic missiles carrying thermonuclear warheads while the United States still relied on manned bombers. Thus Russian superior military might could be used to further their foreign policy. The fear of "atomic blackmail" drove the United States to an all-out effort to develop its own missile force, to a reexamination of its strategy doctrines, and to a renewed effort to contain the rise of Soviet influence in the underdeveloped world.

Time was to prove that the "missile gap" and its handmaiden, "atomic blackmail," were specters that never materialized. The crucible was the Cuban missile crisis of 1963, which brought the superpowers into direct confrontation. That episode ended with the Soviet Union

---

1. Message of President Harry S. Truman to Congress on March 12, 1947. *New York Times*, March 13, 1947.

agreeing to withdraw its missiles from Cuba, but not before President Kennedy had threatened atomic retaliation if the United States were attacked.

At the time, the crisis appeared to confirm the prophecies about Soviet behavior, and the policies adopted on the basis of those prophecies seemed relevant and appropriate. But the self-congratulations had hardly died away before the deepening involvement of the United States in Vietnam began to raise doubts about American foreign policy and the conventional wisdom of the previous decade. At first these doubts were expressed only by members of the antiwar movement, but as American participation in the Vietnam War widened from providing logistic support and military advisers to full-scale intervention with ground, air, and naval forces, these doubts spread throughout the full spectrum of American life. They were fueled by a growing realization that the Vietnam War had become meaningless. Once the image of a monolithic communist bloc was erased, it became apparent that the Vietnam War was a regional conflict whose outcome would have very little impact on the power relationship of the superpowers. Paradoxically that view of the world began to change just at the point when American participation had escalated from providing advisers and logistic assistance to assuming a major combat role. The impetus for a change in the American perception of the world had its roots in the decay of the Chinese-Russian alliance, which forced a fundamental reassessment of the structure of the international system. That impetus was reinforced by the increasing evidence that tensions within the North Atlantic Treaty Organization (NATO) were eroding the Western alliance. This changed perception led editors and TV commentators to ask: "Can the United States continue to police the world?" An increasing number of Americans came to reject the idea that a single nation—no matter how powerful—could maintain law and order in an unruly world, and they increasingly ignored the subtle and complex issues involved in that rejection. The upshot was, then, the first full-scale debate of fundamental issues and assumptions of American foreign policy in twenty years.

The Nixon Doctrine

The Nixon doctrine emerged out of that fundamental debate and represents a far-reaching reassessment of the nature of the international system and the role of the United States in international affairs. The doctrine begins with the premise that the bipolar world that emerged after 1945 has undergone a fundamental structural change. That change has had two important results: (1) a change in the strategic relationships between the United States and the Soviet Union that demands new doctrines; (2) the development of polycentrism in the communist world, which presents the United States with new challenges and opportunities. The other basic premises of the doctrine are that the major American role in international affairs is imperative, and that other nations can and must assume larger responsibilities for their own defense and for assistance to the underdeveloped world. The changes that President Nixon and Secretary Kissinger have made in American foreign policy have flowed from these premises. Let us trace the outlines of those changes.

Détente

The bundle of strategic and tactical policy shifts in the relations of the United States with the Soviet Union has been christened "détente." But détente is as much a psychological frame of mind as it is a set of policies. At a primary level it recognizes the achievement by the Soviet Union of nuclear parity with the United States and the need to cope with that development without recourse to violence. At still another level it symbolizes American acceptance of the postwar power structure of Eastern Europe including the division of Germany. Finally détente stands for the idea that the relationship between the Soviet Union and the United States is not a "you win, I lose" relationship. At the same time it does not stand for the proposition that there is no fundamental conflict of interest in that relationship. It stands for a concept of cooperation within a general matrix of conflict best described by Marshall Shulman's phrase, a "limited adversary relationship."[2] A "limited adversary relationship" recognizes that the parties are ideological adversaries, that they are political and military competitors, that each has a number of allies who are dependent on it for defense against thermonuclear attack and in some cases for economic assistance, that each has global interests that cannot be lightly sacrificed, and that each has at its disposal awesome military power. It also makes allowances for these conflicts and yet provides for cooperation where mutually beneficial, and offers inducements to the parties to widen the areas of negotiation.

This psychological attitude has led to a number of agreements. The most striking result of détente has been the agreement to limit some

---

2. "U.S.–Soviet Détente?" in *Soviet and Chinese Communist Power in the World Today*, edited by Roger Swearingen (New York: Basic Books, 1966), p. 84.

forms of strategic military arms. The initial Strategic Arms Limitation Talks (SALT I) that led to these agreements are notable not only for the substance of the agreements but also because they symbolize the realization by both superpowers that strategic arms control is a continuing process that must be a matter of constant concern to both nations. It is on the willingness to continue the discussion that hopes for the future of arms control must be based, for the failure of SALT I to limit the development and deployment of warheads with multiple bombs[3] for use with existing missiles forces has assured the continuation of the arms race, at least in a qualitative if not in a quantitative sense.

Perhaps the most optimistic hopes raised by détente have been those in the economic area. American businessmen have long speculated on the potential of the Soviet Union as a market for American exports. On the surface détente seems to offer at least an opportunity to explore that potential market. Yet it is the prospects of increased trade between the Soviet Union and the United States that have highlighted the complexities of the "limited adversary relationship" on which détente rests.

If trade with the Soviet Union were to expand rapidly in scope and size, the United States would have to grant most-favored-nation status to the Soviet Union.[4] It is clear that the Soviet Union wants this status as soon as possible, and that the Nixon administration was prepared to meet that request. Furthermore, this seems to be an issue that falls into the area of cooperation foreseen by détente. But it is not that simple, for there is still a large conflictive area in the U.S.–USSR relationship, and the trade issue has been forced into that conflictive area by Senator Jackson's efforts to make most-favored-nation status dependent upon revision of Soviet emigration policies that make it difficult for Soviet Jews to emigrate to Israel. Thus what appears on its face to be a rather straightforward economic issue is transformed by the nature of the "limited adversary relationship" between the U.S. and the USSR into a complex political issue with far-reaching ramifications. This dispute over the most-favored-nation issue is ample evidence that within the present meaning of détente there are no purely economic or technical aspects: all are tainted with politics and, ultimately, ideology.

---

3. The technical designation for these weapons is Multiple Independent Re-entry Vehicles (MIRVs).

4. This would mean that import duty on Soviet goods entering the United States could be no higher than the lowest duty now levied on the same goods imported from members of the General Agreements on Tariffs and Trade.

Détente has a Chinese as well as a Russian face, and of the two the Chinese is the more spectacular. There have been continuous diplomatic relations between the Soviet Union and the United States for some forty years. Those relations have endured despite the breakup of the World War II alliance and the tension of the cold war. American-Chinese relations have not yet reached the stage of full diplomatic recognition; they appear to be cordial now mainly by comparison, because for twenty years the Chinese denounced the United States as the epitome of imperialistic-capitalistic evil, while the United States branded the People's Republic of China as the spearhead of communist aggression in the Far East. The denunciatory rhetoric on each side created the impression that only the elimination of the other from the world scene would satisfy its foreign policy demands. Speculation in the United States about recognizing Red China always ran afoul of the refusal of the Chinese to be recognized, and of China's nonnegotiable demand that the United States recognize Peking's sovereignty and rule over Taiwan. For twenty years Chinese-American relations rarely rose above insult and invective; not even the informal discussion that the two governments held in Warsaw improved the official relations. What event, then, brought about the dramatic change symbolized by President Nixon's trip to China in 1972?

It is true that the United States had made some changes in its Chinese policy prior to President Nixon's trip. These included liberalization of restrictions on trade with the mainland and permission for U.S. citizens to travel to China. It is also true that Henry Kissinger had long believed that the success of a negotiated settlement of the Vietnam War depended more on Peking and Moscow than on Hanoi. But we will miss the significance of the president's visit if we look solely at American-Chinese relations for the reasons that made the trip possible; they must be found in Chinese-Russian relations. President Nixon's visit, then, is not so much an indication of American willingness to view the Chinese in a new light— although there is much of that attitude in the reasons behind the visit—as it is an indication that the Chinese have radically reassessed the nature of the international system as well as their own national interests.

Almost immediately after the communist victory on the mainland, Mao Tse-tung announced in his colorful rhetoric that his government would lean to one side; that the east wind would prevail over the west wind. That announcement characterized Chinese foreign policy for the coming decades. But gradually Chinese political, military, and economic interest began to erode the bonds that had made Peking and Moscow allies. The Chinese finally abandoned the policy of leaning exclusively to one side and turned first to isolationism and then to eventual détente with the United States when it became clear that the Russians would not assist the Chinese in developing nuclear weapons. From that point on the Chinese began to challenge the leadership of the Soviet Union in the communist world, to carry on a bitter propaganda war against Soviet leadership, to assert more vigorously their claims to territory along the Chinese-Russian border, and to push their own efforts to develop nuclear weapons. The Russian reaction was to denounce the Chinese as ideological heretics and to respond in kind to the attacks on Soviet leaders, but most important, the Russians began to increase their armed forces along the Chinese border and to explore the possibility of détente with the United States. When the implications of these Russian initiatives became clearer, and as the Cultural Revolution in China lost its momentum and China began again to turn its attention to the external world, the Chinese leaders began to reassess the isolationism of the Cultural Revolution, as they had earlier reconsidered the policy of leaning exclusively to one side. Although the details of that internal policy debate are not available, the change in policy which soon followed suggests that the Chinese leaders reached a fundamental decision that Moscow, not Washington, presented the most direct challenge to Chinese interests. Moreover, to keep from being completely isolated, given the American-Russian rapprochement then taking place, they would have to initiate their own détente with the United States. That decision brought President Nixon to Peking to explore the challenges and opportunity that the schism in the communist world presented to the United States.

America's World Role

Despite the successful efforts of the Nixon administration to end American involvement in the Vietnamese conflict on terms that cannot be described in any sense as a victory for American arms, the Nixon doctrine is not a return to isolationism nor even to the halfway house of neo-isolationism. It foresees a continuing major role for the United States in world affairs. What is changed is not the content of policy but its emphasis. Although President Nixon has committed the United States to fulfill its existing treaty obligations, and has reaffirmed American intention to *"provide a shield if a nuclear power threatens the freedom of a nation allied with us or of a nation whose survival we considered vital to our security,"* he has laid down limits to American assistance where allies or friendly nations are threatened by other kinds of aggression.[5]

---

5. *U.S. Foreign Policy for the 1970s: Building for Peace* (Washington, D.C.: U.S. Government Printing Office, 1972), p. 13. Emphasis in original.

In such cases the United States, Nixon has said, will provide military and economic assistance "appropriate to our size and our interests."[6] That promise of assistance does not include American manpower, although the president did not completely rule out the use of American armed forces in repelling aggression against another nation. But by raising the threshold of that possibility and by placing the primary responsibility for emphasis on self-defense, he served notice that future Vietnams were highly unlikely.

The role of the United States in international affairs foreseen by the Nixon doctrine is illustrated well by American policy in the Middle East crisis of 1973. American interests in the Middle East center on continued access to Arab oil and on the economic and political independence of Israel. In the past these goals have been potentially incompatible, but in practice they have not been so. The United States has been free to provide Israel with a continuing stream of economic and military assistance without the threat of an Arab oil embargo. Arab unity in the 1973 crisis forced an end to that balancing act, and the United States was faced with a dilemma that seemed insoluble.

Secretary Kissinger's successful "shuttle" diplomacy in the Middle East is a remarkable personal achievement. But it would have been impossible if the objective conditions in the Middle East had not created a policy environment in which the secretary could work his personal magic. The 1973 war forced both the Arabs and the Israelis to recognize that only the United States could help each of them gain its policy objectives. The Israelis needed continued military assistance if they were to deal successfully with growing Arab military strength and effectiveness. Only the United States could provide that assistance. The Arabs needed diplomatic assistance to induce the Israelis to accept a cease-fire and ultimately to consider surrendering land taken from the Arabs. The Soviet Union could provide military assistance, but military might alone could not advance these Arab policy objectives, and the Soviet Union could not provide the missing diplomatic pressure. Only the United States was in a position to induce the Israelis to give serious consideration to Arab demands. Simultaneously the Arab oil embargo forced the United States to reexamine its own interest in the Middle East and to review carefully what set of policies would satisfy American interests and at the same time advance the prospects for a lasting peace in the Middle East.

This review led in the first instance to a reaffirmation of the American determination to avoid a direct confrontation with the Soviet Union in the

---

6. Ibid., p. 14.

Middle East. Hence the United States rejected the Russian proposal that the two nations send troops to the Middle East to police a cease-fire. Furthermore, President Nixon ordered a partial mobilization of American armed forces when it appeared that the Soviets might move unilaterally to police a cease-fire. The real reasons behind that alert have been hotly debated. Some critics of President Nixon have alleged that the alert was more in response to the president's domestic ills associated with Watergate than it was to the Soviet initiative in the Middle East. Although the president may have welcomed the opportunity to demonstrate his continuing ability to act vigorously in foreign affairs, Watergate does not appear to have been the major factor behind the alert. American policy has consistently opposed participation by the major powers in the U.N. peace-keeping forces, and the Soviet threat to take unilateral action ran directly counter to that policy. Whatever the reasons behind the alert, its message was clear to the Soviet Union: détente did not include a carte blanche for Soviet policy in the Middle East.

Once the Soviet Union had abandoned its plans for unilateral action in the Middle East, Secretary Kissinger turned his attention to the task of negotiating a cease-fire on terms that would not only bring an end to the fighting and offer prospects for meaningful negotiation on the issues, but would also assure the United States of access to Arab oil without abandoning its support for Israel. He was able to achieve those goals because the 1973 war substantially changed the psychological climate in the Middle East. It created an environment where a statesman with a sure grasp of the immediate issues as well as a clear concept of the relations of those issues to the larger world scene could take advantage of the opportunities these changes produced. It is difficult in the short run to know which factor weighed most heavily with the parties: Kissinger's personality, or the content of the policy he proposed. If the cease-fire, the prospects for negotiations, and the apparent trust in the good will of the United States which now exist in the Middle East rest on the personal authority of Secretary Kissinger, his departure as secretary of state might bring down the whole structure. If they rest on a conviction that the United States is committed to a long-range stable policy of "even-handedness" in the Middle East, Secretary Kissinger's achievement will endure beyond his term of office.

Alliance Politics

Although the Nixon doctrine has been carried out with substantial success in the Far East, in the Middle East, and in American-Russian relations, paradoxically these successes have increased the tension between the United States and its closest allies—Western Europe and Japan. Irony abounds in foreign affairs, but still it is striking that Secretary Kissinger, whose reputation as a foreign policy analyst was based largely on his critique of American policy in Western Europe, should experience his most significant failures in maintaining good relations with Western Europe. "The Year of Europe"—that was to be 1973. What that phrase meant to its authors, President Nixon and Secretary Kissinger, was a period in which the relationship between the United States and Western Europe would be strengthened as the Atlantic partners explored the ways in which their common interests could be intensified by expanding cooperation. That was the hope; the reality is that the "Year of Europe" has become instead the year in which Washington's relationship with its European partners has struck an all-time low.

What is true of Western Europe is also true of Japan even though it is on the other side of the globe. The Japanese are no less dependent on the United States for defense than are Western Europeans; they, too, are neighbors to a large, dynamic, continental communist power; they, too, are materially affected by American economic and monetary policies. Their alliance with the United States has made them brothers under the skin with the Western Europeans; when the United States sneezes they both catch cold.

The paradox of American–Western European relations is that détente, which reduces the Soviet military threat and thus assures European territorial integrity, has increased Western European fears of Soviet political domination. This paradox reflects the fear that détente will undermine American willingness to maintain a significant military presence in Western Europe. An American military withdrawal, Europeans argue, would leave Western Europe exposed to Soviet political pressure that Western Europe ultimately would be unable to resist. The result would be the "Finlandization" of Western Europe. This metaphor creates an image of a Western Europe that is neutral but in fact dependent— as Finland now is—upon Soviet approval for all its international arrangements.

Among Europeans détente recalls too vividly the specter of Yalta— the superpowers agreeing among themselves about the future of the world without consulting their allies—to be fully welcomed. They suspect détente means that while the United States is more willing to negotiate with the Soviet Union it is at the same time more willing to dictate to its allies.

Despite Secretary Kissinger's long familiarity with the problem of American-European relations, and despite his criticism of the Kennedy administration for failing to establish authentic cooperative relations with NATO members, the Nixon administration has shown little understanding of these fears. At the outbreak of the 1973 Middle East crisis, American policy makers took for granted Western European support. That expectation seems less than realistic, given the policy independence NATO members had shown in the Vietnam War and in view of Western Europe's substantial dependence on the Middle East for its oil. Western Europe could not, therefore, afford the luxury of supporting Israel, for the price of that support was an oil embargo that would bring Western Europe's major industries to a halt with resulting unemployment and economic chaos. It is not surprising then that the Europeans broke ranks to seek bilateral arrangements with the oil-exporting nations of the Middle East, or that they tried to disassociate themselves from American policy. The Germans protested the use by the United States of German airfields to transship military assistance to Israel, and Great Britain refused permission to use Cypriot airfields for reconnaissance missions. These policy decisions by our NATO allies drove Secretary Kissinger to complain that they were acting as if the alliance were nonexistent. Yet a few days later, the United States did not consult its NATO allies before placing its armed forces on alert, a neglect that led Western Europeans to counterattack with their own complaints about noncooperation.

The feeling of each side that the other side is ignoring the logic of the alliance stems from a subtle but sharp shift in the priorities of NATO members.The North Atlantic Treaty was originally proposed as a mutual defense pact to secure Western Europe from Soviet aggression. For the next decade defense issues were the overruling concern of member states and generally there was a willingness to subordinate other issues to the demands of mutual defense. In the early sixties, when European fears of a Soviet military attack began to decline rapidly, economic and political issues within the alliance became dominant rather than subordinate themes. The process of reversing the relationship between defense and economic problems has continued apace. It is true that during the period of conflict between the United States and the Soviet Union, NATO members have tended to present a united front, as in the Cuban missile crisis of 1963. But following each crisis, problems created by intra-alliance conflicts have again become the dominant concern of NATO countries.

What emerges from the past twenty-four years of alliance experience is the impression that when the outside threat is high, cooperation within the alliance is also high. By the same token when the pressure of an outside threat is low, cooperation declines. Furthermore, intra-alliance cooperation is most responsive when the outside threat is perceived as being military in nature and is initiated by the Soviet Union. If this model of intra-alliance behavior is accurate, it explains why the United States and Western Europe chose unilateral measures in response to the Middle East war. That crisis contained no Soviet threat to the territorial integrity of Western Europe; but the Arab oil embargo threatened to wreak severe economic damage in these countries. Hence the American policy of military suport for Israel pleased only the Dutch, and the reluctance of the United States to consult its NATO allies before alerting its military forces for a possible confrontation with the Soviet Union over the Middle East pleased no one in Europe. Furthermore, the consequences of a progressive reduction in oil shipments to Western Europe were so threatening to those countries that not only did they refuse to cooperate with the United States in its search for a policy that would satisfy both Israelis and Arabs, they also declined to cooperate with each other to deal with the impending reduction of oil shipments from the Middle East. Instead they rushed off to make bilateral deals for oil, thus offering the oil-producing countries an opportunity, which they did not miss, to divide and conquer.

Economics and Defense

The altered set of priorities within NATO so starkly revealed by the Middle East crisis are also reflected in the continuing debate among the allies over their foreign trade relations and reform of the international monetary system. The energy crisis and the possibility of shortages of food and other raw materials underlie the emergence of economic issues as the paramount concern of international affairs. For the last twenty-five years students of international relations were forced to learn the language of military strategy; deterrence in all of its theoretical ramifications had to be mastered if one wished to enter the foreign policy dialogue. That language is still very much with us and will be for the foreseeable future. But now the student of international affairs must add to that knowledge an understanding of international economics. Economic issues have always been part and parcel of international affairs, but they have become crucial in a world of growing interdependence. An increase in the price of oil not only means that the consumer in Western Europe and the United States must pay more to operate his automobile but also represents a substantial transfer of wealth to the oil-producing countries. That transfer of wealth, if it is not reinvested in Western Europe and the United States, may well bring in its wake severe economic disruption. Already Italy has had to restrict food and other imports to pay for its oil imports. Inflation is no longer a solely national problem, because many of its causes have their roots in the patterns of international economics and its impact does not stop at national frontiers. The American decision to devalue the dollar in the spring of 1973 led to substantially larger purchases of American products by Japan and Western Europe. This coupled with the ill-fated sale of large quantities of American wheat and with the emergence of the energy crisis triggered an inflationary surge in the United States that is far from running its course.

These examples illustrate the importance as well as the complexities of the problems that economic issues will pose for foreign policy makers over the next twenty-five years. The challenge for the United States is how to provide foreign policy leadership to its allies that will assure cooperation in the solution of intra-alliance economic and political problems. "It is not war that brings the moment of truth," Stanley Hoffman has written, "it is economic or monetary or environmental disaster."[7] Security problems have been the major focus of foreign policy for so long that concentrated effort by policy makers and public alike will be required to recognize the emergence of a new set of problems that must be dealt with if a stable international system is to result. The task ahead is to maintain and strengthen the impetus toward stability in our "limited adversary relationship" with the Soviet Union while learning to cope with the economic and political problems of growing interdependence not only with our closest allies but also with our erstwhile adversaries.

Questions

1. Describe in your own words what is meant by a bipolar world.
2. Identify the changes in the international system that led to the Nixon doctrine.
3. What does the term détente mean in a discussion of contemporary American foreign policy?
4. Why does the author believe that American–Western European relations were strained during the Nixon administration?
5. . List some examples, other than those given in the article, of the economic interdependence of the world and its consequences for American foreign policy.

7. "Weighing the Balance of Power," *Foreign Affairs* 60 (July 1972): 633.